TRULY BLESSED

THE JOURNEY OF THE AFRICAN AMERICAN FAMILY OF SYLVESTER & BILLIE MCCLEARN

OHIRO D. ONI-ESELEH

CHOICE PUBLICATIONS

NEWBURGH, NEW YORK

Choice Publications
P. O. Box 7159
Newburgh, NY 12550

TRULY BLESSED:
THE JOURNEY OF AN AFRICAN AMERICAN FAMILY
OF SYLVESTER AND BILLIE MCCLEARN

ISBN 0-9715552-0-6

Printed in the United States of America

Copyright © 2003 by Sylvester and Billie McClearn

Published by Choice Publications
P. O. Box 7159
Newburgh, NY 12550

All rights reserved. No part of this book may be reproduced or transmitted in any form or by any means without the prior written permission of the copyright owner, except brief quotations used in connection with reviews in magazines newspapers, and other media.

To God, the McClearn family

and

to all who see beyond their difficult moments
and maintain hope for a future yet unknown

Introduction

This book is the biography of a man, Reverend Sylvester McClearn, who was born on a farm in North Carolina, lived a life of poverty as a child, and moved from that to attain tremendous heights despite the odds that were clearly stacked against him. The road from the farm of his birth, through the bright lights of Washington, DC, to the once unheralded place known as Newburgh in New York was an extraordinary one, not because it was long but for the following two reasons. First, because every step on that road was significant and left lasting memories that have become more than the story of one man. Secondly, the subject of this biography believes that every step in his journey was ordered by a power higher than he. He has no doubt that God was with him every step of the way, even when it seemed that he might be lost.

The process of putting this book together was detailed and the end product is, I think, a fascinating read because, again, an exercise that began with the goal of writing one man's biography has resulted in a story that most African Americans can relate to. It is a biography that is rich with lessons and revelations about culture, survival, race, the history of a family, and indeed the history of a people.

The story of the McClearn family neither begins nor ends with this or any book because it is a family that will continue to evolve. I know this because, following in the heels of the McClearn giants of yesterday are tomorrow's McClearns who will learn about the wealth of their family's history from this book and, hopefully, take up and fly the family's flag way into the future. The only people that could inhibit them and make it impossible to accomplish this bold prediction are themselves. Otherwise, the McClearn name will shine forever.

This biography is presented in twenty-two chapters, beginning with the birth of Sylvester on a North Carolina farm off Angel highway into a large family whose patriarch was an abusive, alcoholic father and whose matriarch was a gentle Christian woman as harmless as an angelic dove. The story takes us through years of Sylvester and his brothers and sisters working as child farmers to the time that he drops out of school in fourth grade, leaves his family in North Carolina and goes to the Washington, D.C. area with his older brother. Why? To continue his life on the labor force, so he can send money back to North Carolina to support his mother. If the story ended here, it would still be a great biography, but it doesn't.

From a life of disadvantage, and with very little education, Sylvester meets Billie, marries her, and proceeds to create with her a beautiful family, and a successful business, while also turning himself into a very educated man. Then he succeeds in creating a great ministry as he leads a big church through challenges into states of accomplishment and leaves his mark in the community that he now calls home. The story of Reverend Sylvester McClearn may be a familiar one for many African Americans, and indeed other Americans, but the road that he traveled is without doubt one that is less traveled.

Reverend McClearn has worked very closely with me in creating this work. His gratitude for his life is beyond compare. It is therefore very fitting that this book should have a page of acknowledgments written in the Reverend's words and name. It is also for this reason that he is personally responsible for chapters twenty-two and twenty-three of this book in which he respectively reflects on his life and presents a sermon to end the book.

I am particularly grateful to the Reverend's son, Sylvester Darnell McClearn, without whom this book would not have been written. Despite his very busy life and work schedules, Darnell ensured that he was available as often as was needed to accomplish our task and, together, we fashioned a McClearn family story that will remain one of unparalleled value to posterity. While working on this project, I found Darnell to be a man with a rare commitment to family, humanity, history and progress. He is also a man whose word is golden and whose character is solid. In these respects, he is very much like his father. Aptly, I requested Darnell to write the foreword for this book, and I am glad I did.

Finally, I am grateful to my editor, Ms. Jill Eisenstein, and to Jonathan Gullery who designed the cover for this book.

Ohiro Oni-Eseleh
Newburgh, New York
July 2003

Foreword

Why would anyone wish to have a book written about his or her family? Why would anyone want to learn about, rehash, or document periods of struggles and pain in his or her family? Why would I choose to conceive of, and finance, a project like this one with the potential of opening old or current wounds in my family that I love with all my heart? Make no mistake: I am very well aware that writing a family history is sometimes like opening a can of worms and aspects of the outcome are bound to be hurtful or painful to various family members. Who wants to recall crisis, pain, humiliation, or the dark periods of the history of the United States from which his family and his race are still reeling?

Before I took on the task of doing this project, I asked myself the same questions. I was never in doubt regarding the value of researching and documenting my family's history. However, I needed to be sure that I, or anyone else in my family, would be comfortable with the facts that would be borne out in the research – regardless of how unpalatable they might be. In this, I wasn't just thinking of my parents and siblings but also of the future generations of the McClearn family. But regardless of how frequently and deeply I explored these questions, my answers were always the same as they are now - simply that this is a book that had to be written completely, openly, and truthfully.

By the time my parents contacted Dr. Ohiro Oni-Eseleh to write this book, I was very certain that it was something that I wanted to do and my entire family was very comfortable with the idea. When my parents put me in touch with him, two of his questions to me during our first ever telephone conversation were indeed very simple ones: "Mr. McClearn", he said, "why do you want us to write this book? In other words, why are you doing this?" My response – almost all in one breath, became the cornerstone of our work together and led to the production of the book that you are reading right now. "Doctor", I began, "First, I am convinced that the African American story is richer than what is out there. I think that not enough good African American stories have been published. Secondly, I need to do this to provide great inspiration to other people, regardless of their race. Thirdly, I believe that, when it's all said and done, my family story is a great one". We concluded that conversation with me telling the Doc: "What I am looking for is not a book that will glorify my father or our family. What I want is a book that will tell the truth about us, whether we like it or not. Anything you learn, please feel free to include it if you think it belongs in the book". With that, the groundwork for our working relationship over the next one and half to two or so years was laid.

In the course of developing my family history with Ohiro Oni-Eseleh, I have learned a lot about my family. I have learned that my family history is much richer than I ever knew. I always wondered why nobody ever spoke a kind word about my paternal grandfather, and why I couldn't find a reason to love him as a grandfather that I never knew. Now I know why. He was clearly a man who lived his negatives and represented all of those negatives that existed, and continue to exist, in the African American family. My father made deliberate efforts not to live like his father, and my siblings and I are the better for his choices.

In those days, our ancestors were denied the right to learn how to read and write. In my father's time and case, his family's poverty forced him to drop out of school as a little boy. But he did not give up. As an adult, he decided to make up for his deficits and used the opportunities that he had to return to school, get educated, and wipe ignorance out of his life. If he could do that at his age and with all of the responsibilities in his hands, then most of today's young people can do the same thing if they choose to – especially with all of the avenues now available to make that possible.

While working on this book, I learned that, as the reader will also learn, my father is only two generations removed from slavery, which makes me closer to the era of slavery than I ever imagined. Considering that fact of history, it is greatly remarkable what my parents have done with their lives, and what their generation contributed to the history of this country and its people.

It must have been very horrible for my parents and their own parents and grandparents to be growing up in this country during the time that they did. Often, I wonder what it must have been like for them, and how psychologically strong they must have been to be able to weather the storm of racial prejudice that defined their times. Yet, I feel no resentment toward anyone for the plight of my ancestors. Instead, I feel very proud that they did what they did, and that I had the privilege to have their blood in my veins.

There comes a point in a man's life when he makes a conscious decision to grow up. My grandfather never reached that point but my father and most of my uncles did. As a race, there was a time in the 1960s and 70s when people felt that we African Americans would never grow in the right direction in this country. They saw us go to church daily while we seemed to be going backwards morally. Then other religions and attitudes came and began to appeal to many of our youths. They were new, creative, and offered hope, unity and self-esteem. It was about one's own culture and self-importance, something that our youths had lacked. Our men and women began to challenge themselves to greater heights and to act on those challenges. Now we are looking back and asking ourselves: What happened then and what is happening now? Who are we? Where have the religion, character and strength of our fathers gone?

But we must not spend time wondering. We must rise and move in the direction of progress, taking everyone along regardless of class or religion. African Americans must unite and, like my father, get involved in building our communities. When we do this, the glory of our ancestors will rise again and our people and we cannot fall.

    Sylvester Darnell McClearn
    New Jersey
    July, 2003

Acknowledgements

I have many people to thank for the life that I have had and for the production of this book. There is no way that I could possibly list the names of everyone who has contributed immensely to my blessed life, but they know who they are and I thank them all from the bottom of my heart. The greatest gratitude of course goes to God, without whom there would be no blessings for anyone to write about. He gave me life and gave me a great mother who knew and worshipped the Lord while also working very hard to sustain her family. I am also thankful to God for blessing me with a wonderful wife and great children to share my life with. My wife, Billie, and our children have enriched my life beyond any expectations I ever had, and I give all the glory for that to God.

The United Methodist Church in Newburgh, which I served as pastor for several years, offered me immense opportunities and provided me with a remarkable reservoir of experiences for which I am very grateful. The congregation with which I was blessed in all of my years as a pastor in Newburgh is one that I would never trade for any other congregation on earth. I am indeed grateful to every member of the United Methodist Church in Newburgh for making my job as a pastor as rewarding as it was. To each one of them, I say: I wish you great blessings as you continue to serve our Father in Heaven with the commitment and dedication that I have seen you demonstrate in the years that I have been your pastor.

I owe a depth of gratitude to my sister, Mrs. Cleo Sanders, who provided some of the information that I had forgotten about our family, and to my cousin, Mrs. Geraldine Smith, who was also very helpful with information regarding my father. Geraldine was also the writer's link to Ms. Irene Thomas, my mother's first cousin who provided some invaluable information regarding my parents. Ms. Thomas was almost ninety years old and on her sick bed when she was interviewed for this book, but I was told that her mind was sharp beyond imagination. Unfortunately, she will not see the finished book because she died shortly after she was interviewed for this book. May her dear soul rest in perfect peace.

My gratitude goes to my mother in-law, Ms. Ada Smith, knows no bounds. A remarkable woman, she provided us very detailed information regarding her family, and she spoke of Billie's upbringing with great pride and happiness. I regret that she too will not see this book because she passed away while this book was still being written, but not before she provided an extensive record in her own handwriting. In heaven, I will see her again and I can thank her once again not only for this book, but also for giving birth to a daughter whose life has enriched and blessed mine.

My utmost gratitude goes to my son, Sylvester Darnell, who made this project possible. He not only came up with the idea for the project but also worked very closely with Dr. Ohiro Oni-Eseleh to develop the story. As if that was not enough, he provided all of the finances to fund every stage of the project from the beginning to the end. He is the embodiment of love and foresight and he is the kind of son that most people can only dream of.

Reverend Sylvester McClearn
Newburgh, New York
July 2003

Contents

Introduction 5

Foreword 8

Acknowledgements 12

1. The Beginning 19

2. Portrait Of A Family 31

3. Discovering The McClearn Clan 41

4. Randolph McClearn, Jr.:
   A Human Enigma 54

5. As Close To An Angel As Any Human Can Be 71

6. From Childhood To Labor Force 84

7. Buddy Leaves Home 95

8. New York Receives A Quiet Arrival 105

9. Two Strangers Meet And Unite 118

10. Conversion To A New Life 130

11. Be Fruitful And Multiply, Said The Lord 139

12. When Parents And Children Grow Together 147

13. From Rags To Business Success 163

14. When Disaster Strikes Without Warning 174

15. When You Are Called, You Are Called 184

16. Billie Steps Forward 203

17. Sylvester And Billie: Partners For Life 214

18. Growing Together 226

19. Pillars of Strength 241

20. A Peek At The Next Generation 252

21. Reflections 260

22. A Sermon To End It 266

TRULY BLESSED

THE JOURNEY OF THE
AFRICAN AMERICAN FAMILY
OF SYLVESTER & BILLIE MCCLEARN

ONE

THE BEGINNING

    I imagine standing before a group of children anywhere in the United States of America and saying to them, "I know a man whose name is Reverend Sylvester McClearn. He was born here in the United States in 1936, but not in a hospital. Instead, he was born on a farm." I expect that such announcement would produce surprise, disbelief or even laughter among the children. How could I expect them to believe that there are people in this great country known as the United States of America who were not born in state-of-the-art hospitals, which we now see everywhere across the land? When they realize that I am making a serious point, then they would probably begin to think that this Reverend McClearn must be either a very old man or a very strange man - or both. But the Reverend Sylvester McClearn is neither old nor strange. He is simply an American man whose life exemplifies much of the history, struggles, and values of Black America.

    In my mind's eyes, I can almost see and hear the imaginary children to whom I am speaking, and many other people who are not even young children, ask questions like: Does this Reverend McClearn feel differently from people who were born in hospitals? What does he think about being born on a farm? What was it like for him to live on a farm when he was a kid? How did he get from living on a farm to experiencing adulthood and being in his current position in life? How does someone that was born on a farm, like you say Sylvester was, grow up into a man like he has since become? Did he go to school? Did he have any fun on the farm? What kind of life can a kid possibly have on a farm?

Admittedly, these are some of the questions that I mulled over and over in my own mind while writing this book about the life of Reverend Sylvester McClearn. The Reverend is a man of few words. The information that he provided for this book about his life was volunteered with mixed feelings, which were obvious as he found himself in the position of having to recall so many of his past life experiences. His feelings were largely mixed not only due to the memories and emotions that the telling seemed to bring him, but also because he is a man with almost no interest or desire ever to talk about himself.

Be that as it may, however, Rev. McClearn was able at various points to find some joy in telling his story, evidenced by the smiles that came across his face so many times in several interviews that he did for this book. Often, those interviews were conducted in his office at the United Methodist Church on historic Liberty Street in Newburgh, NY, which Sylvester pastored at the time of the interviews for this book.

Going to meet with the Rev. for an interview, as I did several times, was always like going to a black pentecostal church in years gone by: you knew when you were going in but you were never sure when you would be getting out. The only thing you were sure of was that you would come out of the church more blessed and wiser than when you went in.

Often, when I went to meet with the Reverend, I would come out of my car, which I would always park in the streets because every space in the church parking lot was almost always taken. Then I would walk across the parking lot toward the massive church building that housed not only the sanctuary to the left but also to the raight, a head start program, a gymnasium, and classrooms for after-school programs run by the church. I would walk into the building, through an entrance in the middle of the huge building, turn right, and head for the door with the bold label **"PASTOR'S OFFICE"**.

I would knock on the door that was always slightly open, hear the calming voice of a man from behind the doors who I would always recognize as the Reverend's say "Come In", and I would step into the room. Often, there would be someone in the office meeting with this busy man, but sometimes he would be alone. Whenever he was alone, he was reading something. I would step in and the Rev. would unfailingly say: "Doc., how are you today", "Fine Sir" would be my response, and he would say: "How have you been"? Then he would beckon to a double leather sofa and say: "Please sit down". Then he would get up from his chair behind his desk and sit in a single sofa-type office chair and the interview would begin. But not before I took a quick glance through the office - at the stack of books on his book shelves and the pictures of his wife and him, as well as pictures of some black historical figures.

We would go over my goals, the status of the book, and the Rev's desires, and the interview would begin. I would watch him attempt to remember some pieces of his life story and he would reach for a small address book and give me phone numbers and names of people whose memory might better inform me. Piece by piece, the story of a remarkable man and a remarkable family is laid out, beginning in North Carolina and continuing far away in Newburgh, New York.

There were many things that Sylvester McClearn did not know about his family before work commenced on this book. This is probably not unusual for many people. We often think that we know ourselves well – until we are forced to confront our lives by telling or reflecting on our life stories. In his case, Sylvester could not even remember many events in his childhood – even things that anyone would have expected him to remember. For reasons that may become clear from reading this chapter, he did not even know the exact location of the farm on which he was born. Thanks to information gathered from the research for this book, Sylvester now knows that that farm of his birth was located on Angel Highway.

One of the best-equipped people to provide good and reliable information regarding Sylvester's childhood was her older sister, Cleo Jane McClearn Sanders. God bless her. Mrs. Sanders was able to re-create some of her younger brother's early childhood by relying on her memory, which, one might add, was very clear indeed. Cleo McClearn Sanders provided much of the information in this book that relates to life within the McClearn home during Sylvester's childhood years.

On July 15, 1936, Sylvester McClearn was born on a North Carolina farm to his parents, Randolph and Martha Jean Hooper McClearn. At the time of his birth, there were not as many sophisticated medical systems and facilities such as we now enjoy in the United States. For example, women did not have the kind of prenatal care now widely available to pregnant women across the country. For black women like Sylvester's mother who lived on farm grounds, the social and medical conditions were much worse. Not only were there no hospitals on farm grounds, there were no medical facilities of any kind. Prenatal medical care simply did not exist for people like Martha. She was black, poor, and therefore considered by the mainstream as undeserving.

Instead of hospital maternity wards, midwives frequently assisted women in their homes when it was time for them to deliver. In the area where Sylvester McClearn grew up, there was only one black physician who provided home-based medical care to black people on farms. Even in that case, the doctor's work with his patients was limited mainly to preventive care and other forms of minor medical treatment. Perhaps for logistic reasons, extensive diagnostic and surgical procedures were not part of the services provided to farm dwellers by this or any doctor, nor did the services often include regular inoculations for children.

When a black child was born in those days, his or her first vaccinations occurred at school five or six years later. This, of course, is quite unlike the system we have today, where so much is available in terms of medical care. Considering all of this, it is proper to wonder sometimes how Sylvester and other children like him survived as well as they did.

On the day that Sylvester was born, his mother, Martha, had gone about her usual tasks though she was aware that the time for her to give birth was very near. Like most women in those days, Martha knew her body very well. Since experience is also a great teacher, Martha who had already had children before Sylvester came along knew exactly what her body would feel like when her delivery time came. She didn't need a sonogram or any sophisticated scientific tests to tell her that. Nor would she have had access to any such systems even if she needed them, since she was black and poor.

As a wife and a mother, Martha went about her usual wifely and motherly duties even as the birth of her child got closer and closer. She cooked, cleaned, and fed her children without telling any of them what she felt. She prepared her home and made sure there was enough food to take care of her husband and children for the next few days, which was how long she expected to be resting following the birth of her baby. Along the way, her oldest daughter, Cleo, remained close to her mother providing whatever assistance she could give to her expectant mother.

Cleo had grown to be very close to her mother, and Martha carefully and fondly cultivated that relationship because she believed that she had a responsibility to teach her daughter how to be a woman. Mother and daughter were so close that, like was common in those days, Martha nicknamed her daughter Cleo as "Sister", a name that has stayed with her to this day. Unknown to Martha, Cleo was herself also learning to be a strong black woman like her mother. When the time came for her baby to be born, Martha was able to count on the guidance and assistance of an experienced midwife who had guided several poor black women in the course of delivery over and over again. The child was eventually born, and he was named Sylvester.

It is important to put the period of Sylvester's birth into historical context in order to achieve a clearer understanding of the limits that the little Sylvester and his family, as well as other black children and families like them faced in terms of medical care at the time. Simply put, they were black, and being black invited an untold degree of deprivation in most aspects of American life. Somehow, for the country's white leaders, being a black person born in the United States of America did not quite have the same meaning as being an American. Even if she were rich or middle class, which she wasn't, Mrs. Martha Hooper McClearn could not have walked into just any hospital or any doctor's office to request medical services for herself and her yet unborn son. And even if the McClearn family could have afforded it, which they couldn't, their skin color and socioeconomic status deprived them of easy access to quality health care.

One of the tragedies in our nation today is that many poor African Americans are not faring much better within our current health care system. Even worse, the silver lining that existed in this regard during the era of Sylvester's birth has since become a thing of the past. In those days, there were physicians like the black doctor who were willing to leave the comfort of their offices to seek out and provide services to poor black families like the McClearns.

Today, not even black doctors are generally willing to do that. One of the consequences is that many poor people in the African American community continue to suffer with limited knowledge regarding health issues.

The African American community could benefit from greater access to health care professionals, who are willing and committed to providing diversified health care services in African American communities, even if it means meeting individuals and families where they live.

One may never know how many American men, women and children lived because of the work of the lone black physician who made it his duty to go to the homes off poor fellow Americans to provide them services – even those who lived on farms. That doctor always religiously made the trip past the beautiful brick houses of farm owners and made his way down the dirt roads to the run-down shacks in which the less privileged sharecroppers lived. He knew that he was doing a service, not for money (God knows he wasn't getting his due), but out of a belief that the sharecroppers and their families were human beings that deserved to be treated with some dignity. That doctor was the only professional man that ever treated most of them with any dignity. It is impossible to learn the name of that doctor, but may God bless his soul as well as his descendants.

Rev. McClearn does not remember as many things about his early life as vividly as many people would expect anyone to. I personally expected to get much of my information directly from him when I chose to write this book. As it turned out, he just did not remember very much. It is uncertain why he remembers so little about his own life, but a reasonable speculation is that it has been easier for him not to dwell on most of the events of his life, especially the unpleasant ones. Besides, he is also a man who spent much of his early life growing up and working so hard on becoming a man. In the circumstances, therefore, it is also reasonable to suggest that in the process he neglected to indelibly inscribe in his own memory some of the key aspects of his childhood and some of the significant events that occurred during that time.

I have heard of some successful African Americans who lament the fact that they were so focused on building careers for themselves that they neglected to participate in the Civil Rights struggles that characterized the history of African Americans in this country, especially in the fifties and sixties. What one does not hear of are adults now in their fifties and sixties who have very little or no recollection of that painful period in the United States. Yet, there may well be some of those. Now, I wonder how many African Americans have truly blanked that period out of their minds, for whatever reason, not the least of which could be the pain that such memories can evoke.

Selective memory or inability to recall pertinent painful experiences may occasionally be a useful coping technique. However, I am not exactly sure that it is a good or a bad coping technique in Sylvester's case, since some of the events that occurred during his childhood, and through his adulthood, were of great significance in our nation's history. For example, several significant events were occurring in relation to blacks in the United States in the decades just before and just following the birth of Sylvester McClearn.

For one, his birth occurred at a time when movements that largely became known as "black nationalism" were gathering momentum across the country. This was a period when blacks living in the South still experienced extreme bigotry and lynching as well as segregation that the Southern leaders often justified in the name of God. Very early in the century of Sylvester's birth – actually in 1901 – the Alabama Constitutional Convention met to disenfranchise blacks. J. Thomas Heflin justified inequality as follows: "I believe as truly as I am standing here that God Almighty intended the Negro to be a servant of the white man…"

The United Negro Improvement Association (UNIA), founded by Marcus Garvey in the decade following World War I, led the way in efforts to denounce the bigotry and oppression that blacks suffered, not only in the United States but in various parts of the world at the time. In a speech delivered at Liberty Hall in New York City in 1922, the UNIA laid out it's mission very eloquently, stating as it did, that: "Wheresoever human rights are denied to any group, wheresoever justice is denied to any group, there the UNIA finds a cause. And at this time among all the peoples of the world, the groups that suffer most from injustice, the group that is denied most of those rights that belonged to all humanity, is the black group ...."

Many would argue that this statement remains true to this day, eighty years after it was made. The United States government determined that Marcus Garvey was too hot to handle, and had him deported to Jamaica in 1927. Thirteen years later, he died in obscurity in England.

This country in which blacks had been legally declared as unequal even in the eyes of God, and where people who dared to stand up against the system were either killed or banished in some way, was the same country and world into which Sylvester McClearn was born in 1936.

The farm on which Sylvester McClearn was born was located on Angel Highway in North Carolina. In those days, farms did not have formal addresses, mail boxes, or street numbers like the mailing addresses that we are all now used to. It is proper to wonder how mail was delivered to farm dwellers in those days, considering how much easier identifiable addresses make the jobs of essential service providers. The reality was that black farmers were sharecroppers, and sharecroppers just didn't write a lot of letters in those days, nor did they expect people to write to them. To be able to write or read a letter, you have to be literate, and sharecroppers were overwhelmingly illiterate.

This is not to say that mail never went to the farms at all. They did, but they often went to the white farm owners who of course had friends and family members who would write them. If a sharecroppers had mail, the white farm owner was also much more likely than not to unseal and read the mail, and to decide whether or not to deliver the mail to its rightful owner. More often than not, the mail never got to the black sharecropper to whom the mail actually belonged.

But why would anyone read mail belonging to someone else? That attitude came with the territory of being an oppressor. People who oppress others, like the white farm owners and even today's dictators, often tend to be very suspicious and insecure beings themselves. The tendency is often for such oppressor or dictator to think that a letter that is most certainly innocent may have some unpalatable information about himself. How best to know than to actually read the letter, especially if you believe that your status in life entitles you to do such a thing that would otherwise be considered a fraud! In the circumstances, even several black sharecroppers who could read, and who knew the whereabouts of their family members, often preferred to receive no mail from anyone as the mere ability to read. In addition, any suggestion that a repressed black individual in a lowly position, such as a sharecropper. had some connection with the outside world were often dangerous combinations for which the farmer could be very easily punished.

In those days, farms like the one on which Sylvester was born were known and described by their locations and the names of their owners. Therefore, the appropriate way to refer to the farm of his birth was to describe it simply by its location, namely *"a farm on Angel Highway"*, or by the name of the white family or the white *"Master"* that owned the farm. Since there were many farms on Angel Highway in North Carolina at the time of the Rev's birth, it was by the white owner's name that the farm was most often called.

A farm in those days was for the most part different from what a farm looks like today. The farm on which Sylvester was born was very much like a typical farm in those days. It was a large area surrounded by fields on which cotton, corn, and tobacco were grown. Typically, a narrow dirt road ran through a farm, leading to the rickety shacks that the sharecroppers and their families called home. That dirt road was also the carriage way for the wagons that were used on the farm. It was not meant for cars, and the sharecroppers did not have cars anyway. When it rained, that road and any like it literarily washed out. On either side of the road leading to the homes of the sharecroppers were animal barns and a well from which Sylvester's family and other sharecroppers drew water to drink and to wash their clothes.

Far across the fields, and far from the life that the sharecroppers lived, one could see the beautiful homes of the white farm owners. Those were mainly brick houses that served as a reminder of the quality of life that the sharecroppers and their children could not have. In contrast, they lived in run down shacks that had no beauty whatsoever, and nobody took any time to repair any damage to those shacks whenever there was one. And in any case, a sharecropper rarely stayed long enough on any farm for him and his family to have the opportunity to put their own personal touches on the homes.

The farm where Sylvester was born still exists but it has undergone such remarkable changes that it is certainly nothing now like it was then. Clearly, it does not even carry the same name anymore by which it was known when Sylvester was just a kid. This is the case because the ownership of the farm and the land has changed hands several times since his childhood and mechanized farming has taken the place of the oppressive manual labor by which the McClearn family was victimized. The farm remains located on the road that was called Angel Highway, which runs between Smithfield and Raleigh in Johnson County, North Carolina.

Of course at the same time that these injustices were occurring here in the United States, bigotry and hate were also being promoted in Europe against a people that had been selected by Hitler for oppression and destruction. Five years after Sylvester's birth, World War II began – a war that he vaguely remembers. That War of course ended when he was eleven years old. Although he was very young at the time of the War, Sylvester believes that he would feel much better if he could recall any events related to the War, since he was alive when they occurred. His position makes sense, considering that World War II was and remains so highly significant that it will forever remain a strong reference point because of the great good that the World War II accomplished for humanity, as it saw the triumph of good over evil.

Even if Sylvester McClearn was a little older during the War, his lack of ability to recall the War period might still be understandable considering that African Americans in this country were fighting for their own survival at the same time. In such circumstances, events occurring in a far away land might not have been of great significance to young African Americans at the time who were busy trying to survive racism and oppression here at home. This was especially so for those, like Sylvester McClearn, who could not even join the military to escape their circumstances because they were too young to serve in the military. Consequently, they had to get up everyday and confront their lives anew. This is rarely an easy task for anyone whose life is replete with challenges and experiences, some of which are not so pleasant.

For any African American male or female that was born in the same era as Reverend McClearn, it is impossible to have lived in the United States without one's life and experiences being affected more by influences in the micro American society than in the macro world of which the United States is just a part. Even if one does not feel the negative influences all around us in this country, the reality is that they exist, and they are powerful. For example, an African American does not have to have directly experienced racism to be affected by the influences of racism. Racism is both insidious and pervasive. Whether we believe it or not, it is sometimes the reason why one black man and his family may be subjected to an eternity on a wretched farm while another man of a similar stature and age, but of a different race, occupies the position of lord over others in the same environment.

Certainly, events of national importance can always be studied from textbooks, but learning about one's life and self is usually something that is not generally known to occur in the same fashion. For this reason, the task of writing about Reverend Sylvester McClearn is a remarkable learning process both for the writer and the subject. One hopes that the picture that emerges from this process is one that is clear, not only to readers but also to Sylvester McClearn himself.

TWO

PORTRAIT OF A FAMILY

By the time of his birth, Sylvester McClearn's parents already had six children - three males and three females. His oldest sibling was Randolph, Jr., named after his father. Being Randolph, Jr. himself, the older Randolph McClearn, Jr. was apparently unaware that he could not name his own son Junior as well. So he did. The second child was Thomas; followed by the first girl, Cleo Jane, fondly known as *Sister*, then Estelle Magnolia, who intensely disliked being called Magnolia. She had been named Magnolia in honor of her father's sister who was so named. Since she didn't like the name, Estelle Magnolia was succeeded in keeping it out of most people's awareness by sticking with Estelle. The fifth child in this McClearn home was Leroy, after who was Lizzie Mae.

Sylvester was number seven in the family's birth order. Although his parents named him Sylvester, his entire family preferred to call him "Buddy" (after his uncle Buddy), and Sylvester is still fondly called "Buddy" in the family to this day. This is why he will also be referred to over and over as Buddy in this book. Clearly, this was a family that tried to maintain close ties between generations within the family. This is obvious in the way that people were named in this family – after members of the generation before.

Needless to say that Buddy comes from a very large family, at least by today's standards. Yet, the above list does not represent the entire McClearn family. Seven more were born after Buddy. The first of the seven was Dorothy, who was given that name by the uncle that the McClearn children fondly called Uncle Buddy. Unfortunately, Dorothy died only two days after she was born. The ninth of the McClearn children was Ella Louise and the tenth was Gertha Lee. After Gertha Lee came Joe Lewis, Roosevelt, Jesse Earl, and Alice Gray, in that order.

It is almost unimaginable in today's world that anyone would even conceive of having as many as fourteen children, as Mr. and Mrs. Randolph McClearn did in those days. It is even difficult to imagine having thirteen brothers and sisters, even from more than one marriage. Yet, it is true that despite its size, this McClearn family was not even the largest family in their neighborhood when Buddy was a child. While growing up, the things that Buddy thought about were often not unlike things that most children in his situation would have been thinking about. So too are the things that he did not think about. For example, as a child, he never wondered how his parents managed to care for so many children, though he wonders now that he is much older That makes great sense, since worrying about such complex tasks as child rearing is really not what children generally do.

Admittedly, Sylvester now sometimes wonders how it was possible for all of his thirteen siblings and himself were able to live in as much peace and harmony as they did in their home as children. This is not to say that there were no arguments or any fighting between siblings. It would be unnatural to make that claim. Of course there were conflicts, as there usually are between siblings, but conflicts did not define existence in the McClearn home. There were many more times than not that Buddy and his siblings were very happy together. These are the times that Sylvester remembers very vividly.

The McClearn family was very poor, but poverty was definitely not unique to them. Of course most African American stories are often replete with tales of poverty at some point in time, and accomplishments that are significant because they tend to represent a rise through periods of inexplicable hardships. The sad fact about this reality is that those stories are often true, and it was certainly true for the McClearn family. In fact, abject poverty was commonplace across the Southern part of the United States in those days, and blacks more than whites were frequently the victims. In such a situation, a child was born into poverty and grew up in poverty.

Society, and perhaps even his own family members, expected an individual from such a family background to grow into a poor adult. The only exception was if the individual had a lucky break or found the right combination of actions to help him break his family's cycle of poverty within which he himself was very often stuck. Reverend McClearn's family was just part of the norm rather than the exception for Southern blacks at the time. Blacks have never had the benefit of easy access to wealth. They did not then, and do not now. In the circumstances, young Buddy had very little or no chance of making it out of the trap of poverty.

The fact that Buddy's parents had so many children and had no money would make them very easy targets for condemnation in today's society. Clearly, they were poor people with many children that had to be raised. Poverty and parenting a high number of children are not a good mix in today's world, nor were they when the McClearn parents had their fourteen children. Be that as it may be, the family in which Buddy was born and raised deserve understanding, not condemnation. This is crucial considering that the actions of times past are not always logical within the context of today's thinking but that does not mean they were foolish actions taken by foolish people.

Thanks to the circumstances of his birth and upbringing, Sylvester is much less judgmental than most people who have and express opinions regarding poverty and the poor. He is well aware that people often tend to judge the poor who have no real knowledge of the individual circumstances of the people on whom they pass judgment. Nor do they know what poverty feels like, since most of them have never experienced poverty and understand it only as an academic concept. But poverty is much more than an academic issue. It is a real-life state experienced by living people.

Sylvester knows that, even with very little or no knowledge of what life was like for poor people when he was growing up, many people today often have a field day blaming poverty in families like his on the choice of the parents to have large families. Undoubtedly, there are people in today's American society who would write off Randolph and Martha as a careless and unreasonable couple who continued to have children despite knowing they did not have the means to provide freely for the children they were bringing to life.

It is difficult to argue against this suggestion, considering that it seems to be based on some humanitarian interest. Yet, as reasonable as it may appear to be, it is a position that must be scrutinized because it is both unreasonable and lacking in understanding of the human and historical circumstances of the period. To understand the circumstances of the McClearn family, it is important to put the period of their family development in American historical context. Certainly, the times were different, and the circumstances of the time dictated the choices that many people made regarding childbirth.

As has been stated in Chapter One, Randolph McClearn, Jr., who was Sylvester's father, was a sharecropper who worked on farms owned by white men. That was the norm for black people across the Southern United States at the time. White men owned the farms and black men, along with their spouses and children, lived and worked on the farms. The common practice was to have one big family to live on, and work one farm. The white farm owners strongly desired black sharecroppers with large families to work for them.

Consequently, the greater the number of children a sharecropper had, the greater his opportunities for employment by white farm owners. The logic was obvious: sharecroppers with large families were more marketable in the farm labor force because having large families meant that they could perform more extensive farm tasks for the white farmer than sharecroppers who had smaller families. The motivation for African American sharecropping men, like their African ancestors on the African Continent, was to have large families to increase their chances of employment and to increase the number of hands that were available to till the farms.

This is exactly the reason why so many Africans of times past became polygamists. Since they depended largely on farming for their livelihood, they also learned the importance of having many hands to till their land and grow their crops. The way to acquire those hands was very often to marry more than one wife because that increased the number of children that they could have, and decreased the amount of time that it would take to have as many children as they desired. Although the African American sharecroppers were operating in an American society that did not sanction polygamy, they were quite aware of the need to survive efficiently within the realities of their lives and time.

For these African American men, therefore, the need for many children was often a product of a need for survival in a sharecropping system that was harsh, cruel, and hard. By no means was it a sign or product of irresponsibility. Some people may argue that the choice to have so many children was a function of illiteracy. That is indeed a very accurate assessment, but we must remember that most of those able-bodies African American would not be sharecroppers in the first place, had they been educated. At the same time, most of them might be educated had they been given the opportunity to do so by an American system that operated on a desire to keep African Americans at the bottom of the social ladder.

Truth be told that the failings of African American sharecroppers were really not as much a failure of morally frail men as they were the failings of a society and system that rejected some of its own. For a large part of his life, Sylvester (Buddy) and his family were part of that rejected bunch – by virtue of the fact that they were subjected to a life of poverty on Southern farms where they received treatment that was very often undignified. But even on those farms, the course of nature, part of which is the miracle of childbirth, was alive for the McClearn family. The evidence is that Buddy was not the only one of his parents' children that was born on a farm. All of his siblings were as well.

Regardless of what one thinks about life in a very large

and poor family, like the one that Buddy came from, it is important to check out the facts from the people who lived that life. For Rev. McClearn, the memories are sweet, although his feelings about his upbringing are deep and very mixed. In his words: "My siblings enriched my life, and I would never trade any of them for anything... And despite our poverty, we were able to experience a lot of love, fun and happiness in our home". This is largely because African American homes have historically been warm and full of love, regardless of what else might be going on outside the immediate family system.

It is impossible for Sylvester to forget what life was like in his family while living a poor life on the farm. For one thing, the McClearn family life went contrary to the conventional thought of what life must be like for poor people. When anyone walked into the McClearn home, the picture that greeted the guest was never one of gloom. Even when they were hungry, Buddy and his brothers and sisters had been raised to be polite to one another and to whoever came to visit. Although they had very little by way of material, Martha ensured that her children were allowed to have in their home any healthy thing that helped them to take their minds off their socioeconomic situation. In this case, that meant pets, cheap toys, and laughter.

For a pet, the McClearn family had a goat that they named "Billy", as well as a big black cat, named Tom, which they all loved and played with, except their father Randolph, Jr. who was by no means a cat lover. He liked dogs instead, and they had one. Although he never spent much time in his home, Randolph seemed to have some emotional investment in the dog, evidenced by the fact that he often seemed to enjoy having the dog around whenever he was home. The cat did not have equal privilege with the dog as far as Randolph Jr. was concerned.

With the pets and each other, the McClearn children and their mother were able to ensure that there was so much to do in their home, and the children kept themselves busy despite their family's socioeconomic conditions. They had fun raising cows, chickens, hogs, and several other animals. They were able to create fun out of everything that they did, including their frequently unexpected relocations from one farm to another, which is discussed elsewhere in this book.

In retrospect, the fun activities that the McClearn children had in ther rickety farm shack might not have been gorgeous or expensive, but they did serve a purpose for this family. For one thing, they helped to divert the children's focus from their otherwise miserable circumstances. The fact that this was a large family also helped immensely, because it meant that there was always something going on in their home and their lives as individuals.

How poor could the McClearn family really be, considering the "good times" that have just been discussed in relation to this family, which has already been described here as a very poor one? To be sure, Sylvester has very strong feelings about his family's poverty and he does not make excuses for it. Nor is it the responsibility of a child, anyway, to move his family out of poverty. And Sylvester does not go out of his way to pretend that he came from a middle-class family. In any case, he is not a man who would ever claim or lead anyone to believe that he is who or what he is not. Instead, he is very conscious of the family that he came from, and he is very proud of that family, but he has not allowed his family's poverty to entrap and define every aspect of his existence. But, how poor could they really be?

Perhaps the point should be made that, when he speaks of his own personal joy in his family home despite their poverty, Sylvester is in fact referring to an emotional state that is not dependent on material possessions. Indeed, poverty made life very difficult for the McClearn family in which Buddy was born and raised. Consider this: This family did not even have regular beds to sleep on because Randolph, Jr. and Martha could not afford to buy beds. So the only choice that young Buddy and his brothers and sisters had was to sleep on straw beds, which frequently attracted bugs that would bite them very harshly whenever the straw beds were wet.

The family could not even afford mattresses for their

straw beds. Instead, the ever-so thoughtful and creative Martha made the improvisations that her family used as mattresses. To avoid the bug bites, Martha arranged for her family to sleep sometimes on cotton layers on the porch. Several other basic necessities were actually luxuries for the McClearn family. For example, they were so poor that they could not afford shoes in any variety. Therefore, they would wear the same pairs of shoes every day. Socks were completely out of their budget. In place of socks, they would cut sleeves off their sweaters and make socks out of them. This practice applied to everyone in the family except, perhaps, Buddy's father, a man who was forever conscious of his appearance and made sure to dress well, even if no one else in his family looked as well.

Anyone would expect that someone living on a farm would have food in abundance. That is a reasonable expectation, but it wasn't the case for the McClearn family that lived on North Carolina farms. Due to their bad financial circumstances, the family did not always have plenty of food to eat. So they ate a lot of pickles, fish, and corn - foods that Buddy really didn't care for, even in those days. It was rarely the kind of food that he and his family would have chosen to eat, but it was food nonetheless, and they ate it and were usually filled.

In a family as large as the McClearns, it is natural to wonder what the children were like while they were all growing up. And seeing the type of man that Sylvester is, it is definitely impossible to wonder what he was like as a child. For him, this is sometimes a difficult question, mainly because he does not generally enjoy putting the focus of attention on himself. His older siblings describe his childhood in several ways, but all positive. For some, he was a quiet and respectful kid with a great sense of responsibility, even at a young age. He describes his own childhood character in the following words: "I was never a mean-spirited child, and I never engaged in fights with my peers, unless I really had to defend myself against attack. I was never a problem for my family. Instead, it was very important to me to ensure that I only did things about which my family would be proud".

As the reader will find through this book, Buddy's desire to do his family proud took him places and through situations that would help shape him into the kind of man that he became and still is. He was determined and very ambitious in his quest to help lift his family up from the economic situation in which no one in the family was either very happy or very comfortable.

Rev. McClearn is one man who will never forget the circumstances within which he grew up. As a result, he cannot help but frequently ponder the damage that poverty tends to heap on a family. He believes that poverty robs a family of its sense of priorities. He should know. In the distressful circumstances of poverty, a family can become suspicious, frustrated or desperate and begin to perceive of potential opportunities and responsibilities as obstacles.

This is often worse when the family either lacks leadership or has to also confront the consequences of alcoholism or other substance abuse. For example, a child that needs to be nurtured gets to be perceived as a problem instead of a responsibility, and societal or systemic requirements begin to be perceived with suspicion – as the family places much of its focus on the addicted family member. To the poor family, such requirements take on the same identity as problems instead of opportunities and/or potential solutions to the family's obvious crisis. From that, the hope is that the children will arise and soar above and beyond heights that their parents ever thought was reachable. Often, that hope never materializes but sometimes, it does. But it is often that hope that makes it possible for strong women like Martha and children like "Sister" and Buddy to wake up every morning believing that the new day will be better than the one before.

This may be the best way to explain why, in spite of the McClearn family's circumstances, Buddy was independent even as a child. This should by no means be interpreted as an indictment on his parents. In fact, Buddy will be the first to tell anyone that his mother did the best that she could in the circumstances in which the family found itself. He and all of his siblings felt that they had a responsibility to work and assist their family both morally and financially. This was just as well, since they had no uncles, aunts or cousins in any position to be of help to them. For young Buddy, all he knew was that his family needed money to meet its needs, and he felt a need to contribute his quota. Nobody asked him what he did so long as he brought money home to help the family. Thank God, he knew enough to earn money through legitimate means.

Clearly, Reverend Sylvester McClearn knows firsthand what poverty can do to anyone because his family lived a life of poverty when he was growing up. He admits that he often finds himself wondering a lot about the causes of poverty and the mechanism that drives it. After so many years of research into this subject, a few things are certain. First, the causes of poverty are rarely as simplistic as the sound-bite explanations that one hears regularly on television and radio talk shows. Secondly, the cause of poverty is not the same for every person or every family or group. Thirdly, poverty is like a terrible sentence on the lives of innocent children.

Social commentators cannot be right when they claim that poverty is entirely a function of laziness, mismanagement, or choice. Neither are they always accurate when they claim that the only explanation for poverty within the black community in America is the systemic unfairness that exists in our society. While one cannot deny that the degree of injustice toward blacks is depressing and sometimes overwhelming, that does not completely explain what Sylvester McClearn saw and felt growing up. For example, despite the oppression that blacks experienced as a people, young Buddy saw some black people who lived very well. They might not have been as wealthy as their white counterparts, but they did not possess the same degree of deprivation that was his family's lot.

THREE

DISCOVERING THE MCCLEARN CLAN

Sylvester McClearn does not recall ever meeting his grandparents. If he did, it must have been when he was very young. The chances are better that he never did. However, he knew his parents quite well and remembers them as great contrasts in many ways. He is not the only person who remembers them in this way. In fact, most people who knew them do. But this is a matter for upcoming chapters.

Not very much is known about the history and evolution of the McClearn family, but the little that is known is highly significant because of what it means for the African American family in the United States. Without a doubt, the McClearn family came from slavery, which means that McClearn was not the birth name of the first patriarch of the family. To understand how the family got its name and evolved into its current state, one must engage in an effort to understand some African American history and learn how a common historical thread runs through so many African American families.

In the case of the McClearn family name, historical records are available at the Family History Centers across the United States, including Wilmington, North Carolina. From those records, we know that the McClearn name originated from Scotland, with genealogical data in that country dating back to about 1610. The original McClearn name and family became a part of the United States as a consequence of immigration. One Daniel McLaurin II was married to Margaret McLaurin in Scotland. Following Margaret's death either in 1785 or 1786, Mr. Daniel McLaurin emigrated from Scotland to Wilmington, North Carolina and later settled in Marlboro County, North Carolina where one of his sons, John, was already established. Descendants and relatives of the McLaurins continue to live to this day in several states, including North and South Carolina, Florida, Mississippi, and Texas.

Another McLaren emigrated from Scotland to Stewarts–ville, near Laurinburg, North Carolina after surviving the battle of Culloden Moor in Scotland in April 1746. Born in 1724, this man, Duncan McLaren, died in 1809 and his relatives and descendants continue to reside in North Carolina, Virginia, West Virginia, Kentucky, Tennessee, and other Southern States.

It is unclear if the McLaurin and McLaren that came from Scotland were related, although it is assumed that they might have been – notwithstanding the different spellings of the name that is evident here. That is not a mistake. The fact that their last name was spent differently does not mean that they were not from the same family.

There are in fact ten variations of the McClearn name, and most of them descended from the same source. Even within Sylvester's father's family of origin, there is more than one variation of the family name, as will be discussed shortly. Those variations are follows: McLaren, McLaurin, McLaurine, McLarin, McLaran, McClaren, McClaran, McClaron, McLearen, and McClearn.

It is uncertain if Sylvester's family came from Daniel McLaurin II or any of his descendants or from Duncan McLaren or any of his descendants. There are, however interesting parallels to consider. First, when he came to the United States, Daniel McLaurin II stayed in Wilmington, North Carolina, where a huge segment of Reverend McClearn's family still resides and calls home. Secondly, when Duncan McLaren came to the United States from Scotland, he settled near Lauringburg, North Carolina. This is significant because some of the members of Rev. McClearn's extended family in North Carolina trace their origins to Lauringburg. They also maintain fairly extensive family relationships in that area. Thirdly, all of Reverend McClearn's family members in the Wilmington, North Carolina area spell their name McLaurin, as in Daniel McLaurin II who lived in that area.

There is a dimension to the McClearn (or McLaurin or McLaren) family story that deserves at least minimal discussion in this book at this time. It is the fact that there is even a suggestion or consideration of the possibility of any kind of relationship between a white family and a black family in the United States. This is clearly one of the major areas in which the social history of white America comes in direct contact with the black McClearn (or McLaurin or McLaren) family history. This is also the point at which all Americans – black or white - must stop to consider their past. This exercise is necessary because of the significance of that past for our own understanding of us as individuals and as a nation.

Again, Sylvester's family name came from slavery. In other words, they were slaves. While working on this book, I had the pleasure of interviewing an eighty-eight year old woman who knew the McClearn (or McLaurin) family well. Ms. Irene Thomas was the daughter of Fannie, one of the older sisters of Randolph McClearn Jr, who was Sylvester's father. When I interviewed Ms. Thomas, she was ill and frail, but her mind was extremely sharp, and I would later learn that she was always a repository of information pertaining to both sides of the Reverend's family. She could do this because, not only did she have a great memory and not only was she the niece of Randolph II (that is, Randolph McClearn, Jr.), she was also the first cousin of Sylvester's mother Martha. The information that she provided for this work was invaluable.

It is a fact of American history that black slaves were routinely made to give up their original last names and take on the names of their masters. Even after the slaves became free they maintained those names for several reasons. One, by the time of their freedom, they had gone through a few generations and lost any possibility of sustained memory or knowledge of their families' original names and/or culture. Secondly, even if they knew what their families' original names were, most of the freed slaves did not know how to go about effecting desired changes to the names. Thirdly, the joy and stress of being free and having to learn so many things about society produced sufficient survival pressure without having to add other "little" tasks like changing a name. As a result, African Americans have gone through generations of their history, carrying names and identities that are vestiges of slavery.

Sylvester's family is one such family. Whether it is spelled McLaurin or McClearn, or McLaren (and all of these variations do in fact exist even within Sylvester's extended family), one of the most important thing to note is that they are all consequences of the family's experience with slavery. During slavery, Sylvester's family, just like most African American families, was stripped of its original name, identity and culture, and what they currently have were imposed upon them. Like most African Americans, none of the living members of the McClearn family remembers what the family's original name was, although some of them in North Carolina remember some of the African cultural practices that they learned from their mothers who learned same from their own parents.

When slavery ended, the McClearn family kept the name (believed to be McLaurin) that it acquired from slavery. As the family evolved, the variations to their name also developed. The three main variations today in Sylvester's family name are McLaurin, McClearn and McLaren. Over the years, the McClaurin and McClearn sides of the family have largely argued about what the correct spelling should be, and which variation is original.

It is also interesting to study how the existing variations developed. It occurred through a process that requires no long, in-depth analysis. Simply, white people in America, or anywhere else, were never interested in the actual spelling of the name of any black person and they could get away with any spelling that they entered for anyone since black people were largely uneducated. The norm for those white people, who were also mostly uneducated, was to spell a name the way they heard it.

The following scene was played out over and over again by African Americans interacting with white folks in this country: The black American individual (usually male) went to apply for a job before a white man; the white man asked him what his name was; and the black man responded with his name. Unable to spell the name correctly, the white man spelled it exactly as he believed he heard it. The only problem for that moment was that what the white man spelled was really not the accurate spelling of what he actually heard, but it became the black man's name for that time. Unfortunately, it also became the name of future generations in that one black man's family as one generation after another was born with a family name that had been inadvertently (but now officially) changed by one white man several years ago.

This is exactly what happened in the McClearn (or McLaurin) family. It is interesting that all members of the family spell their last name as McLaurin except for Randolph McClearn II and two of his other siblings who, like Randolph II, moved away from North Carolina and resided in Washington, D.C. Naturally, the descendants of Randolph II (like the Reverend) and the descendants of those two siblings are the ones in the family who now spell their names the same way that their own fathers had them spelled - McClearn and McLaren.

Randolph II was a very uneducated man and one of the ways in which he was victimized by his illiteracy was in his name. Without formal western education, he did not know how to spell his last name, or even his first name. Therefore, he, like some of his other siblings accepted their name as it was spelled by whatever white man they were dealing with.

What is in a name? And to what degree did this little name switch affect the identities of African American individuals and families in this country? The story of the impact and meaning of names in African American life is best told by the children of William McLaurin of Wilmington, North Carolina who was the uncle of Sylvester and his father's brother. Named William at birth, Mr. McLaurin acquired the nickname "Duncan" by which he became known to everyone in the community. During the births of his own children, the midwives who made entries in their birth certificates identified the children's father as "Duncan McLaurin" instead of William McLaurin, which was his real name. One of the interesting things about this story is that those midwives were not always white. Instead, some of them were black women who knew Mr. McLaurin well in the community, but knew him as "Duncan". To this day, William "Duncan" McLaurin's children's birth certificates identify their father as "Duncan", a name that was clearly not given to him at birth.

Several years ago, Mr. Robert McLaurin, then in his sixties, went to the Office of Vital Statistics to have his birth certificate replaced. They were unable to find the required records with the information he initially provided them - until they asked him and he responded in the affirmative that his father was Duncan McLaurin. This, clearly, is a story that is being told and re-told across the United States and it has everything to do with the impact of slavery on African American history and life in this country.

Sylvester comes from a long line of people with a tremendous history. There is still a remarkable degree of self-discovery that needs to occur in the family, largely because of the existence of missing links that need to be bridged. This is a huge family in which gaps have developed through the years, but it is also a family that is blessed with a great number of people who are very open and willing to develop relationships with one another. For anyone who wonders how big this family really is, read on. Before you do, however, you should be informed that Shiloh Missionary Baptist Church in Wilmington, North Carolina has at least fifty young and old McLaurins in its congregation, and that is not the only church in that town that has McLaurins in its membership. The Union Baptist Church is another.

The Reverend's grandparents were Randolph and Florence McLaurin who had nine children, including Randolph, Jr. – Sylvester's father. The children of Randolph, Sr. and Florence McLaurin were born in the following order: J.W., who was nicknamed "Brooks" because he worked for several years in a produce company, called Brooks; Lola; Fannie; Cora; Elliot; Betsie; Tina; Curly; Randolph Jr.; and William, who was nicknamed "Duncan".

Sylvester's father and all of his brothers and sisters listed here have passed on, but they leave behind many living children and grand and great grandchildren who now reside in various parts of the country. A few reside Overseas and some have served the United States extensively in various capacities. Some of these will be discussed shortly.

J.W. had no children, and Curly had a son and a daughter. J.W., Curly, Tina and Cora eventually moved to Washington, DC where they lived until they died. Except for J.W. who had no children, all of these siblings raised their children in Washington, DC. Lola had eleven children and Fannie had fourteen children. One of Fannie's children, Melvina is now an eighty-six year old woman who, along with her sister Ruth and some of her brothers, continue to reside in the Leland, North Carolina neighborhood famously known as McLaurin Hill. That was the neighborhood in which Randolph II and his siblings were born. The significance of that neighborhood to the McClearn-McLaurin family history, and indeed African American history, is discussed in some detail in the next chapter of this book. William McLaurin had ten children, and Randolph Jr. and his wife, Martha Hooper McClearn, had fourteen children including Sylvester.

Sylvester's children have hundreds of cousins that they have never known or even heard of. This is one fact of their family's history that they will all learn about from reading this book. For example, many of the cousins are football fans, but they never knew that the Michael McClearn of Newburgh, New York who was drafted by Cleveland Browns and played for the Washington Redskins was not just a great football player but is also their cousin.

From Duncan's line of the family alone, there are tens of children, grandchildren and great grandchildren who know very little or nothing about their other cousins. The story is the same with most of the McClearn and McLaurin cousins residing in various parts of the country. Just attempt to do the calculation from the the Duncan and Randolph II lines alone: Duncan and his wife had ten children who now have several children and grandchildren of their own. Randolph II and Martha had fourteen children who also now have several children and grandchildren of their own. Then attempt to add up all of these children and grandchildren. The number that you will come up with will be just plainly amazing.

Take a look at William "Duncan" McLaurin's lineage: He and his wife gave birth to ten children who gave birth to other children as follows:

William: He served the United States in the Airforce for several years and settled in Brooklyn, New York almost thirty years ago, following his retirement from the Force. He has three children.

Alonzo: He has two children, both of whom live in Wilmington, North Carolina.

Robert: He is a highly respected community and church leader in Wilmington, North Carolina. For decades, he owned a very successful business (a store), but his community service remains unparalleled. From his own resources, he serves free meals to the poor in that community to which he is a great blessing. He has seven children, five of whom live in Philadelphia. Two reside in Wilmington, North Carolina.

Thomas: He was the fourth black police officer enlisted into the Wilmington Police Department since Reconstruction. His enlistment occurred in 1963 and he retired from the Police Department in 1985 after a distinguished career that spanned twenty-three years. Then took up a position in the Security Department of New Hanover Hospital, where he also retired in 1995 after ten years of great service. He has five sons and two daughters.

Geraldine: She had a remarkable career as a nurse for twenty-seven years – until 1994 and is enjoying her retirement in Wilmington. She has two sons, Johnnie Laval Smith and Vernon Pierre Smith, both of whom reside in Wilmington. Vernon Pierre maintains a professional career at Dow Corning.

Donald: Died in 1994.

Sarah lives in Wilmington. She has three biological and two adopted children. Four of her children live in Wilmington while one resides in a different North Carolina town, where he is on the management staff of MCI Worldcom.

Kenneth: He was the first black principal of a senior high school in Wilmington, North Carolina. After serving in that position for several years, he retired only to return to public service years later. In 1975, he became the first black City Councilman in Wilmington and won re-election by sixty-six per cent of the votes. His entry into politics was not really by design. He had gone in to complete the term of a man that had died in office as a Councilman. Then he got elected in a general election following the end of his term. Altogether, Kenneth McLaurin served in the City Council for seven years and believes that he would not enjoy being in politics today because he would rather perceive of himself as a servant than as a king. Kenneth is back working as a high school principal, this time in South Carolina. He has one son, who resides in Kenya, where he works for an American company. That son is now married to a woman from Kenya, and they have one child.

Evelena has no children. She resides in Wilmington, North Carolina.

Gloria also resides in Wilmington and has three biological children and one adopted. One of her children, Cheryl, had some contact with Reverend McClearn while she was studying for her Master's degree in Psychology at Boston University, but she has never had any contact with the Reverend's children.

To get a sense of how large the McClearn (McLaurin) family is, one should note that the above list relates only to one line of the family and, as has been stated, that there are also several grandchildren in the lives of the children of family members listed above. In addition, the contributions that the McClearn (McLaurin) family has made to this country go way beyond what has been stated above. For example, Jesse, son of Randolph II and Martha, who is also Sylvester's younger brother, served in the United States Military from 1965 to 1969. The son of Randolph Jr's nephew, named Leo, not only served the United States with honor but was also killed in Vietnam while fighting on behalf of the United States. Therefore, if the discussion is ever about an American family that has taken more from this country than it has ever given, let it be known that that is a discussion that does not apply to the McLaurin (McClearn) family.

As has been stated already, the McLaurin family lived in a place still famously known as McLaurin Hill in Leland, North Carolina. That was indeed the official name until a white man by the name of Butler moved into that neighborhood. The home into which he moved still stands today as the first house to the left on that road as you pull in from the direction of Wilmington. Once Butler moved in, the name of the neighborhood was officially changed to Butler Road, after him. Although that change occurred a long time ago, the area is still popularly known in Leland, North Carolina by its real name, McLaurin Hill.

It is on McClaurin Hill (or Butler Road, as it is officially known) that Randolph II and all of his siblings were born. His uncle, James, also lived there until his death. James had five children - Nora, Annie, Lizzie, Clara, and Booster, all of who have also since died. McLaurin Hill is a vast area in Leland, though it would seem that it has become quite small largely because of the social networks that have evolved there. Due to the historically deep family relationships that have been built in McLaurin Hill over the years, nearly everyone who lives there now is related. What this means for young people growing up now in McLaurin Hill is that they have to go outside of the area to date or marry. The people in McLaurin

Hill are all parents; uncles, aunts, nieces, nephews and cousins of one another, and therefore all have family relationships with Reverend McClearn.

In years gone by, McLaurin Hill was a wooded area and everyone in the family had fields on which they grew food and catered for farm animals. Randolph II was born on one of those fields. Today, McLaurin Hill has several houses, all owned by members of the family. The field on which Randolph McClearn Jr. was born now has a beautiful brick house built on it, owned by the Leo's son. Across from this is another beautiful house that is owned by another one of Leo's sons. Then to the immediate east of that house is situated the McLaurin Family Cemetery, located on Leo's Drive – named after the nephew of Randolph II.

The McLaurin family had a remarkable degree of land wealth that they received at the end of slavery. Some members of the family proceeded over the years to do a great deal of community good with what they owned. For example, James McLaurin, the Reverend's great uncle, donated the land on which a church called Hooper Chapel was first built. That church actually still sits on that land. Subsequently, white people deceived various members of the McLaurin family into signing bogus contracts for small loans and succeeded in stealing much of the family land from them. This was of course a very easy thing to do, since so many of the McLaurin/McClearn family members at the time were illiterate.

Geraldine Smith, who is the daughter of Duncan, recalls her mother telling her that a member of the family once bought a car but was unable to make his payments regularly. As a consequence, his white creditor took from him and his family several acres of land that they owned. Of course that was not a fair trade, considering that the value of his debt was very highly unequal to what he was dispossessed of. But stories like that were rampant in those days, and it is not just a McClearn family story. Instead, it speaks to the plight of African Americans in this country - including the American history that they have had to live.

In terms of the general African American history as it relates to the loss of material that they suffered at the hands of white people in this country, one thing has been different in the case of the McLaurin family. Younger generations in the family have fought back. Using the legal system against the white establishment that oppressed their families before their own time, members of the McLaurin family that remained in Leland have sued scored tremendous legal victories against the establishment. Although they have not been awarded any monies, they have succeeded in regaining an estimated five hundred acres. Although this is less than half of much more than one thousand acres that the white establishment is believed to have stolen from this family, the victories are highly significant indeed.

These legal victories have tended to re-define relationships in the larger McLaurin family. For example, those who stayed behind exclude from the gains the other McLaurins (or McClearns) whose parents or grandparents moved away from Leland for other places several years ago. Even those who live less than thirty minutes drive away in Wilmington are excluded from gaining from the benefits of these victories. On their part, none of these other McLaurins/McClearn is asking to be included, or unhappy about their exclusion. Instead, they are clear that they expect nothing from the victories. They are just very happy for their family members in Leland, and for what the victories mean for the memory of the family's ancestors. The Wilmington part of the family has lived in Wilmington for sixty-eight years and has done very well. So have most of the others, including the Reverend and his siblings, whose sides of the family moved to other parts of the country.

The McClearn family is very large and members are now spread across the South and Northeast United States. It is believed that some of them have in fact intermarried over the years, without knowing that they were related.

In 1998 for example, the wedding of a young couple in Philadelphia was almost put off when they learned that their families may have originated from the same McLaurin family of North Carolina. One of the two young couple was the child of Robert McLaurin, the son of Duncan. Following a period of uncertainty and research, the older people advised that the wedding should proceed, and it did.

THOUGHTS:

A lot of damage was done to the African American family by slavery here in America. The scattering of family members and the destruction of family cohesiveness are just two of the many lingering and unforgettable consequences that slavery heaped on the African American people. Regardless of the victories that African Americans may win in the corporate world or in the legal and sociopolitical arenas, the damage to the African American cultural identity will forever remain immeasurable. Sylvester McClearn's family was not spared the impact.

FOUR

RANDOLPH MCCLEARN, JR: A HUMAN ENIGMA

Mr. Randolph McClearn Jr. deserves to get a special chapter in this book. This is not because Randolph was a major superstar for which he needs to be singled out for commendation. Far from it! However, Randolph deserves the attention because he was an embodiment of something that requires greater scrutiny. Simply put, he represented many things to many different people. That is evident in the degree of passion, compassion, memories, and impact that the mere mention of his name still evokes among his people in Wilmington and Leland, North Carolina.

I did not realize the meaning, depth, and value of the name Randolph McClearn, Jr. until I traveled to Wilmington, North Carolina to research him in May 2002. That visit was made possible by his niece Ms. Geraldine Smith, at the time a 63 year-old retired nurse. Although I had never met her before my trip to Wilmington, Ms. Smith was very caring, very loving, very warm, and kind enough to make all of the necessary arrangements to make my stay and research work in the Wilmington area as productive as it became. I will return to discuss Ms. Smith and the rest of her family later on in this chapter. For now, the writer's spirit demands that the light should shine on Ms. Smith's paternal uncle, Mr. Randolph McClearn, Jr. who was the father of Sylvester McClearn.

Randolph McClearn, Jr. has already been referred to as

Randolph II several times in this book. And from this point on, he will be referred to both as Randolph II and as Randolph McClearn II, to distinguish him form his own father and son, both of whom were also called Randolph. As has been stated elsewhere in this book, Randolph McClearn, Jr. also named his son Randolph Jr., like himself, because he did not realize that the existence of two juniors in a family was a practice that was not only uncommon but was also largely unheard of. It was very rarely done.

Randolph II was the oldest of ten children born to Randolph and Florence McLaurin, both of who lived and raised their children in Leland, North Carolina. That was a time when the area of Leland in which the McClearns (McLaurins) lived was still called McLaurin Hill. It remained McClaurin Hill until well into the nineteen-thirties. Of course, many African Americans in that area sill refer to it as McLaurin Hill but, as anyone can deduce from the discussion in Chapter Three, that is now much more a product of history and a consequence of emotional sentiments than it is a matter of law. This is because, once the white man named Butler moved into the neighborhood in the thirties, the name of the entire neighborhood was legally changed from McLaurin Hill to Butler Road, which remains the legal name to this day. Although he has long died, the house in which Mr. Butler lived remains in its location – as the first house on the road that was once McLaurin Hill, Leland, North Carolina.

When African Americans in the Leland area – even those who were not yet born when Mr. Butler was alive – speak today of that area as McLaurin Hill, it is certain that they are stating what was once fact by repeating a name that has been transmitted from generation to generation. What is unclear however, is how much of the area's history has been so transmitted to younger generations. It is also unclear what it must feel like for so many members of the McLaurin family who still live in this area, knowing that this was a neighborhood and a street that once carried their family name.

Yet, as tragic as it may seem, this is all part of the victimization of African Americans families that has occurred through history in the United States. Some may argue that this is a matter for history, by which they mean that it should be put aside and forgotten, and we should all move on from "the past". The question that must not be put aside, however, is: How do you truly move on when, everyday of your life, you wake up in a neighborhood with replicas that constantly remind you of how your family was robbed and victimized in their own homeland? How do you truly move on when everything around you reminds you of how your family had to become subservient to the people who came to your homeland to victimize you? We must never forget that the McLaurin family never invited Mr. Butler or any white man to go to McLaurin Hill and take over their neighborhood and their acres of land, and make their family members servants in and on their own land.

It was on this land, and in these circumstances that Randolph McClearn II was born in 1898. Most members of the McLaurin family took the loss of their land and status in strides, and they were able to do so for several reasons. First was because the circumstances at that time were such that a black man and his family were completely powerless in the face of oppression. Secondly, the McLaurin family was never one to buck any part of the white system, except Randolph II who was prone to do so in his own way. Thirdly, most of the McLaurin family members were very concerned about their own families and knew that they stood in danger of having their family members harmed should they challenge their white oppressors. Fourthly, even in their circumstances, the McLaurin family did not consider itself poor. They had food and had a lot of love on McLaurin Hill, and that was enough to satisfy them. Fifth, they had a white physician in Leland who rode to their homes on a white horse to provide them medical care. Dr. William Moore was his name, and he was a very good man who cared for the people of McLaurin Hill, regardless of the times. And the people of McClaurin Hill loved him too. He represented hope to the McLaurins of McLaurin Hill, and his presence in their lives took off some of the emotional pressures that they might have been feeling as a consequence of their oppression. One McLaurin who did not seem to care very much about the calming effects of Dr. Moore's interactions with his McLaurin Hill environment was Randolph II, Sylvester's father.

The Reverend knows much less about his father than he does about his mother. Initially, this may seem to anyone as strange, considering the fact that both parents were married and lived together as a couple in the same home as their children. However, a closer study of Sylvester's parents and family of origin reveals exactly how he and/or any of his siblings could have known so much about their mother and so little about their father.

Perhaps the point should be made from the outset that Mrs. Martha Jeane Hooper McClearn never discouraged her children from knowing or developing a relationship with their father. On the contrary, she wished and encouraged her children to be close to their father and to try to develop their own individual and collective relationships with him. Whatever happened contrary to her wish and desire was completely outside of her power, and the reasons will become clear as the reader progresses in reading this book.

WHO WAS RANDOLPH MCCLEARN, JR.?

Opinions and descriptions of Randolph II vary widely, depending on who you ask. Interestingly, different generations of the McClearn (or McLaurin) family remember him differently, although there are some common threads in the descriptions that they give of this man who remains a towering figure in the family's memory, almost forty years after his death.

Several members of the family (including those who were not fond of his ways) recall Buddy's dad as a robust, tall, jolly man who loved life and sought to enjoy it in a way that seemed right to him. One of his nieces remembers him as "a giant with a big strong laugh that would rattle you". A nephew remembers him as "a very big and friendly man who could have used his great physical potentials to his family's advantage but didn't because he was too busy doing other things". Another niece describes Randolph II as " a great man to be around, an uncle with whom we always had a lot of fun. He would get down on the floor and clown with us (his nieces and nephews. To him, everything was funny."

One thing that is interesting in learning about Randolph II is that, although his nieces and nephews – especially those younger than Sylvester - have several fond memories of him, others who are older do not. Neither does any of Sylvester's brothers and sisters, except Joe Lewis who saw his father as a role model and lived his own life doing some of the things that his father did.

For Sylvester himself, daddy was physically a big man who really did not make himself well known to his family. Part of the evidence that supports this characterization is that none of the Reverend's siblings or the Reverend himself has a photograph of their father. And none of them knows of anybody who has one. Not even his nieces and nephews who have some fond and not-so-fond memories of him have pictures of him.

To Sylvester's younger brother, Jesse, "Dad was a big man in stature. The house shook when he walked in, and he ruled our home with fear". But even inherent in the following ongoing description that Jesse offers of his father is the challenge for anyone who desires to study Randolph II. According to Jesse, "Dad was unapproachable, though he loved a lot. He was very distant from us – his wife and children". To be loving and be distant, and to be unapproachable at the same time that one is both loving and distant are really not terms that are used in the same breath in describing anybody. But Randolph McClearn, Jr. wasn't just anybody. In life and in death, he was, and remains an enigma.

Shaking her head and looking the other way in deep thought, Melvina, an eighty-seven year-old niece of Randolph McClearn II, summed up the impressions of the older generation of the McClearn (McLaurin) family and, perhaps, of some in the Reverend's immediate family in this way: "Uncle

Randolph could have done a lot for himself and his family. He had the strength and he had a wonderful wife. He really could have done a lot, but he drank himself to death". This is a characterization with which Sylvester and his siblings would readily agree. To this day, it is impossible for the Reverend to even guess what his father's triumphs and struggles may have been, or why he did anything that he did.

Randolph II was in and out of his family's life pursuing a life of fun. He whole-heartedly loved blues music and seemed completely given to it. This shouldn't really sound that unusual, since blues music was a favorite of blacks in those days. That was the music that spoke to the true spirit and struggles of a black man, and those were struggles with which Randolph II identified. In his own way, Randolph II was very much a part of that consciousness.

There is no disagreement in the McClearn (McLaurin) family that Sylvester has great physical (including facial) resemblance to his father, though his approach to life is so much different. Randolph II was a big man who seemed quite conscious of his size and he was often influenced by that consciousness, sometimes to his detriment and that of his family. He was about six feet and four inches tall and quite strong. His employers always loved and tended to take advantage of his physical size in much the same way that they took advantage of his lack of formal education.

Anyone who has ever worked in the manual labor force understands that physique and physical strength are characteristics that are much sought after. Randolph II's physical size ensured that no employer was going to assign easy jobs to him. Fortunately, he was a great worker and was always up to the task. For as long as he was able to perform physical tasks for those employers, Randolph McClearn II always remained a favorite employee to white farm owners.

RANDOLPH MCCLEARN, JR. AND THE SHARECROPPING SYSTEM

After slavery was abolished, blacks in the South were moved from slavery to sharecropping. Unlike slavery, sharecroppers were not supposed to work for free. Instead, they got paid a percentage of the farm's proceeds at the end of the year. That percentage always depended on the contract that was developed between, and agreed upon by, the farm owner and the sharecropper.

When the time came to review the account books at the end of the year, it was common that the farm owner and the sharecropper would disagree so intensely that they would separate. Since Randolph II could neither read nor write, he was always a victim of the dishonesty that characterized the business dealings of many of the white farm owners who hired sharecroppers at that time.

At the end of the year, when it was time to review the accounts, the white farm owner would always claim that Randolph II was not entitled to any compensation, but was in fact in debt to the farm owner. After working so hard all year without being compensated, Randolph II was told that he would have to keep working to pay back what he allegedly owed the master. In every case, his reaction was to challenge the farm owner and then pack up and move.

There may have been other farmers at the time who were also terribly victimized by this system and yet kept their cool, but Randolph II was not one of them.

Tact was not in the vocabulary of Randolph II, nor was cowering to anyone. Instead, he stood up to the white farm owner and demanded fairness whenever he was a victim of the same kind of injustice and fraud by which most black farmers were victimized as a consequence of the sharecropping system. Each time he stood up for himself, Randolph II, and consequently his family, was kicked off the farm.

The sharecropping system was not exactly like slavery, but the conditions under which the black sharecropper worked and related with the farm owner were reminiscent of the kind of master-slave relationship that characterized slavery. Sylvester and many people who lived the sharecropper life often think that the primary difference between slavery and the sharecropping system was the absence of a contract in slavery. Although there was a contract involved in sharecropping, it was often based on a fraudulent premise and became the cause of many a conflict between the farm owner and the sharecropper. The conflict often resulted from the manner in which the contracts were structured and implemented.

In slavery, the slave belonged to the master and did whatever the master ordered, without remuneration and without contract. In the sharecropping system, the sharecropper was expected to work for the farm owner and receive a specified percentage of the proceeds from the farm at the end of the year. However, it did not always work out that way.

In reality, the white man kept the books and, even when he allowed the black sharecropper to also maintain a record of his activities and transactions, the black worker's records were usually meaningless in the end. At the end of the year, some well-meaning white farm owners allowed the black sharecropper to compare his books with those of the farm owners', but this was not the norm. More often than not, the white master used only his own books at the end of the year.

Regardless of how hard working the sharecropper had been during the year, the white master always maintained at the end of that year that the sharecropper was in deficit and needed to pay the white farmer some money, which the sharecropper of course did not have. This usually committed the sharecropper to the white farm owner for another extended period of service – really, servitude. Unfortunately, the same abuses are still occurring today on migrant labor farms in America's new South. These abuses were documented in a CNN report just a few years ago.

Although the sharecropping system was fraught with abuses and dishonesty, many black sharecroppers were able to benefit economically from it. Some black sharecroppers had personal goals and were fortunate enough to have responsible and honest white masters who not only respected them as human beings, but also believed that people who had worked for them deserved to get paid. Many of such fortunate sharecroppers were eventually able to buy their own property through the sharecropping system. Sylvester's family was not as fortunate, largely because they had at their helm a man (Randolph II) whose choices were rarely responsible, but also partly because they were not fortunate enough to meet many hearty white farm owners as they evolved as a family.

The McClearn family under Randolph II moved so frequently that it is difficult for Sylvester to remember all of the places where his family lived when he was growing up. One of the reasons for this memory lapse is also because he was very young when most of the moves occurred. Another reason is that the moves occurred with great regularity, and to several different locations. However, Sylvester remembers four different places to which his family moved before their final monumental move to the city of Smithfield, which occurred when he was about ten or eleven years old. Prior to this big move, the family lived on various farms, two of which were the Fleming Farm and the Arnold Farm - both named after their owners, as was the practice in those days.

Since he was very young during most of the moves, Sylvester has had to depend on his siblings over the years to explain to him what was going on in the family in those days to make so many relocations necessary. One of the Reverend's brothers has a simpler and more direct explanation for the family's frequent moves. According to him, "Daddy was a trouble maker. He would always cause trouble and we would get kicked out of the farm".

Regardless of what one thinks of Randolph McClearn II, one thing is certain: he was not a conformist. He had no problem challenging what he perceived as unfairness perpetuated by a white establishment represented by a white oppressor. Whether in labor fields, in politics or in business, non-conformists tend to get in trouble and the case of Randolph II was no different. Being a non-conformist tended to get him in trouble frequently. At least, that is one of the interpretations that can be offered to explain the plight that the McClearn family faced. There are others. Darnell, one of the sons of Reverend McClearn, offered one of those others.

Darnell suggests that reasonable non-conformists consider how their actions will affect their families and themselves before they act. In his grandfather's case, there is no evidence that his family was ever forefront in any consideration he ever made. If he did, he would have known a few times that his actions would get his family and him kicked out of their homes as frequently as they did. And he might have acted in ways that would have guaranteed, or at least helped to gain, some stability for his family.

Sylvester's sister Cleo offered a reason that is both historically reasonable and socio-politically apt. According to her, the reason the family moved so frequently was because, being such a large and hardworking family, they were always in great demand. In other words, Randolph II moved his family so often because he was conscious of his resources and was trying to take advantage of the opportunities that existed for large families on the farms in those days.

On the surface, this suggestion sounds as though the relocations were often the products of rational calculations by a man who wanted a good life for his family. That would be inconsistent with the kind of man that Randolph II was. He was certainly not a very rational man who carefully thought out his moves. So many of the things that he did actually suggest that he was an impulsive and irrational man who acted without any consideration of thoughtful planning and consequences. That also is the story of Randolph II that is told by most people who knew him.

Generally, stories about Randolph II point to the fact that nearly all of the relocations occurred as a consequence of Randolph being kicked out of the farm that he and his family had been living on. Yet, Cleo's explanation does make sense when one considers the fact that Randolph II was a man who was quite conscious of sociopolitical events in his society at the time. In fact, some of the names that he gave to his siblings - such as Roosevelt and Joe Lewis - were evidence of that consciousness. For such a man, chances are that he was well aware of the opportunities available to him as a farmer who was the head of a large family. Such a man was also most unlikely to be one that would cower to a white authority that he considered to be oppressive – even if he thought that his family's well being was at stake.

The McClearn family of Randolph II moved every year, and there were some years when they moved two times. In most cases back then, when a sharecropper and his family were kicked off a farm, they were not allowed to take anything with them. This meant that every time the McClearn family relocated, they practically had to start life all over. This was unfair, but that was the way the system worked. Without money or moving trucks, the relocations occurred on mule wagons that traveled very slowly by today's standards.

The family always received very short, if any, notice from Buddy's father that another move was about to occur. But since the moves were never planned, Randolph II himself almost never knew when he and his family would be packing up to move again. The process mostly took this form: He had words with his boss who owned the land on which the McClearn family lived and worked; his boss told him to get out; Randolph II refused to negotiate and went out instead to arrange for a wagon to move. The night before the move, he told his Martha that the family would move at sunrise, and Martha informed the children. Then Randolph went out to drink or gamble while Martha stayed home and helped the children get together what little possessions they were allowed to take with them from the farm.

Considered against the background of today's technological developments, it has to be baffling how a family's relocation from one farm always ended on another farm, sometimes twenty miles away. How did they know that an opportunity was available so far away? There were no telephones for striking contractual deals or newspapers advertisements to alert them that a farm somewhere else was in need of workers. Yet, somehow, it was always possible through word of mouth to know of a farm that needed workers. His shortcomings not withstanding, Randolph McClearn, Jr. was always able to get news about the need for his services and was able to effect relocations successfully.

Another fact of interest is that Randolph II, who was illiterate, was always able to strike contract deals that were legally binding, although his employers broke those contracts quite commonly. In those days, a man's word was very valuable, and people could stake a premium, even their own lives, on their word. In the circumstances, contractual deals were often sealed with handshakes even for people like Randolph II who could neither read nor write. Yet, it was common then, as it is now, for a man – very often the white farm owner – to eventually deny that he actually had anything to do with what he had said, offered, or agreed to when the business relationship began.

Sylvester is still unsure how much, if any, psychological impact his family's frequent moves may have had on him or anyone of his siblings. If there was any significant psychological impact, he was not conscious of it. Instead, his consciousness regarding those moves revolved mainly around economics. Every time the family moved, young Buddy hoped that the new place was one where he could make more money from working. Yes, even at a very young age, his concern was often not to make new friends or to start a new life in a new school. Instead, his main concern often focused on the job opportunities that might be available for him, and what the chances were for increasing his income.

Randolph II's lack of education became a huge problem for him after he decided to move his family to the city after decades of living and working on farms. Like nearly everything else that he did, Randolph's decision to move his family to Smithfield, a bigger city by the standards of the farms, was not a product of any responsible calculation. He woke up one day and told his wife, "We are getting out of here. We are moving to the city. We are moving to Smithfield". Smithfield was of course a much bigger town than anywhere the family had ever been to, and it is located off the US Interstate 40, between Raleigh and Wilmington, North Carolina.

Being an obedient, dutiful wife, Martha did not question the wisdom of this decision, nor did she challenge her husband to tell her why that was a necessary thing to do at that point on their lives. Martha knew that Randolph had just again lost another job on the farm and it was indeed time to move on. She also thought that, being as hard working as he could be, Randolph would have more opportunities for work in the City of Smithfield, to which they were moving.

For Randolph, that was indeed true, but it was also true that the bright lights of Smithfield were bound to provide Randolph more opportunities for partying, gambling, womanizing, and the various vices that Randolph II had become accustomed to. To that extent, Smithfield was a great attraction to Randolph II, even before he moved his family there. What Smithfield was not going to provide was a skilled job for a man who had no real skills. In a city like Smithfield, work was scarce for a big man who had only worked on farms all his life. For one thing, there were no farms in the city. The forms of labor available were somewhat alien to him.

Besides lacking in skills, Randolph II came to the city with a bad back that was going to make life difficult for a man with such pronounced shortcomings. Randolph II shot a man during the time that he and his family were still living and working on the farm. For this incident he was prosecuted, convicted, and sentenced to prison. While in prison, he hurt his back, and his ability for much physical effort was seriously curtailed. That further damaged any major opportunities he might have had to be gainfully employed in the city, and compounded the problems of his lack of skill and lack of formal education.

This is not to say that there was nothing that Randolph II would have been able to do in the city, if he wanted to. A bigger problem than his bad back and lack of skills was that

Randolph II did not seem to want to work. If he had wanted to work, he certainly would have been able to find something to do in Smithfield. For example, just because of his size, he could have gained employment doing some manual labor, but he chose not to do so. Most men who cared about their responsibility to cater for their family would have made more responsible choices. Unfortunately, this was not most men; this was Randolph McClearn, Jr.

Sometimes when Sylvester thinks about his family's experiences with the oppression and victimization that sharecropping represented, the mere thought almost brings tears to his eyes. This is because it reminds him of how difficult things were for his family specifically, and African Americans as a people. Sometimes, however, the thought makes him smile or laugh because it reminds him of how far his people have come in this country.

The Rev. has often wondered what would have become of his family, both as individuals, and as a family, had his father always accepted everything rather than argue and disagree with the white farm owners. There is, of course, no way to ever be sure of what would have been. However, it is proper to speculate that, had he been passive in the circumstances, he may have been able to have some stability and security in his life, but he would also have been used up and eventually discarded.

As often as he has thought of his father, Reverend McClearn has reached the conclusion that, at times when he could have reached inside of himself to identify and employ whatever other strengths lay within him, he went instead to his weaknesses and employed them to the utmost. At a time when his family needed him to be a leader and provider, Randolph II chose to accentuate his personal weaknesses. Thanks to his wife, Martha, the family stayed intact even through the most difficult times.

But who really was the person, Mr. Randolph McClearn

Jr.? Nobody is really sure what lay in him and what made him the kind of man he was. He had many friends. He loved to party, and would do that as often and for as long as he had money. Whenever he had money, he went partying with his friends and would return home after the money was finished. Sometimes, he would go from the city to sell tobacco on the farms, return two days later without any money. There were also times when he would stay away from home for two or three days without leaving any information regarding his whereabouts. His wasteful expenditures meant that his family was perpetually broke – a state that caused the entire family much agony and frustration.

THE MISSING AND FINAL YEARS OF RANDOLH MCCLEARN, JR.

There are several years of Randolph McClearn, Jr.'s life that are unaccounted for. Now we know that, for some of those years, he was running from the law after committing a crime. The most serious of his crimes was shooting a man on the farm and spending time in jail. Some of his crimes were petty, such as stealing liquor and chicken from the homes of white people. This is interesting since Randolph II was a bootlegger and made and sold his own liquor. It is uncertain if he did some of those crimes because he was just a criminally minded man or because of a desire to irritate white people. The truth is probably somewhere in the middle, or a combination of both possibilities. For several other crimes, Randolph II served prison terms, sometimes in Wilmington while his family was in Smithfield.

There are other things for which he could have been arrested and prosecuted, or assaulted by his some of his children that were often so frustrated with him that sometimes they felt like turning on him and kicking him out of their lives so their mother could have some peace. But his wife was always the buffer. He protected and cared for her husband, but she was also often the first and the main person to receive the brunt of her husband's violent and often baseless temper. Randolph II was largely an irrational man and he often made his wife pay for his irrationality. For example, while still living in Leland, Randolph, II would get drunk and force his wife to walk with him through the neighborhood all night. Whenever he got tired of walking, he made her sit with him by the rail tracks for the rest of the night. Why did she oblige? She did because she wanted to keep him quiet, and because the alternative was getting beaten by him and disturbing their children's sleep.

On one occasion, Sylvester and two of his brothers went home to visit his parents and found their mother badly beaten. Her face was seriously bruised and there were pieces of shattered glass on her face. The young men were very angry and their mother, seeing their faces, knew that they would find and hurt their father who had run away from the home to Wilmington when he knew that his children were coming. To this day, Reverend McClearn remembers her mother's words: "That is your dad. You must not lift your hand up to him". They obeyed.

Randolph II spent his final years in Wilmington, North Carolina, one of the places where he had moved back and forth while his family lived in Smithfield. There were times when he walked out on his family and didn't return for a long time. His family in Smithfield thought he was either in Leland or in Wilmington, while the family in Wilmington thought he was in Smithfield. Nobody recalls him talking about his wife and children when he returned to Wilmington for the last time. His final years were spent there, and nobody in Wilmington is sure if he returned to them directly from Smithfield, or if he lived elsewhere before his final return to Wilmington. What is known is that, upon his return to the area, he worked for the white Butler family in Leland, and then moved on to Wilmington where he spent his last years working at a grave yard. When he wasn't working, Randolph McClearn was drinking and spending time playing with his nieces and nephews who loved him dearly.

There is a strong belief that Randolph McClearn, Jr. may have had other children from extra-marital affairs. Nobody is certain if this is true, but nobody is willing to deny that this could have happened. There is a general belief, even in his extended family, that he was probably capable of this, especially since there were some periods that his whereabouts could not be accounted for. Whatever the case may have been, the reality, however, is that there is no known conclusive evidence that Randolph II had children from other women besides his wife, Martha Hooper McClearn.

Despite their feelings about their father, the McClearn children never forgot their mother's admonitions that they must honor their father, regardless of what he was. When they heard that he was ill, Sylvester and Thomas and Randolph brothers drove to Wilmington to see their father and found him in a very broken state. They took him to Washington DC where he later died. Randolph II died in 1964 from cirrhosis of the liver, following years of alcoholism and a lifestyle that kept him distant from his family – even until his death. He lays buried in Smithfield, North Carolina.

FIVE

AS CLOSE TO AN ANGEL AS ANY HUMAN CAN BE

In 1909, the world received a beautiful, strong, African American child through the family of Mr. and Mrs. George Hooper who at the time were officially listed as residents of Hooper Hill in Leland, North Carolina. Their daughter, however, was born in Wilmington, which is now about a half hour's drive from Leland. In those days, that journey took much longer to make because much traveling occurred on foot, since the kinds of transportation we now have were largely unavailable at the time.

If Mr. and Mrs. Hooper were residents of Leland, why would they have chosen Wilmington as the place where their child would be born? The quick thought might be that the quality of life in Wilmington, and therefore health care services, were much better in Wilmington. But this would actually be a thought that does not quite take into consideration the historical and social circumstances of the time. For one thing, that was not a time when blacks in the United States were allowed access to medical or any such services, whether they were in Wilmington, in Leland, or anywhere else in the South.

Therefore, it would not have mattered where two black people desired to have their child. It would only have been a desired hatched in their minds and killed by the realities of the society in which they lived. A desire tends to become a choice in a situation where options exist. For African

Americans in the United States in those days, that evolution often did not carry on to any logical end. In the circumstances, a choice regarding where the Hoopers would have their child would have been a luxury for them. The country was segregated and blacks were not allowed access to decent public facilities. In fact, they were not perceived as complete human beings deserving of the same rights and quality of life that was accorded to other human beings with a different skin color.

Attempt to imagine the picture of a young black man walking along the road from Leland to Wilmington with his young wife, who is nine months pregnant, in the warm North Carolina weather, so she could have a baby in Wilmington! Well, that is not exactly what happened with Mr. and Mrs. George Hooper. They and their daughter were products of the history of the moment in their own country. At the time of their child's birth, George Hooper was working as a sharecropper on a farm in the Wilmington area and he and his family resided on that farm.

Although he and his wife always perceived of Hooper Hill as home and longed for a time when they would return there for good, the will to survive ensured that, for now, they would be sharecroppers in a place that was removed by distance from their home town. Although they lived and worked in Wilmington, they never felt that they had indeed moved away. Their hearts remained in Leland, as did much of their loyalties for a very long time. No wonder they were regarded in recorded official documents as residents of Hooper Hill, though they were actually living and working in the Wilmington area. In those days, you were always a native of Hooper Hill and Hooper Hill never gave you up, however long you stayed away. Regardless of where you made your home, you were always welcome to think of yourself as being home away from home, home being Hooper Hill.

Like any new baby getting his or her first introduction into the world, the young Hooper parents had no idea what lay in store for their new daughter, who was also their third child. By the time of Martha's birth, her parents already had two sons, which made her the youngest of three. Her brothers were called James and George. George was actually a Junior, in the sense that he was named after his father. After Martha, these parents chose to have no more children.

Though his wife was twelve years younger than he was, George Sr. was not only very dedicated to her and to their children, but he was also very respectful of her. They were very conscious of the very harsh realities in which African Americans lived in the United States at the time, but they were very happy to be blessed with a new child. In private discussions with one another and with other family members and friends, Martha's parents often spoke of a future in this country that they hoped would be much better for their children that the circumstances that defined their own time. They were almost certain that no man could make the change occur. Instead, they hoped and prayed in faith for divine intervention. Unlike many people around them, these parents were hopeful that the world would be better for this new child and her older siblings when they all got older. Full of hope and prayers for their child's future, Mr. and Mrs. Hooper named her Martha Jean Hooper.

The Hooper family from which Martha came was quite unique in many respects, which came together to make Martha a very unique woman herself. Martha came from a highly religious Christian family. Her parents were a very Godly couple and her father was in fact a Baptist preacher. Their religion perhaps explains why nobody in Leland speaks ill of that couple or of the daughter that they raised – Martha Jean Hooper. They were guided by their religious values and principles and they made sure to pass those values on to their daughter. The fact that she was a girl made them even more conscious of, and careful about what they were doing as they raised her. They did not want her to be swallowed up by the world and they made a concerted effort to raise a daughter that would grow into a virtuous woman.

One thing that is very rarely mentioned in discussions about the Hooper couple is their racial composition. It is actually something that is generally not discussed, either because people have forgotten, don't know, or just have developed widely held but erroneous assumption over so many decades. Martha's mother was in fact an Indian woman who married George, a black African man. This fact is significant because it speaks to several factors: one, it explains the degree of open-mindedness that was very evident in Martha's life as she lived her own life and raised her children. Two, it may explain the degree of open-mindedness that the Hoopers' grandson, Sylvester McClearn, exudes in his own life, perhaps without even knowing it. It seems reasonable to contend that the seeds for such character were sown several years before he came along, by his grandparents who saw love rather than just race as they bound together to fulfill God's purpose for their lives. Thirdly, this fact should inform us of a major aspect of African American history, as indeed the history of even white people in the United States. Clearly, a remarkable degree of interracial interactions have historically occured in this country and, regardless of what people are willing to accept, those interactions will continue to occur. Therefore, those who think they are only white, only black, or only Indian may indeed be mistaking.

A close look at the history of the Hooper family reveals an open-minded family and provides us a good way of understanding the influences that helped Martha develop the loving, caring, and nurturing character that she had toward all people regardless of race, ethnicity or class. Besides coming from a racially mixed background herself, Martha was conscious of her parents' values and their desires for her and her brother. Obviously, her parents were both people who were determined to raise their children with a good knowledge of, and commitment to the gospel of the Lord Jesus Christ. They did very well. Their daughter Martha not only knew the word of God but like her father, became a preacher herself.

Like Martha herself, her grandfather before also had two siblings. Unlike Martha, however, her grandfather was denied the right to grow up in his family home with his parents. In those days in America, no African American had that right. The opportunity to be raised by one's family was a privilege that was dictated by white people and dished out at will. Martha's grandfather was not allowed that right, or even the privilege to live as a free person in his family's home with his parents in his own country. Instead, he and his two siblings witnessed their parents get sold into slavery. Following this tragic incident, Martha's grandfather and his siblings were left to drift until some unidentified people picked them up and raised them as their children.

It is unclear who picked up and raised the young Hoopers but the Good Samaritans clearly did a good and Godly thing for which no amount of gratitude can ever be enough. As a human being, one cannot help to wonder what kind of evil possesses any person or group to forcibly dispossess children of their parents. Yet, what happened to Martha's parents also certainly happened to an uncountable number of African American families in the United States. It was a product of institutionalized oppression whose consequences continue to be with every African American individual or family to this day. To this end, it is a fact of Sylvester McClearn's life that he has to live with, just as it was a fact of the life of his mother's life that she had to live with. It is also an African American story, with which every black person in this country or elsewhere ought to be able to identify and relate. Black people who either deny or lack knowledge of the impact of slavery on their lives do a great disservice to themselves and deprive themselves and posterity of the opportunity to achieve a level of completeness that is only possible through knowing the details of one's self and history.

On the day that Martha's grandfather and his siblings were sold into slavery, that family's history was altered and the fate of their offspring was severely impacted – even before they were born. It is difficult to imagine how any offspring whose life has been so impacted can still be full of love rather than hate, respectful toward all rather than to her race only, and Godly rather than angry toward God. Yet, this is what

Martha Hooper was. She was a lively and loving woman with a remarkable sense of commitment to family. People who knew her well often like to think and speak of her as a woman who had a life that was bigger than her family life.

Martha grew up in Wilmington, North Carolina, where her parents raised her on a sharecropper's. She had no formal western education, thanks to the realities of racial oppression at the time. It was on the farm that most crucial decisions would be made that would impact the rest of her life, as well as the lives of her own children that she would eventually have. Perhaps the most crucial of such decisions was her romantic involvement with, and marriage to, Randolph McClearn, Jr. who would become her husband of several years and the father of her fourteen children.

Martha Jean Hooper was a young teenager when she met and fell in love with Randolph. They were both children of sharecroppers and both lived with their parents on the farm. That was where and how they met, and that was where they developed and grew their relationship, first as friends and then as lovers. Though they were still young, several people on the farm, who were equally young, considered Randolph bad for Martha, and some of them actually took steps to attempt to dissuade her from carrying out a romantic involvement with him. One of those concerned people was Ms. Irene Thomas, Martha's cousin who died in 2002 at the age of eighty-nine.

Like Cousin Irene, most of Martha and Randolph's contemporaries were put off by what they perceived as Randolph's "smooth, insincere, dishonest, cheating, lying" personality and they were convinced that she was not the type for Martha. But Martha was a woman of her convictions, who was not easily swayed by people. She was always a loyal person to her friends and family, and this quality that she developed as a very young person never left her for as long as she lived. One of the consequences was that she loved and agreed to be courted by smooth-talking Randolph and then married him in Wilmington.

Besides being a loyal person, it is unclear what else encouraged Martha to marry Randolph II. To this day, it remains a subject of discussion among many family members who knew them both. Among the reasons offered is that, being from the kind of background from which she came, Martha may have taken sympathy on Randolph II who, for all practical purposes, was a lost man, considering that hardly anybody liked him. In the circumstances, Martha may have agreed to marry him in the hope that she could help him straighten out his life. Unfortunately, relationships that are begun and led against such background of hope and expectation often turn against the tide of the original hope and expectation.

By now, the story of the life Randolph II is well known, having been detailed in Chapter Four of this book. He was the complete opposite of Martha's father. Randolph II was a cruel alcoholic who was mean to his wife throughout the duration of their marriage. Despite this, Martha was the buffer. She attended church regularly who guaranteed that their children would maintain some respect for their father and acknowledge him as dad, even when he wasn't acting like one.

Several people wondered then and now how Martha could have accepted her husband's abuses and continued to be a wife to him. The truth is that she lived with the abuses and took them but did not accept or approve of them. She knew that it was wrong for a man to abuse his wife, and she knew the pain of the abuses because she felt them. Yet, the question is still an interesting one, considering that the same phenomenon occurs today, even among so-called modern women.

To understand Martha's options and choices, it is important to put the family's circumstances in social and historical context. First, that was a time when divorce was something that most people just didn't do. You went into a marriage and you stayed there. Consequently, society didn't look with remarkable kindness or respect on single women who had been married and divorced.

Secondly, Martha was the mother of several children – fourteen altogether. Though her husband was no good, she knew that the most important consideration that she had to make was to focus on caring for her children rather than focus on developing any kind of anger toward her husband. She made that choice and lived with it. Thirdly, Martha truly loved Randolph II, though it is still very difficult for anyone who knew Martha and Randolph II to understand how that could be. There is no argument that Randolph II did nothing to deserve his wife's love, but Martha saw it differently. She believed that she had a responsibility to love the man that she had chosen to marry for as long as she lived, regardless of the circumstances. That, truly, was unconditional love. Fourthly, Martha was a very devout Christian, and a traditional one at that. That also meant that she did not believe in divorce. So she stayed married to Randolph II for as long as it took.

Martha loved the Lord with all her heart, though she was married to Randolph II who didn't attend church, didn't practice Christianity, and lived recklessly on the edge. She also believed very strongly in the Biblical admonition in Proverbs chapter 22, verse 6: *"If you bring up a child in the way he should go, when he is old he will not depart from it."* Therefore, being a very religious woman who considered obedience to the scriptures to be the paramount responsibility of any Christian, Martha mother took his children to church frequently. She wanted to ensure that her children did not get lost in a world that was becoming increasingly dangerous even at that time. Besides, she knew the importance of deliverance and the value of Christianity, and she wanted that experience for her children.

Although she was a quiet woman who rarely said what she was thinking, Martha may also have been thinking of how terrible it must be to suffer oppression and untold hardships here on earth as a black and then die and still suffer in hell. That was certainly not what she wanted for her children, so she did whatever she could to guide them in the way of the Lord and be guaranteed eternal life in heaven.

Perhaps the attempt should be made here to put into perspective the role that religion may have played in the McClearn family that Martha was matriarch of. It is generally expected today, as it was in those days, that people go to church all together as a family. But that has always been an expectation rather than an absolute reality. In this regard, my family was no different, for although my mother went to church often and took us with her, my father stayed away from church. Yet, in spite of the fact he did not attend church, he must have known the value of what my mother was doing because he never stopped her from going, and did not oppose her taking us to church as often as she did.

In Martha's time, and when Buddy was growing up, marriage relationships were much different from the way they are these days. Since that time, the institution of marriage has certainly gone through an evolution of sorts in this country. It is uncertain if the evolution has been all good or all bad, but it is certain that marriage is much different now from the way marriage used to be. For one thing, most people who got married in those days remained in the marriage through thick and thin. Regardless of the quality of their marriage relationships, couples believed that they were in it for the long haul and they tried to live that belief. The marriage between Sylvester's parents could be perceived as an example of that kind of marriage, except that only one person in that union was making the decision to stay, and that was Martha.

Like many marriages in those days, Randolph II was clearly the head of the household, despite his moral shortcomings. This meant that he made all major decisions, often without consultation with his wife. Notwithstanding any contrary opinions to his decisions, Martha and he knew that their children had a responsibility to comply with whatever decisions he made. Martha lived much of her life as a single parent, even when her husband was at home. Then, as now, life as a single parent could be extremely difficult, especially when one parent has to be responsible for as many children as Buddy's mother was. She would leave for work early in the morning, return late at night, and try to catch up on things that had happened at home while she was gone. Often, this meant having to referee or resolve fights that had occurred in her absence.

It was of course natural that fights would sometimes occur between siblings. The reason for this was not far-fetched. Naturally, since there was no parent in charge of the home while mom was out working, some of Buddy's older siblings would feel a responsibility to step up and play the parent's role. Often, this was not welcomed by some of the children who felt that the older ones were over-stepping their bounds and would therefore refuse to give them the respect that they were demanding. This clash of egos often led to conflicts, which mother had to settle when she returned home after a hard day's work.

As she struggled to raise fourteen children by herself, there was no doubt that Martha experienced some untold hardships and frustration. It did not help that she had many physical ailments as well. Sometimes, her physical pain was excruciating, but there was never a way to tell how much emotional pain she was in. The only indications would sometimes reveal themselves in Martha's prayers that young Buddy would sometimes overhear. According to him, mother would pray aloud sometimes, and the content and nature of her prayer would reveal the degree of pain that she was in.

Although she had many physical ailments, Martha was always there for her family, and they could always count on her. Even at his current age, Sylvester's eyes still well up with tears when he thinks of his mother. He wishes that she had lived longer than she did, so he could at least make some effort to reward her for what she did for her family, just as his own children reward him now for parenting them the way he did. In Sylvester's estimation and words, "mother was a good woman who was caught in a hard web with many children and not enough physical strength to love each child individually. In the circumstances, she loved us as a group".

Clearly, Martha was the backbone of the McClearn family from which Sylvester came, and her strengths became even more evident during the stressful periods that the family experienced as a result of father's behavior. But for Martha's strength and sense of purpose, Randolph II's behaviors could have destroyed the family, or any other family. In talking with Cleo Sanders (that is, "Sister") about their parents, she had this very succinct description of what and who they were: "Mama was an evangelist and daddy was a drunk." For those of them who were raised by these parents, and many others who knew Martha and Randolph II well, that characterization speaks volumes.

Sylvester and most of his brothers and sisters can clearly recall several times when the family ran out of food and had nothing to eat. Things seemed to get better on this front when mom began to work in the kitchens of white people. She would bring some food home at the end of her workday, and the children always looked forward to the bread and cooked flour that she brought because it filled them. To make ends meet, Mama also began to launder and iron clothes for people. Among the things she did at this time was to wash the clothes of someone who was a first cousin to the famous actress Ms. Ava Gardner.

The point must be made that the McClearn home was not one dark roller coaster of stress, even if it was not like some other homes. In spite of the difficulties, there was a great deal of love in the McClearn home, which made it possible for all of them to stand up to the test of survival as individuals and as a family. The values that they developed were rooted in hard work and a sense of normalcy that maintained a presence in our hearts, even when the going was rough. For example, it is impossible to forget the big gardens that the family had, and how they raised hogs.

Of course it wasn't just the parents that did this task, or any task for that matter. The responsibilities belonged to everyone in the family, and they pitched in. For example, Martha had chickens that the family raised and would sometimes slaughter for meat, and they had a cow that was milked by Randolph Junior twice a day. This part of the family's existence, causes smiles because it brings memories of Junior (that is, Randolph III) drinking the milk after milking the cow. Cleo in particular was particular about not drinking the milk until their mother had strained it.

Sylvester has always been one of the quiet ones in his family. His feeling of connection with his mother is stronger than he has words to express. Prompted to express some thoughts about his parents, he had the following to say: "Oftentimes, I feel a need to ask my mother, how did you do it? How and why did you feel that you had to accept everything you went through, just to ensure that your children did not become negative statistics? From where did you get your strength, courage, and determination? What was it like living with my father? At the same time, I sometimes feel a strong need to ask my father several questions, such as Daddy, why did you love to party so much? Did you do your best for your family? Daddy, what really happened? In fact, I have a much longer list of questions that I would like to ask each of my parents but I cannot ask those questions now because none of them is with us anymore".

When Martha died in 1956, she was only forty-seven years old and she had finally succumbed to several years of physical illness. Perhaps the beatings that she received from her husband and the stress of being married to him took a toll on her. This is not something that the McClearns discuss, even if any of them has ever wondered. Be that as it may, his mother's death was very painful for Sylvester, and it continues to be a major loss for him. Of course he knew she would not live forever, but she wanted her to live longer than she did and enjoy as much of life as possible, considering how much she had labored to raise the family.

Until she died in 1956, Martha maintained regular contact with Cousin Irene and was able to discuss her private inner-thoughts and pain, but she was also always able to share her triumphs. She considered it great pride that her son, Sylvester, was on the right path and predicted to Cousin Irene that Sylvester would be a greatly accomplished man. Though she never met Sylvester until she died in 2002, Ms. Thomas felt as though she knew Sylvester, largely because she heard his mother speak fondly of him.

In the circumstances in which Buddy's family lived, they could have been sentenced to a life of eternal misery, however hard they tried. But fortunately, they had a praying mother that, more than anyone, believed it important that her children never saw her with her head down in defeat. Therefore, with her head up in hope and determination, she went about the business of almost single-handedly parenting all of her fourteen children. By so doing, she guaranteed that the values that were being instilled in them were such that they would forever feel influenced by, and grateful for, having her in our lives.

Once the daughter of a Christian preacher became "equally yoked with the unbeliever" the consequences were set in motion, both for her and the future generations of her offspring. However, as her complete story shows, Martha, who also became a preacher, anchored her family in the hands of the only sure Marina because she knew that this was the only way to guarantee their future. She never stopped praying for her children and their families, and she never gave up on her husband.

The current and future generations of the McClearn can be rest assured that the prayers of their mother, grandmother and great grandmother, Martha Jean McClearn, cover them. But they must also be aware that they owe her memory a duty to maintain the legacy that she picked up from her own parents, built in her own life, and handed to her own sons - Sylvester and Jesse: A legacy of faith, preaching and prayer. Although she is not here anymore, there are three words all of the living McClearns would like to say to her: "Thank you mom."

SIX

FROM CHILDHOOD TO LABOR FORCE

Sylvester McClearn and all of his siblings were not only born on farms, but they also worked faithfully on those farms, the last of which was a thirty-acre cotton farm. It was very important that they worked as hard as they did, even as very young children. That was one of the expectations that guided the execution of the sharecropping system. Children were part of the package in that system. When a farmer was hired to work on a farm, it was understood that he was being hired along with his entire family, including his kids, however young they were.

Therefore, children had the same responsibility to the farm owner that their parents had. This did not mean that the children were paid separate, additional wages for their labor. In fact, they often did not receive separate incomes from the farm owners. Whatever wages accrued to the father was considered payment for his entire family's labor.

When young Sylvester was about ten or eleven years old, his family was kicked off another farm for the last time and his father made the decision to move his family to the Smithfield, North Carolina, which was a big city. As the Reverend recalls it, this move to the city was the product of yet another conflict that ensued between his father and his boss at the time. By this time, young Buddy had become so used to moving from one place to another that, although he did not consider it pleasant, he did not feel that the family had any choice. It was just the way they lived – a somewhat nomadic existence.

It was in the city of Smithfield that Buddy began to learn a lot more about his family, his potentials, and about a life that was completely different from that which he had known all along. For example, he was amazed to find that there were black people who did not live on farms. He was surprised to see black people who did not have to focus entirely on farm work. Instead, they emphasized education and ensured that they and their children were educated.

For the first time, Buddy also realized that the various relocations of the family carried grave consequences both for the family as a whole and for them as individuals. First, the relocations caused great damage to the education of Buddy and his siblings. By the time they got to the city, they were all behind other kids in their education and, on his part, Buddy found out how bad a student he really was. It was a culture shock indeed, but also one on which he did not dwell very much.

Although Buddy and his siblings had attended school when they lived on the farm, their attendance was very spotty because the farming season always took priority over their schooling. For instance, Buddy could only go to school about half to three-quarters of the school year because the farming tasks had to be given precedence. For his older siblings, it was even worse. As a result of the relocations, they would sometimes miss entire academic sessions. In retrospect, that was indeed an existence that was both tragic and unfair. It was a system that produced only one result of note: keeping down the children of poor black people who worked to uphold the survival of white America, while the children of white people went to school to be prepared for potentially notable and meaningful lives. In the circumstances, the distance to be covered in the race toward hope and destiny was never the same for black and white children, or for their families.

Another shock of city life for Buddy was socialization. Social life was practically non-existent for his family and him when they lived on farms. Even now, he does not recall having any friend until the family got to the city. One reason for this was that they were always so busy working on the farms that they had no time left to socialize with anyone. The other reason was that the farms were big and far apart from each other. They would have had to walk at least a mile to be able to make friends.

In Chapters One and Two, the degree of poverty in the McClearn family was discussed. The way it impacted the family was also discussed. Thanks to the poor choices that the family's patriarch, Randolph II continued to make, the family almost never had any money at all. That alone might not have been so bad if the family had had food most of the time. As it turned out, they frequently lacked food in their home.

It is very difficult to imagine an American family of fourteen children and their parents staying in their home and looking at one another without food to eat, or money to buy basic necessities. The hopelessness of the family was felt very deep in Buddy's heart as perhaps all others in his family, except of course Randolph II who obviously had no trouble carrying himself as a patriarch without a conscience.

At no time in his growing-up years did Sylvester feel that the end to his family's poverty was anywhere in sight. Without question, his family's situation deteriorated to the point where the children and their mother had to make very critical decisions to sustain their family. Since Sylvester's father did not seem to care very much that his family was wallowing in deep poverty, someone had to do something to try to stem the tide of the seemingly unending slide. It is difficult to imagine that a husband and father would let his family struggle as much as Buddy and the entire family struggled without doing anything to alleviate their suffering. But that's exactly what Randolph McClearn did to his family.

In some situations where there is such a high degree of poverty as was present in Sylvester's family of origin, more privileged family members have historically come to the aid of the less privileged. For this McClearn family, that was certainly not the case. It is uncertain if the family of Randolph II made a conscious decision not to assist him and his family, or if they were themselves too poor to provide needed assistance, since poverty was and still is a major bane of the African American community. Two things are clear however. First, as I found out while working on this book, the family from which Randolph II came was a very loving and generous one. It still is. It is unthinkable that they would have stayed uninvolved had they any knowledge of the sad plight of some of their family members – unless of course they were themselves not in a good enough position to offer any assistance.

There is indeed a second reason to consider: For whatever reason, Randolph II kept his nuclear family alienated from his own brothers and sisters and their families. One of the consequences of that action is that most of his grandchildren across the United States do not even know of one another's existence, or of the existence of their cousins. And most of the McClearn children and grandchildren around the country have very little or no knowledge regarding the importance of Wilmington and Leland, North Carolina to their family history. Most do not even know that that area is the original home of the McClearn family that has now extended all across the United States and beyond.

Sylvester does not recall any aunt or uncle ever being involved with his family when he lived at home. This supports the position already expressed above that Randolph II kept his family alienated from the extended family. Sylvester's older brother Thomas seemed to be much more aware and more conscious of the responsibility to help the family than anyone else, including their father. In retrospect, Reverend McClearn often thinks that his brother may in fact have neglected his own family in his effort to lift up his family of origin - that is his parents and siblings, including Sylvester. For this, Sylvester feels both guilty and exceedingly indebted to his late brother.

The need to survive as individuals and as a family became so strong in the McClearn family that Sylvester and his siblings had no choice but to enter the labor force at very young ages and become very hard working individuals in that arena that is theoretically reserved for adults. Thomas was a particularly hard worker. Thomas and Leroy gave their father much of the help he needed on the cotton fields on which he worked.

Working with Randolph II was not always easy. He expected Thomas and Leroy to work as grown-ups, and it did not matter to him that they were kids. Being a man of unpredictable moods, Randolph II would yell at his children when he thought they were not working fast enough to suit his expectations, but would sometimes become very friendly when they did not expect. Even to everyone else in his family, Randolph II's mood was often unpredictable. But Leroy admired and looked up to dad, and he wanted very much to be like him. However emotionally painful it might have been to work with dad sometimes, Leroy always looked forward to going back and working side-by-side with him.

As young children, Thomas and Leroy each developed a remarkable degree of knowledge regarding things like the weight and prices of cotton. Naturally, Thomas who was very strong, and a great leader eventually took on the responsibility of running the farms where his father worked for almost as long as he, Thomas, worked there.

Although his family was always poor, Buddy only began to realize the extent of their poverty when they moved out of the farm and into the City of Smithfield, North Carolina. For one thing, there were bigger and better things available in the city, and it was impossible for Buddy not to notice the purchasing abilities of the people around him. Those abilities were quite evident in the material things that surrounded him. In the circumstances, it became practically impossible for Buddy not to realize and be conscious of the fact that his family did not possess similar abilities. Instead, being in the city opened the eyes of Buddy and perhaps some of his siblings to the realities of their family's circumstances and helped them to realize just how little they had and how much they lacked. Suddenly, in the city, the extent of the poverty of the McClearn family became magnified against the status of everyone else around them. In that city, it became commonplace for the family to run out of food with greater frequency than ever before. For the first time, Buddy began to see family members crying because they had no food to eat in their home.

As turning points go, it was this move to the city and the realizations that he suddenly acquired that propelled Sylvester's ambition into higher gear and led him to join the labor force at a much younger age than most people in today's America can ever imagine. He loved his family dearly and was greatly aware of their circumstances, including their dire need of survival.

The recognition of the need for survival meant that, from a very young age, Buddy and each of his siblings had to work a lot to help their parents support their family. To be sure, the reference here is not to work within the home, which is the common type of work that very young children do in today's society. Instead, the reference is to hard work outside of the home - the same work that many adults did at the time and still do now.

Buddy had to go out and work for money to help support his family. The initiative to join the labor force at a very young age of nine certainly did not begin with him. With so many siblings older than he was, it was just natural that they would set the process in motion and Buddy would do exactly what his older siblings before him had done. The only way he would not have done the same thing would have been if his family circumstances had gotten better, which they did not before it was his turn to go out and get a job. By going to work when he did, Buddy was not making a decision to do anything; he was just following the footsteps of his older siblings because it was the only thing he knew.

If he spends any time thinking about his childhood, Sylvester has very good reasons to be angry with his father for keeping his family in the conditions described in this book. Some people would reasonably expect him to condemn his father each time he speaks about him. Although he can do any of this, Reverend McClearn chooses not to. Instead, he insists as follows: "I can't condemn him; I can't hate him. He was my father and he was deserving of my honor".

As terrible as the family's situation may have been, some silver lining could well be found in the circumstances. Sylvester believes that, according to him, "Our poverty created for my siblings and me a value system that grew up with us into adulthood. We all developed a strong work ethic, a great understanding of the human experience, and a sense of compassion for others as a response to our circumstances". Better than anyone else, Sylvester should know.

Regarding the structure of the labor force in those days, it is interesting

now to see how much has changed. Today, there are laws against child labor in this country and around the world. It is either that those laws did not exist when Sylvester was a working child, or nobody cared to obey or enforce them. Or maybe the laws just didn't cover black boys and girls in the labor force. Consequently, it was a very common thing to be working before one was even nine years old, especially if you were black and poor. That was exactly what Sylvester did.

Today, young people who take up employment have entry-level positions from which they begin, and they receive varying entry-level wages for their work. In those days, it was a little different. There was no minimum wage standard. Therefore, employers paid whatever wages they felt like paying to their employees and did so for as long as they wished. For example, when

Sylvester's sister Cleo began to work on a farm as an employee in her own right, she received the exact amount in wages that her mother and father did though they had been working on farms for what seemed like an eternity. As Sylvester also had to do later, Cleo always gave her income to their mother to take care of the family's needs.

Considering how much Cleo, Sylvester and their other siblings contributed toward the support of the family, one can only wonder how much the family's economic situation was impacted after Cleo (that is, *Sister*) got married in 1948 at age eighteen years old. Perhaps nobody will ever know exactly how negatively the family's finances were affected by Cleo's marriage, but it is certain that *Sister's* own life changed for the better once she got married. To this day, *Sister* herself reports that her problems ended when she got married. For one thing, she never again had to work any more than she needed to.

The man that Cleo married in 1948 was a man named Ison Sanders. Mr. Ison Sanders was a very good and hard-working man with a strong sense of responsibility and respect. He never posed any problems to Cleo or to the McClearn family during their courtship or after they got married. Besides their father, Randolph II, everyone in the McClearn family liked Ison very much, and he received instant acceptance. Nobody is sure why Randolph II had great difficulty accepting Ison as his future son in-law, but then again, nobody is sure why Randolph II ever did most of the things he did. Cleo and everyone else learned to ignore their father's dislike of Ison and she carried on her relationship with him regardless.

Ison Sanders was always a compassionate and great family man, and once he married *Sister*, he never stopped being a big help to the family. He and Cleo have since built a wonderful family together. There was never a doubt that they were a perfect fit for each other. Reverend McClearn speaks very fondly of *Sister*, who anyone would be glad to have as a sister, and of her husband, Ison. Cleo is now paralyzed, but that is only a physical limitation for her. Her spirit will never be broken.

As has been discussed, Sylvester McClearn was still a very young boy when he began to work. He was less than nine years old. Like his other siblings, Sylvester's first job was on the farm with his parents and siblings. His responsibilities included ploughing, cultivation of crops, and everything else associated with crop growing. The farms were always set up in such a way that there were tasks for adults as well as tasks for children. His tasks, therefore, were those that supposedly belonged to children.

Although the tasks were separate for children and adults, that separation seemed to have existed only in principle and did not go all the way. For example, there was no expressed consciousness regarding the hazards of child labor on the farm, nor were there any special provisions in place to protect working children who worked on the farms. Of course those were overwhelmingly black children – not the special concern of any United States government on those days. The only thing their parents could do was to pray that nothing bad would happen to their children while they worked. As it turned out, physical injuries to children were quite commonplace on the farms. Undoubtedly, the farm was a dangerous place for children to work, and the absence of safeguards for working children was all part of a system that was clearly designed with an oppressive intent.

By the time the McClearn family moved from the farm to the city of Smithfield, Sylvester was already in the process of being established as a working man, even though he was only about nine years old. As a worker by this time, moving to the city opened an entirely new world for him. With so many job opportunities being so clearly available, he felt like a kid who had just found himself in a toy store. He suddenly realized that he could make a whole lot more money than he ever made by doing the same jobs that he always did on the farms, and more. Again, he was only just about ten years old.

In the city, Buddy was able to work shining shoes, raking leaves, and cutting grass for people, but these were not the only jobs that he did. Regardless of the nature and intensity of the employment that he had at any time, the intent was exactly the same: to make as much money as he could to help support his family. This need became more urgent when they moved to the city and Buddy felt it very strongly. This became especially the case after much of the responsibility for caring for the family fell squarely on the shoulders of his mother.

To fulfill this responsibility, Mrs. Martha Hooper McClearn held steady employment for much of the time that the family lived in the city. Regardless of the amount of work that they did, Buddy and his family just never seemed to earn enough to take care of all of the family's needs. Food was still very scarce, so Buddy and his siblings often found themselves anxiously waiting in hunger until their mother returned home after work and brought them something to eat. She also had an account in the neighborhood store, which enabled her to purchase food on credit and pay the bill once she received her wages from her place of employment.

Since she often did not have money, Martha would go to that store anytime she was in great need of something to feed her family, have her name written down in the storekeeper's lined and faded black notebook, and then go back to the store to pay the tab after she got paid at her employment. Several times in her life as a wife and mother, Martha felt that it was humiliating to have to buy food on credit but, rather than get angry or sad, she approached her realities with a sense of gratitude. She was grateful that I was possible to purchase food for her family even when she had no money, and she was thankful that there was an entrepreneur that was willing to offer such credit opportunities to people like her without any fear that someone would run out of town without paying him. That degree of trust is largely lacking in today's world, though there are still merchants, though few, in local communities that are willing and do maintain this age-old practice that is based completely on trust and some belief in human goodness.

Even as a little boy, Sylvester did not like the fact that his mother had to work as hard as she did, or keep a credit account at a store, just to be able to keep the family's health going. He wondered why his father couldn't have been doing that, which was certainly what she saw the fathers of most boys doing. It was, in that tradition as it is in any other, the role of the man to care for his family with his sweat. That fact was never lost on Buddy, and it was certainly something that nobody needed to teach him. To help alleviate his mother's suffering, Buddy and his siblings all went to work very young and it was particularly important for Buddy to will relief for his mother without any delay. No wonder he was very determined to find work, go to work, and make money for his family. In this role, he had a few good examples: his older brothers and sisters.

SEVEN

BUDDY LEAVES HOME

As if it occurred yesterday, Sylvester remembers very clearly the day his second oldest brother, Thomas, came home from Arlington, Virginia, where he had been living for about two years. Thomas felt it necessary to visit because he knew that the family was experiencing severe financial crisis. He was the kind of man who seemed to have powerful premonitions and always knew when something was either happening or about to happen to members of his family. This time, his premonitions were about the family's social and economic conditions. His body was speaking to him and, without malingering he got on a bus and traveled from Arlington, Virginia to Smithfield, North Carolina.

When he was not sleeping on that bus, Thomas was looking out the bus window at the farmlands that reminded him of his upbringing in North Carolina. He could see vast, cultivated lands and, in some cases, a house that looked small from a distance and he never had to be told that the house he was looking at in each case was the white master's house. He wondered about the black faces behind those farms, the anonymous black farmers who, along with their children were in the business of feeding America without getting paid for their labor. Thomas and his family had lived their lives on the farm, forced by the realities of their race to engage in such business as well. So he knew that his thoughts were without basis. He knew that the children growing up on the farms he was looking at were doomed unless someone showed them a way out of those farms.

Although some black people had begun to own farms at

that time, Thomas' American experience taught him that blacks did not own farms as large as the ones he was looking at in that Southern part of the United States. As his bus made its way further and further into the South, Thomas increasingly thought of himself as one who had escaped the harsh realities of the South and he felt a strong desire to help his entire family escape as well.

On the evening of his arrival in Smithfield, the McClearn family members, with the exception of their father Randolph II and *Sister*, who had already married and left home, and perhaps one or two others all sat down in the living room and began to discuss the state the family. It is unclear who exactly was present or absent at this discussion, but Sylvester clearly recalls that informal meeting. Martha began to talk about the state of affairs in the family and Thomas began to recall the farmlands and the thoughts that he had been having on his way to Smithfield. At that point, Thomas, who was obviously moved by what he was hearing, suggested that one of his siblings should return with him to Arlington, Virginia and work there.

This was a very wise and generous suggestion, since Arlington, being closer to Washington D.C., offered more employment opportunities than Smithfield where the rest of the family was living. His brother's exact words have remained unforgettable to Reverend McClearn even to this day. As he recalls them, the exact words were "Someone can come with me to work in Arlington and send money home". Without thinking, Sylvester volunteered to go with his older brother; and without taking any time to consider his offer or the fact that Buddy was only a kid volunteer, his family agreed that he should go with his brother to work in Arlington and send money home to assist his family.

Several times in his life thus far, the Sylvester has wondered why nobody in his family raised any objections to his offer to go with his brother. After all, he was only fifteen years old, and kids that age were supposed to be in school, not working to care for their families. On that day, nobody raised any concern that going with his brother and joining the labor force in Virginia would take him away from school. Nobody asked Sylvester or his brother if he (Sylvester) would attend school in Virginia, and nobody expressed any concerns regarding the fact that a lack of education could negatively impact him for the rest of his life. On his part, Sylvester never even thought about it. He had only one desire - to assist his family in getting out of the severe financial hardships that they faced. Here was his brother offering what seemed like a good opportunity to achieve this desire. So, Sylvester was happy to be able to take up the opportunity and do what he knew needed to be done to lift his family's circumstances.

This is an otherwise tragic development for any child or family in the United States or anywhere in the world. For any child or family to have to choose between a family's survival and the child's education speaks volumes, not just about the family's condition but also about the society that creates an environment where such choices have to be made. It should never be the case, but that was the lot of many African Americans and their families in years gone by, and it is one of the often-unspoken reasons why so many African American men and women around the Reverend's age are illiterate today. As we see later in this book, Reverend McClearn was fortunate enough to be able to direct his life in a different course.

Buddy was always aware that Thomas was very concerned about the family, and would have taken care of the obvious responsibilities of the family all by himself, without getting any of his other siblings involved. Thomas was that kind of man – a compassionate and thoughtful man whose sense of responsibility was unparalleled. However, he was a married man, and had his own family, which made it a little more difficult to stretch his finances as far as he might have wished.

Within days, after his brother's visit home, Buddy traveled back to Arlington, Virginia with his brother and began to live with him and his family. This was the first time buddy ever left his family home, and one thing was different from what normally happens. In most cases, when children leave their parents' home for the first time, it is usually a temporary departure and they return in due course. In Buddy's case, that did not happen. When he left home on that day with his brother, his departure was for good and he never went back, except for occasional visits.

Thomas got Buddy a job, charged him no rent for living in his home, and placed no demands on him. The only thing Thomas requested of Sylvester was to send some money home to their family in Smithfield, NC every week. For this family, that was not an unusual request

One time that Sylvester gets emotional is when he speaks of his brother, Thomas. He is eternally grateful to Thomas who, despite his own circumstances, took him in and fed him so he could effectively carry out this new responsibility that Sylvester took on. To this day, the Reverend frequently wonders why nobody in his family or society forced him to go to school, instead of watching him labor and make money in the work place. He has never asked that question of anyone in his family, but he does not expect that he will ever get an answer directly from anyone's lips. Instead, he is satisfied with what he believes to be the reason: his family needed all the money they could get in order to achieve and maintain a bare survival.

For that to be achieved, responsibility and conscience dictated that Sylvester had a role to play in ensuring that his family had enough to sustain them. His age notwithstanding, his role was to work, earn money, and contribute his wages to help his family. In retrospect, Sylvester performed that responsibility quite well and made a contribution that was highly beneficial to his family. Of this, there is no doubt.

LIFE IN THE CAPITAL CITY FOR A COUNTRY BOY:

From an income ranging between thirty and thirty-five dollars, which Sylvester earned per week at his first job in the Washington, DC area, Thomas was able to get him to agree to send twenty dollars to the family back home on a weekly basis. Buddy had never made so much money, and it never even occurred to him that that was possible. On the day he got his first check, he didn't know what to do with himself. He had looked forward with some anxiety and had even played through his mind several times what that day would look like, and had even tried to estimate what the exact amount of his check would be. When the day came and he received the check, he realized that taking out twenty dollars for his family back in Smithfield still left him a lot more money than he needed. He was now the man!

With so many job opportunities in the area, Sylvester was able to acquire varied work experiences. For example, his first job when he got to Virginia was as a bus boy in a restaurant known as Ryan's Grill. He held that job for the first one or two years that he lived there. After that he worked for the next two years at a black construction company that was known at the time as Barnett Brothers.

Every employee in this company was black. In fact, Buddy worked predominantly under black supervisors throughout the time that he lived in the Virginia/Washington, D.C. area. This was a very memorable experience for him because it showed him some of what was possible, rather than what was impossible, for black people like him. Coming from his North Carolina home, there were vivid reminders all around him of what was impossible if you were black, and especially if you were black and poor. Here in the capital city area, things were different.

For the five years that he lived in that area, from 1952 to 1957, Buddy was never out of work. Besides working in a restaurant and with a construction company, he also held positions at what was then known as the Durbar Hotel, a club that hosted black entertainers in those days. As an employee in that hotel, he had the opportunity of seeing and attending to stars like Ella Fitzgerald and Little Richard, among others, who used to come through the Durbar Hotel in those days.

There was a reason why the Durbar Hotel was popular. At that period in our nation's history, Blacks were denied a right of access to most places in this country. Although prominent black entertainers were allowed to perform before white audiences in posh clubs, they did not possess the right to stay in the hotels that housed those clubs. There were only a few places where such entertainers could stay before and/or after they had performed. The Durbar Hotel in Washington, D.C. was one of those unique places.

Another place of prominence for black entertainers at the time was the Howard Theater, also in Washington, D.C. Both the Durbar Hotel and Howard Theater have since closed, though it is uncertain when these closures occurred. This is a particularly sad thing because both places of entertainment carried with them a highly impressive amount of African American history and culture. They were there before the beginning of the civil rights struggle and opened their doors when most doors were closed to black people in America, and they continued with their mission throughout the period of the civil rights struggle.

Often, one wishes that every place that catered to blacks the way Durbar Hotel and Howard Theater did would still exist today, if only as historical landmarks of what it once meant to be an African American in this country. Their continued existence would also serve as a good reminder of how far we have come as a people and as a nation. But then again, maybe God intended such places to exist only as a succor for His children until they attained the state of freedom that we now have. If that was their only purpose for existing, then the Durbar Hotel, the Howard Theater, and many such places in this country at the time certainly accomplished their purpose, and much more.

Sylvester moved frequently from one job to another

because he always wanted to do more than he was doing, and he knew that the opportunities to fulfill that desire were plentiful in Washington, D.C. Although the jobs that were available to him were neither career-oriented nor permanent in nature, Sylvester was always convinced that he could do better. For example, when he washed as a bus boy, he did not wish to work as a dishwasher all his life. As a result, he always kept his eyes and mind open for better opportunities.

What was it like to be a black employee in a place like Washington, D.C. in those days? That is a thought that very rarely crosses Reverend McClearn's mind, yet it is an important issue for exploration. It also became important for the Reverend to consider the question when he was directly confronted with it while being interviewed for this book. Even then, as he thought about that period of his life and everything he had to do, Sylvester could not recall experiencing any racial problems at any of his places of employment in the Washington, D.C. area.

It is of course possible that Sylvester would have been more cognizant of the existence of racial problems on the job if he had been more educated or more aware of the social and political problems of the day. As it turned out, his low level of education and lack of social and political awareness guaranteed that he was not a threat to anyone and was not highly conscious of the social events of the day. The fact that he always got paid for the work that he did also had a tremendous impact on his outlook and perception of the labor force. He was not trying, neither was he going to pry open or knock down any doors. Instead, he was just happy to do any job that was available and was not a threat to the white establishment in any way.

To be sure, the point being made is not that a white person at a place of employment never disrespected Sylvester. This is certainly not the inference that any reader should draw from the discussion here, since that would be an inaccurate claim for most black employees of white organizations anywhere in this country to make, even today. At various places of employment, Sylvester was in fact the object of racist jokes and insults by white people who desired to box him into the kinds of categories that racists often tended to want to put black people. It was also quite common for white employers and fellow employees who were white to attempt to take advantage of people like Buddy in any way they could. For example, they might try to make him and other Blacks do more tasks than they were paid for, or tasks that had not been assigned to them in the beginning of the contractual relationship.

Although these situations often angered Sylvester, he was prepared for them, thanks to his parents' frequent reminder while growing up that "sticks and stones may break your bones but words can never break your bones." Therefore, even when he was angered by these incidents, he never felt injured by them. Instead, they just made him want to do better.

The incidents that Sylvester considered as injuries on the job were actually perpetrated by fellow blacks. One of those incidents remains very fresh on his mind to this day. A black man who was known to his family had approached Sylvester's mother and told her that he needed some to work for him on his farm, and he wondered if Sylvester would. As remuneration, this would-be employer promised an acre of tobacco farm. When Sylvester's mother told him about this request and offer, he jumped at it and worked very hard because he saw it as an opportunity to assist and also please his mother. When he finished the assigned work, the man and his wife refused to pay him anything for the work. They did not pay him the remuneration that he had been offered or anything at all. To support their position, the couple concocted a story, claiming that Sylvester did not deserve to get paid because he had been disrespectful to them. He felt injured and so deeply hurt that he is not likely to ever forget the experience.

This type of oppressive exploitation was certainly not unique to black employers at the time. However, Sylvester did not spend as much time with white people as he did with Blacks. As a result, his chances of getting so emotionally injured by Whites in the workplace were limited. This, of course, cannot be said of Reverend McClearn's father and other Blacks who experienced remarkable injustices working for white people. In this case, it does appear that what made this experience so hurtful for Sylvester was that the perpetrators of the injustice were black people like him, who should have understood his situation and protected him from the kind of experience that they handed to him.

Later in his working life, Reverend McClearn realized that there were remarkable differences between working under a black supervisor and working under a white supervisor. For example, he learned that a black person working under a black supervisor did not often feel as though he was being treated with prejudice when he was wronged or made to work harder than he should really be doing. Instead, it was often easy to explain away the supervisor's attitude as "a bad mood".

Secondly, he found that it was always possible for a black subordinate to interact freely with his supervisor and, thirdly, black supervisors sometimes acted as though they had a brotherly responsibility toward the subordinate. As a result, they would often go beyond the call of their duty to help the worker in his personal life and even to encourage the worker to save his earnings.

As he would find later in Newburgh, New York, the relationship between a black worker and a white supervisor was much different. There was no running away from prejudice because there was no way to work in the City of Newburgh without feeling the prejudice. He began to wonder why black employees all worked in one area, separate from white people, and why the patterns of promotion were stacked against black employees. It was only a question of time before Sylvester would lead a challenge against the systems of hiring and employment at his place of employment in Newburgh. Fortunately, he won the battle and caused changes to occur. Since that challenge that he led, labor relations have not been the same in Newburgh, New York.

It is possible and easy to look back today and think of Reverend McClearn as a man who had no childhood. Of a fact, much of his early childhood was spent either working in the fields or in the streets. His later childhood was spent working at jobs that are now reserved for adult men rather than young boys. Since he was a kid who did tasks that would have belonged to men, Sylvester became an adult very quickly – well ahead of his chronological age. With the tasks and responsibilities that he was expected to accomplish, he became at a very young age a notable contributor through his sweat and labor to the development of his family and his country. Of course this occurred by default, since he was only a child who was forced to begin to play in the adult labor league due to circumstances that were clearly beyond his control.

EIGHT

NEW YORK RECEIVES A QUIET ARRIVAL

Fate made Buddy leave his family's home for the Arlington, Virginia at a very young age. Eventually, he landed and lived in Washington, D.C. The goal was to engage Buddy in a productive economic life from which his family back home in Smithfield, North Carolina was expected to benefit. This is certainly the kind of responsibility or pressure that should never be placed on the shoulders of any American child. However, Buddy was not just an American child; he was black – which put him in a different category. For African American children, the same rules that applied to other American children did not always apply.

As an African American child, Buddy had a responsibility to contribute financially to the survival of his family. The issue was survival rather than an effort to help his family "move on up". That was not a responsibility that generally belonged in the arena of kids, but it was one that fate thrust on African American kids in Buddy's situation. Buddy embraced that responsibility with an open mind and open arms, probably because he knew no better and because his family's survival was more prominent in his mind than trying to determine what was right and what was wrong.

As a good child, Buddy did exactly what he was expected to do in Washington, D.C. He worked very hard and, true to plan, his family benefited from the fruits of his labor. Buddy's brother, Thomas, was very proud of him and remained so even when he became somewhat concerned about Buddy. At that point, it became necessary that a decision be made to get Buddy to relocate from Washington, D.C. The decision that was made was for Buddy to move to the State of New York. That decision had very little to do with Buddy, and almost everything to do with his brother, Thomas. More than any other human being in Buddy's life, Thomas was a great influence, which is why Reverend McClearn will forever speak fondly of his brother who he describes as "my guiding post".

Thomas was the brother who, several years earlier, had moved Buddy from Smithfield, North Carolina to live with him in Arlington, Virginia. Throughout the duration of his stay in the Washington D.C, area, Thomas never left Buddy to his own desires that, for him and for any young man, were not always pure. Thomas was conscious of the potential challenges facing a good-looking young man like Buddy. As a result, he was always there to guide and support his younger brother. Clearly, Thomas was much more of a father figure to Buddy than his father ever was. It was Thomas that provided both the structure and the foundation for the conscience that Buddy needed for his life as a young man.

It is impossible to tell what would have become of Buddy had Thomas left him to traverse life without guidance. Roosevelt ("Velt") McClearn put this very succinctly when he stated in an interview with me: "I think we all had pieces of my father's bad stuff in us – all of us, including my brother Buddy. Some of us have since been able to shed those pieces but some of us still have them. Thomas did very well for Buddy. He was very influential in helping Buddy find a path for himself". In other words, Sylvester was not always a man with a stellar character. As he himself would acknowledge, he did things that many men still do at a young age. However, he was wise and responsible enough to allow himself to be guided by Thomas - an older brother who clearly had his family's best interest at heart.

Reverend McClearn and people who know his family well

understand why he can never say enough about his brother, Thomas, who was really one of a kind. He was a very caring and very thoughtful man with a heart that was completely full of love. If there are ever any hearts that are made of gold, Thomas had one. There was no doubt that he often thought a lot about his family and he often wondered how he could make Buddy's life and the entire family's life better. Incidentally, Thomas was as gracious and compassionate toward everyone else as he was to his own family. Like his mother, nobody has ever been known to speak ill of Thomas.

Thomas was a man with great foresight. Years before, he had seen his family heading dangerously down the spiraling road of poverty, and he intervened to rescue the family by moving Buddy to Virginia to live with him. Now in Washington D.C., he saw his brother Buddy heading dangerously down the spiraling rails of an out-of-control life, and felt that he had to intervene to save Buddy from himself. To achieve this, he believed that he needed to take Buddy out of the fast lane of Washington, D.C., and move him to a slower lane, wherever that was.

Thomas would often inquire into Buddy's well-being and thoughts, as well as the plans that he was making for his life. Thomas was never afraid to ask Buddy any questions that might have been on his mind at any given time. He was clearly the best example of what an older brother was supposed to be. It was always important to Thomas that Buddy should take advantage of the opportunities that were available. He wanted Buddy to live a responsible life and to maintain a lifestyle and choices that were both healthy and purposeful. Even after Buddy began to live alone in Washington D.C. Thomas checked up on him as often as he could, just to make sure that all was well with his brother. Without a doubt, Thomas' concerns were well placed.

Although we often tend to look with disdain at the lifestyle choices that surround us in our society today, the truth is that many of the behaviors that we now condemn also existed a long time ago. Many of the young men and women of Buddy's teenage years, who we now consider as today's old men and women, were active participants in the now-criticized actions of those years. For example, there were always young ladies who were willing to invite young men to move in with them, and there were always young men who were just very happy to make such a move. Therefore, it was common for unmarried young men and young women to live together in romantic relationships without getting married. Such interactions were often like contracts without serious emotional strings attached.

Young men and women would live together and do what couples usually do; then they would move on to other willing partners and start new relationships once the reigning one was over. For many of those young men and women at the time, this was just the way life was, and therefore the way they lived. Consequently, there were always young men and women who lacked needed stability in their lives. Instead, the young people were often like transient nomads whose homes were temporary abodes with whomever men or women they were with at the time.

Like most people his age at the time, Buddy did not lose much sleep analyzing the moralistic value of the choices that he made, especially in regard to the common practice that has just been described. In fact, it is doubtful that there were many people in his peer range who spent much time analyzing such moralistic issues. That was not just what young people did then, nor is it what most young people do today. To them, there was really nothing wrong with actions, which in their eyes and minds were essentially a rite of passage.

The only major thing that young people really worried about was the challenge that they often faced each time they made the choice to move in with the young ladies that they were romantically involved with. That challenge often had to do with striking the necessary balance between giving the kind of relationship that the ladies wanted, and keeping one's independence at the same time. How could you really be independent of someone with whom you were living? How could you actually maintain a long-lasting romantic relationship that was based on convenience rather than love? The challenges were indeed always very difficult but for that moment at least, that was the way Buddy and most of his peers lived. Clearly, their concerns mainly had to do with survival rather than saving the world from itself.

Through his calm eyes and mind, Thomas had seen and seriously thought about the way that young people like his brother were living and he was both very concerned and scared. After several nights of thinking about Buddy's future in the midst of what he considered to be the craziness that was increasingly characterizing Buddy's era of youth in Washington DC, Thomas decided to act. His first move was to travel from his Arlington home to visit Buddy in Washington and confront him directly with his thoughts. When Thomas stepped into Buddy's well-kept cozy apartment, he looked troubled. He was clearly unhappy and dissatisfied with the way Buddy was living and what he was doing.

Thomas was a straightforward, sincere man who never minced words. You could always count on him to say exactly what he thought and to mean what he said. He was both honest and courageous, and he always called anything as he saw it. On that day in Buddy's apartment, his dissatisfaction with his younger brother seemed clearly written all over his face. He saw, rightly, that Buddy was a young man living life on the edge of a very fast lane and he seemed quite pained that Buddy seemed to be on the verge of wasting some of his youthful potentials. Buddy had known his brother long and well enough to be able to read him sometimes – even before he said anything. So on this occasion, he was able to read the expression on Thomas' face and he knew instantly that his brother was not pleased.

At some level in his own subconscious, Buddy knew that the way he was living was not very good for him, but he had neither plan nor desire to undergo any reformation. Although it was wild, dangerous, and careless, his life seemed like fun to him – as it would to anyone in his shoes who spent so much time partying when he wasn't working. This is the kind of lifestyle that Buddy's brother Velt calls "the piece of Daddy in all of us". Here in Washington D.C. was Buddy living the piece of his father that was in him. Now that he is much older, Reverend McClearn looks back at those years of his life and he doubts that he would have lived much longer had his brother not intervened at the time that he did.

That day of Thomas' visit to Buddy in Washington D.C. remains as clear to Reverend McClearn now as if it had happened only yesterday. He had no idea that Thomas would be visiting that day, but it was quite typical of Thomas to just show up unannounced. That was also not unusual in those days. Family members and friends did not need any special invitation to visit your home. They could always expect to be received whenever they showed up, and they knew that they could in turn expect the same open acceptance if they decided to visit the same family members. Of course that is no longer the way family interactions occur in our society. Everyone is now too busy to have people drop in on them unannounced. Besides, we have become a society in which independence and individualism are emphasized above the values of friendship and family unity.

This is probably what happens whenever the marketplace begins to determine how people live their lives. In that sense, it is a development that can probably occur anywhere. It is the case in the Western world now, but it is a change that the rest of the world can expect to experience as they increase in economic and technological development. In that sense, there is often a high price to pay for advancement and, in the case of nations the chief culprit is sometimes the family system and values.

Thomas visited Buddy occasionally - usually after he had not seen or heard from him for some time. But there was something different about his visit on this day that was to be one of his last visits to Buddy's home. As soon as Thomas walked in, Buddy noticed him looking around the apartment, stopping momentarily, and then looking very directly at Buddy before sitting down. No sooner had Thomas sat down than he said to Buddy in his usual caring and down-to-earth fashion: "Buddy, you need a change of location". Without waiting for Buddy to respond, Thomas continued: "How about going to New York?" He did not wait for a response from Buddy before he continued: "If you get a job in New York, will you go?"

Instantly, Buddy thought of the bright lights of New York that he had seen so frequently on television and in pictures, and it occurred to him that New York was a dream place to go and live in. Almost immediately, it also occurred to him that he was having fun in Washington, D.C where he was currently located. On the one hand, he wanted to remain where he was, but on the other hand, he had utmost trust and respect for Thomas and he knew that his brother always meant very well – even now.

Since he wasn't expecting this proposal from his brother, Buddy decided to give his brother a response that would satisfy him for the moment. So he told his brother that he would indeed go to New York. Even a man like Buddy who knew his brother very well did not expect that his brother would pursue that conversation beyond that point. Instead, he expected that the discussion would end as soon as Thomas left his apartment. That was in fact Buddy's desire but unknown to him, his brother took Buddy's word seriously and chose to act on it after he left Buddy's home. In essence, he proceeded to call Buddy's bluff.

Once Buddy agreed to his brother's suggestion to move to New York, Thomas took care of everything else, as was his nature to do. As soon as he got home, he contacted Randolph, Jr., who was living in Newburgh, New York, and requested him get Buddy a job and take him into his home. About three weeks later, Thomas returned to visit and informed Buddy that a job was waiting for him in New York, courtesy of his brother, Randolph, Jr. Before he left on that day, Thomas gently informed Buddy that he expected him to make the trip to New York within the next two weeks.

Every time Thomas visited Buddy, he left him with words

that were clearly words of wisdom. For example, he met Buddy hosting a party during one of his visits and he told him before he left, "You won't make it like this." On the day he returned to inform Buddy about his new job in New York, Thomas said: "When you go to New York, you will meet the same kind of people there that you have here." He paused briefly, then, he added: "But you will have the opportunity to decide whether to start on a new path. I wish you would choose a different path, find a church girl, and live well." With that, he bid Buddy farewell.

In retrospect, Reverend McClearn is not sure why he agreed with his brother's suggestion that he move to New York. As it turned out, he did not only agree with Thomas, but he obeyed. Left to him, he was satisfied living by himself and making his own independent decisions in the District of Columbia, which usually involved working and enjoying what he considered to be the good life. Most of the time, he lived in a room that he rented for between fifteen and twenty dollars per week. Occasionally, he rented an apartment for about fifty dollars per week.

The type of apartment that commanded such rent, which was considered high in those days, was usually a two-room apartment - meaning a bedroom and a kitchen - and the rent included heat and housekeeping, which was done by the landlord. Although fifteen dollars or fifty dollars doesn't sound like a lot of money to many people today, it was certainly a whole lot of dough in those days. Certainly, things are more expensive now, but there is also much more money floating around now than there was in those days.

With only two weeks to prepare for the move from Washington, D.C. to Newburgh, New York, Buddy created a long mental list of things that he needed to accomplish. The most significant on that list had to do with the friendships that he had established since living in Washington, D.C. He knew that, if he moved to New York, proximity would become a detriment to the continuation of those friendships. Yet, he knew that he had to move because he had already given his word to his brother. The way he resolved the internal conflict was to convince himself that New York might not be suitable for him after all, and he might have to return to Washington, D.C. in a little while. So, he told some of his friends that he was only going away on vacation, and he left some of his clothes behind in Washington, D.C. He did that just in case things did not turn out well for him in New York and it became necessary for him to return.

Buddy began his journey to Penn Station, New York, from Washington D.C.'s Union Station on a very cold February morning in 1957. From Penn Station, he took a taxi to Grand Central, also in Manhattan, and from there he took another train to Beacon, New York. At the time, there was no bridge, as there is now linking Beacon with Newburgh. So it was impossible to travel by road from Beacon to Newburgh, which is now less than fifteen minutes by road. When he arrived in Beacon, Buddy traveled from there to Newburgh by ferry, which was the only means of transportation available at the time. Once in Newburgh, Buddy walked the short distance from the ferry dock to his brother's house. As he walked, he looked around the surroundings of what he didn't know would become his home for perhaps the rest of his life. He wasn't very pleased with what he saw.

Buddy was disappointed when he arrived in Newburgh because it was very different from the expectations that he had always had regarding New York. Those expectations were based on ideas that Buddy had formulated about New York City - ideas produced by widely held opinions about New York that were certainly not unique to him. Like so many people, Buddy imagined that New York was a community of bright lights. It did not occur to him that New York was actually a big state rather than one beautiful, fast city. But, again, that impression was not unique to him. Even today, he sees so many people outside of New York State who think that New York means New York City. Of course, it is understandable why the term New York would be synonymous with New York City, since that city has everything - enough to make up an entire state.

Buddy was twenty-one when he arrived in Newburgh. He had no idea what awaited him, except that he was there to work and make the best of his opportunities, whatever they were. But Buddy's first impressions of the town were quite bleak. Compared with Washington D.C., Newburgh seemed like a ghost town. After getting off the ferry at the Newburgh Landing, Buddy began the walk up the hill into Newburgh, o his brother's house. Although he had never been to Newburgh before this time, he had received instructions from his brother on how to get to his house, and Buddy felt as though he knew exactly where he was going. But Newburgh also seemed to him like a very small place compared to Washington, D.C. and he knew that he couldn't get lost in Newburgh. As he walked to his brother's home, he looked around in disappointment and with some regret that he had chosen to leave Washington, D.C. Buddy was disoriented and unhappy for sometime, and he felt as though he was being punished by having to live in a "dead" place like Newburgh.

In the absence of bright lights and glitter in Newburgh, Buddy preferred Washington, D.C. and began to miss it. Washington was much bigger and more beautiful, and it certainly had all of the city-features that he had now become accustomed to. Although he had been convinced that he needed a change from the life he had been living in Washington, D.C., and hoped that Newburgh could provide the opportunity to achieve that change, Buddy was nevertheless disappointed with the contrast of Newburgh and the city he had just left behind. It was certainly a culture shock.

Several times during that initial period of his stay in Newburgh, Sylvester felt like leaving and returning to Washington, D.C. The only thing that kept him from doing so was hearing the tape of his brother's voice over and over in his head: "You can decide to go back where you came from, but you should want to change your life." Buddy knew that his life needed to change, and he made the decision to remain in Newburgh. By so doing, he gave himself the opportunity to achieve the changes that he needed to make in his life. In the end, he decided that it might be worthwhile to remain in Newburgh and change his life. That decision turned out to be highly rewarding for Buddy.

Randolph, Jr. had been so named by his father who was himself named after his own father. As has been explained in a previous chapter, this situation guaranteed that there were three Randolphs in the McClearn family, two of who were Randolph, Jr. In Chapter Four, a conscious decision was made to refer to Buddy's father as Randolph II. In this and subsequent chapters, the Randolph, Jr. who was Buddy's brother will be referred to as Randolph III or Randy – the name by which he was known by many people.

Randolph III was the oldest of the McClearn children. He was also the first to get married and the first to leave the South. He chose to migrate to Newburgh, NY because his wife had some relatives in Newburgh, NY through whom they found out that life was much better in New York. He was a very big man who maintained his great looks throughout his life. As an adult, he weighed between 400 and 500Ibs but was a great dresser and never sloppy. Despite his weight, Randolph III was very light on his feet and would move with much more grace and speed than most people who were much lighter in weight. He was extremely intelligent and hardworking, and a great family man. Randy worked for several years as a cook in Newburgh. Later, he worked for forty years in a tile-manufacturing factory, also in Newburgh. Randy was blessed with a great wife, two daughters (Shirley and Gloria) and one son (Jimmy).

Families do not always welcome new arrivals with open arms – until they develop a good level of comfort. In the case of Randy's case with Buddy, there was no such honeymoon period. From his first day in their home, Randy's family received Buddy very warmly and they were forever wonderful to Buddy. Randolph also sang in a quartet that rehearsed regularly in his home and it became Buddy's routine to go with his brother to rehearsals and performances. At nighttime, he frequently went to the bars to see what the nightlife in

Newburgh was like. Certainly, it was nothing like nightlife in Washington, D.C.

Randolph, Jr. and his family went to church every Sunday, and Buddy went with them. They gave Buddy a room in their home and he worked at the same tile factory at which his brother was employed. The factory operated twenty-four hours a day, and work shifts were scheduled accordingly. The system was such that they worked one shift for a month and then another shift for another month. In this way, the shifts rotated continuously. Although he missed his friends in Washington, D.C., Buddy was able to make friends very quickly in Newburgh. Most of his initial friends were his brother's friends and his colleagues at work.

While he was living in New York, and now in Newburgh, the mother and siblings that he left behind were missing Buddy very much at home in North Carolina. He was an extremely hardworking and generous so and brother of whom everyone was very proud. In the same way in which he speaks glowingly of Thomas, Buddy's siblings also speak very highly of him as well. He had been a loving and nurturing big brother all along, sometimes putting himself in the line for his siblings' welfare. His sister, Gertha Lee, regarded as "Baby Lee" by everyone in the McClearn family, has very fond memories of one of the roles that Buddy played when he lived at home.

During an interview done with her for this book, Baby Lee spoke of how a very young Buddy would often take on the role of getting food for his brothers and sisters when there was no food at home. At some point, Buddy realized that while his family starved, a local bakery there in Smithfield always had enough food to throw away at the end of their business day. Once he figured this out, Buddy began to go to that bakery to get food (mainly baked goods) from the dumpster to feed the family.

One day, Buddy's younger brothers and sisters were very hungry and he knew it. He was a young man who was very sensitive to pain and could tell if someone close to him was having a bad time, even before a word was expressed. He remains that kind of man even in adulthood. On this day, Buddy knew that his siblings needed food, so he went to the bakery's dumpster as he had done several times before and brought home some soybeans. After cooking them, Buddy offered to eat the soybeans first, to be sure that they were ready for his siblings' consumption. Unfortunately, neither Buddy nor any of his siblings did realize that the soybeans were not edible. As Baby Lee tells it, "What happened is funny now, but it was very scary at the time. Buddy became very sick. The soybeans swelled up in his stomach and he was rolling. He looked pregnant". This was clearly a case of a young child who not only saw it as his responsibility to fend for his siblings when they were hungry, but was also always ready to put himself on the line for them, even at the risk of getting hurt.

Buddy's family in Smithfield missed him greatly, but they also knew that he was looking out for them, and would always be willing to do so, however physically distant he was away from home. Moving to Newburgh moved him even farther away from home but his success and, consequently, enhanced relief of his family's plight, was going to depend on how resilient Buddy was and how willing he was to change his life.

With many things that don't start out quite well, a turn for the better tends to occur if we only give ourselves a chance to succeed. When we do, we can ride out the difficult and lonely times and embrace our blessings that lie on the other side of the hill. Buddy gave himself a chance in Newburgh. The result is an amazing story of a life that responded to a call to change and did his part to lift himself and future generations in a small New York town in which most people in his shoes might have refused to spend more than one lonely night.

NINE

TWO STRANGERS MEET AND UNITE

This section is devoted entirely to Sylvester's recollections of the early life of his relationship with Billie, his wife of over four decades. Since there are usually at least two sides to any story involving two people, Billie's perceptions, experiences and feelings regarding that early time and their life together are also discussed in a subsequent chapter. It is only fitting that a woman who has walked on Buddy's side for so long and has played a tremendous role in his life for as long as she has should step forward and speak about what she has seen, felt, and thought through the years.

When Buddy arrived in Newburgh and began to live with his brother Randolph III, he realized that his brother, who was always sociable, had not changed very much. He had several friends who came frequently to visit him. Named Randolph, Jr. after his father, this Randolph was very different from his father in many ways. Unlike their father, Randolph (referred to as Randolph III in this book), was a deeply religious man who maintained remarkable commitment to his church. He loved God with all his heart, loved people, loved the church, and served on several church committees. To most people, Randolph III was not just plain old Randolph. Instead, he was Randy, an identification that signified his connection to people, his entire environment, and the times in which he lived.

Gospel singing was Randy's chief love and he was a member of a singing quartet that rehearsed regularly in his home. It was only a question of time before Buddy himself became an active part of the quartet, singing and traveling with the group. One member of that quartet was a man named Mitchell Elliot. Mitchell was very well known in town, and he seemed to take a liking to Buddy very soon after he arrived. When Mitchell came to visit one evening during Buddy's second month in Newburgh, he informed Buddy about a young lady that he wanted Buddy to meet. That was in March of 1957.

It is uncertain what the exact motive of Mitchell was, or if there was even any motive or goal behind his kind gesture. Certainly, Mitchell saw a young man who was new in town and he thought that the new arrival might benefit from some female companionship. Mitchell also knew that Buddy still had not developed a high level of comfort with his new environment, so he felt that a romantic involvement with a woman might help Buddy become more accepting of Newburgh. Whatever the case might have been, Mitchell was a nice guy who was trying to do a nice thing for a nice young man.

As it turned out, Buddy wasn't looking to settle down with any woman at that time. First, he knew that he was still very young - and young people just didn't look to settle down with a woman. Secondly, Buddy was still in shock about being in Newburgh and was wondering how he could live in a place that seemed and felt so remote. Yet, he knew that Mitchell might be right – that he might indeed benefit from some close friendship with somebody, preferably a female companion. He obliged Mitchell, not because he was desperate for female companionship, but because he was somewhat bored and felt that he needed to fill his time with something, or someone.

Mitchell spoke very highly of the young woman that he wanted Buddy to meet. As it turned out, the young woman was herself a new arrival in New York. The words that Mr. Elliot spoke of this young woman left Buddy in no doubt that she was a special lady, at least to Mitchell. Later, Buddy would learn that the woman was indeed a special lady to everyone, and Mitchell's words did not in fact tell all. She was from Texas, where her parents lived, and she was visiting with family members here in New York.

Although Buddy was uncertain why Mitchell thought of him as the person to introduce to her, he knew enough by now to assume that this must have been part of God's special plan for his life. However, to say that he was completely certain of the meaning and content of God's plan, or even of the concept, would be claiming too much. The reality is that he was not completely certain of this at the time, since he had not as yet developed a personal relationship with God. The concept and its meaning fact became clearer and clearer to him over the years. That unfettered knowledge came after Buddy accepted Christ, following the religious experience that will be describe later in this book.

Without much thinking on his part, Buddy accompanied Mitchell Elliot to the home of the young lady about whom he knew very little. When they got there, they rang the doorbell and waited for just about a minute that felt like an eternity to Sylvester. When the door was eventually opened for them, they walked into a living room where they were welcomed by the sight of three young ladies, whom Sylvester later learned were all living in the house. One of them was braiding the hair of another, while the other sat with other members of the household as the adults all chatted.

No sooner had they received their warm welcome that Sylvester from the introductions and especially through Mitchell's body language that the woman he was there to meet was the one that was on her feet braiding the hair of one of the ladies. Right at that moment, her beauty struck Sylvester. His focus was instantly turned to her. This is in itself probably evidence of predestination, since young men in such situations often tend to be attracted to someone else when they get to their destination and find more than one woman. In this case, Sylvester found this woman to be a very attractive lady and a very good person, even before he spoke any words to her. Conventional wisdom tells us that we cannot tell a book by its cover. In other words, we cannot tell a good person from physical appearance or at a first meeting. But conventional wisdom certainly flew out the window when Buddy met Billie. He had a very strong feeling that he had just met a very good person that he would actually love to have a relationship with.

Like most first such meetings tend to go, the first meeting between Sylvester and Billie had nothing extraordinary to it. The entire visit was quite casual and they did not engage in any discussion related to the real reason for his visit with Mitchell. And there is no reason why Billie or anyone in her family would have suspected that this was anything other than just a visit. After Billie's aunt and her family knew Mitchell and it was not unusual for him to visit the family in their home. Since nothing stood out in this meeting, besides the woman that he was just about to become interested in, Sylvester does not recall the exact content of their conversation that visit night. All he remembers is that she was introduced as Billie, and he thought that was a beautiful and uncommon name for a woman. Greatly memorable and life-changing events would however begin to occur afterwards.

About a month after he accompanied Mitchell on the visit to Billie's home, Sylvester contacted her by telephone and asked if she would go with him to see a movie at a drive-in theater, the only one in Newburgh at the time. She agreed but, when the day and time came, she had her friend accompany her on the date. That move was interesting because, as Sylvester found out very quickly, Billie was not interested in him and certainly did not wish to have a relationship with him. Instead, she was trying to push her friend on to him but it was obvious that her friend didn't want Sylvester either. Sylvester knew exactly what was going on, and it was quite disturbing to him. But young men have always found themselves in situations like this, and always will. One thing that Buddy had learned in his young life so far was never to give up. As a result, he was able to believe that the rejection he was experiencing from Billie was only temporary. There was also no doubt in his mind that, although Billie's friend seemed like a good person too, the woman he really wanted was Billie. So, he persisted with the kind of determination and zeal that produces desired results. Eventually, Billie agreed to become involved in a romantic relationship with him.

For much of his life, Buddy had been in the labor force and was always an employee who was very committed to his tasks. The level of responsibility that he brought to the performance of his duties had always been his hallmark at every place where he had worked. Now, he found himself in a romantic relationship with a woman that he cared very much, but it was also important for him to keep his job. It became necessary for him to find a good balance between his responsibilities to his job and the effective maintenance of his relationship. The fact that he worked at one instead of multiple jobs offered him several advantages. For one thing, it afforded him a remarkable amount of time for their courtship, once Billie eventually agreed to engage in a relationship with him. In addition, his job was such that he did not have a permanent shift. Instead, he worked on rotating shifts that could otherwise have impacted the courtship negatively. As it turned out, Billie and he were able to use even the rotating shift schedule to advance their relationship.

In terms of material possessions, Sylvester had very little at this time. He was a twenty-one year old man with one job and an income that would be considered meager by today's standards. But he was also now a happy man who knew the value of what he now had in his life. He had never felt for any woman in his life the same way that he felt for Billie. It became highly essential to him to ensure that he handled the relationship in a highly responsible manner. He did whatever was possible to make the relationship a success.

In retrospect, Reverend McClearn realizes that he did his utmost in the necessary balancing act and they were able to maintain a happy and eventful relationship without disrupting other aspects of their lives. This is certainly a lesson that young couples need to learn especially in light of our increasingly capitalistic world where financial accomplishments appear to be taking precedence over the development and nurturing of relationships.

COURTSHIP

Today, Reverend McClearn often hears young people say that there is too little – or nothing- to do in Newburgh. He understands the sentiment very well because he once felt the same way. It is true that Newburgh is nothing like New York City or any of the big cities in this country. Newburgh is a small town located about 90 miles north of New York City, and removed from the bright lights and entertainment of the big City. It was, and still is not the place to choose to go to in search of fun. But many changes have occurred in Newburgh since Buddy first arrived there in 1957. There is much more to do in Newburgh now than when Sylvester and Billie were courting. Compared with any major city, there was almost nothing for young couples to do in Newburgh in those days - although at the time, Billie and Sylvester did not see it as such. They always made the best of whatever was available to them.

This means that Billie and Sylvester courted in a manner that was quite reminiscent of what country life courtship may still be like today. They would walk up and down Broadway in Newburgh and stop at the stores to buy ice cream. Sometimes, they would walk to Billie's home from his, or vice versa, then walk the distance back and forth a few more times before separating. They did so much of the same thing daily, only breaking the monotony of walking by going to see movies at any of the two or three theaters that existed on Newburgh's Broadway at the time.

Just in case the reader is thinking that the Sylvester-Billie courtship period was one of uninterrupted fun, let it be known that it was by no means a picnic. Although their relationship produced highly positive emotions for him, Billie and Sylvester were both strong-willed people who clashed frequently. When they were not having a great time in one another's company, they were arguing over little things. At one time after their engagement, their argument was so strong that Sylvester demanded that she return to him the engagement ring that he had given her. In turn, she was stubborn enough and proud enough to refuse to beg him to reconsider. Instead, she returned Buddy's ring to him. As he looks back now, he is glad that that crisis did not last very long. People who know them now would certainly share this same sentiment when they learn that this model marriage of over four decades almost didn't happen.

As they both grew emotionally, Sylvester and Billie learned to have mutual respect for one another. He realized that he had some growing up to do, and that included learning to respect a lady as well as increasing the degree of patience that he possessed. In due course, he became more patient and mature, and he began to apply his new qualities to his relationship with Billie. Buddy was even able to handle, appreciate, and honor Billie's desire to keep their relationship chaste until marriage. Although that was difficult for him to accept initially, it became a very strong part of his beliefs once he became a born again Christian. From the time that experience occurred, every desire that was contrary to chastity died in Sylvester "Buddy" McClearn as he became a completely new person.

Like many people who know a good thing and refuse to give it up when they have it in their hands, Sylvester had a good woman in his hands, and he was never going to give her up. Therefore, within a few months after they started dating, he asked Billie to marry him. This was of course completely consistent with the practice of the times. In those days, courtship did not drag on indefinitely. Unlike today when people meet and date each other for several years before they get married, courtship in those days was often brief, although some also lasted for extended periods. There were just no hard and fast rules, and people believed and trusted in each other, even if they had only been dating for a very short period of time.

There is another significant difference between the way courtship and marriages occur today and the way they occurred in those days. That difference was in the age of couples then and now. In those days, it was very common for teenage women to marry and it was quite common for men to marry as teenagers or in their early twenties. That is almost unheard of in today's world, but it was almost the norm in those days. Therefore, nobody told Buddy that he was too young to get married when, at age twenty-one, he began to think seriously of marrying Billie. She was a woman whose entry into his life was special enough to make him want to alter his life in ways that he had never thought possible until then.

Once Billie accepted his marriage proposal, Sylvester wrote a letter to her mother in Texas and asked her permission to marry her daughter. He did not say much in the letter, but he made sure to tell her that he would be dedicated to her daughter, and he would do his best to ensure that she was happy if she married him. He also assured Billie's mother that she would never regret allowing her daughter to marry him. In his letter, he enclosed a picture of himself, so she would see what he looked like. It may not have been a sophisticated letter, but he knew what Billie meant to her mother, and he meant every word he wrote in that letter. He was also determined to ensure that he would be the best husband that any woman could hope for, and the best son-in-law that anyone would like to have in his or her family.

As far as he was concerned, making this kind of request of Billie's mother was one thing. Being guaranteed a positive response was another, and there, he was not so confident. First, Billie was an only child, and Sylvester was sure that her mother had great goals for her, as well as very high expectations regarding the kind of man that she hoped Billie would marry. He wasn't sure that he was that type of man. Second, Billie had a high school diploma and he did not. It was clear that if Billie's mother wanted her to prosper materially, he did not possess the material qualities. Third, their upbringing was quite different. In other words, they came from two different backgrounds, and she was definitely from a higher social class than he was.

As it turned out, Billie's mother was not one to be

impressed by material possessions. She was more impressed by the heart of a person than what the person possessed materially. As a result, she saw through his letter a young man with genuine intentions and a solid moral character that approached her from his heart. As a result, she responded to his letter by agreeing to have her only child marry him. To the day that she died in 2001, Mrs. Ada Smith remained consistently accepting and supportive of her daughter and son in-law, and she has never presented them with any problem. Sylvester is sure that not many men can claim to have had wonderful mothers-in-law, but he is one of those few who can make that claim and mean it from the bottom of his heart.

Since Billie was raised strongly committed to the Christian faith, exemplified by church attendance, there was no question that she and he would continue to go to church after their marriage. While they were courting, she continued in her church while Sylvester remained in the church he had attended prior to their meeting. Fondly called Holy Temple, the complete name of that church was United Holy Church of America. After they became engaged, however, she joined him in his church.

HERE COMES THE BRIDE...AND THE GROOM

In November of 1957 - eight months after they met - Billie and Sylvester got married in the home of the pastor of their church, Reverend J. C. Watson, who is now deceased. They had a small wedding, but one that was both very meaningful and unforgettable. Reverend Watson conducted the wedding ceremony. Sylvester would be the first to admit that he was in a daze during the ceremony, only to snap out when the pastor said: "You may now kiss the bride."

He had given his life to Christ four months earlier and, Billie and he remained devout members of Holy Temple for twenty-five years after their wedding. All of their children were in fact born while they were still attending that church. Their wedding day was quite exciting for Buddy and it remains one day that he will never forget. Randolph III and his family attended the wedding and were very happy for the very beautiful couple, both of whom they loved very much. Randolph and his family had been very supportive throughout the course of the relationship between Billie and Buddy as it was developing and there was never a doubt that they were in complete approval. Most members of their church congregation also attended the wedding and wished Billie and Sylvester very well. As if only yesterday, Sylvester vividly recalls working the overnight shift, getting a haircut, and then a short nap just before the wedding. As a result, he was slightly late for the wedding. When his bride, a very beautiful woman in a blue dress, came in, accompanied by her friends in the bridal train, her entry was itself an unforgettable moment.

After leaving the church on their wedding day, Billie and Sylvester stopped at a photography studio and took a photograph that still adorns their home and his office to this day. After that, they went to their reception in the home of his aunt in-law, Mrs. Ruby Nichols. The reception was filled with laughter and fun, all of which he was able to handle, since he was in great physical shape. After the reception, the young couple went to begin their lives together in the place that would become their first apartment.

Many people talk about the challenges that confront newly married couples. No doubt, there are challenges but Sylvester prefers to think only of the blessings that Billie and he experienced in the early years of their marriage, and the lessons that they learned. Those lessons shaped and strengthened them as individuals and as a family and brought them even greater blessings.

Most certainly because they were two young people who truly loved each other and were prepared to work and live together for the rest of their lives, many lessons were easy for them to learn. Perhaps because they learned those lessons together, they received many great blessings as a couple. Very early in the life of their marriage, they learned that they would have to work together as a couple if their goal was to achieve matrimonial, material and emotional success. Therefore, they proceeded to do just that.

One of the first things that Sylvester and Billie began to do was to pull their money together and develop a budget to guide them. At the same time, they knew that it was not enough to just have a budget. Instead, they recognized that it was even more important to follow that budget very closely. Therefore, they were very economical with their finances. They knew that, based on what they had and what their goals were, they could not even consider shopping in designer stores. Of course they could have made the choice to do that, but they were conscious of their means and the importance of living within rather than above their means. If they went to designer shops, they would most certainly have been broke a lot. Thanks to that realization, Sylvester and Billie shopped prudently.

It is impossible for any man to take this approach to life unless he has a spouse that understands and accepts the individual for what he is and is willing to work with him, even if that means suffering for the moment as a sacrificial step to future gains. In Buddy's case, he was very blessed to have his new wife, Billie, on the same page with him. Their circumstances, including their choices, were made much easier by the fact that Billie and he were people who were never moved to the point of jealousy or anxiety by whatever someone else had. In other words, they never felt the need to compete with anyone, or to keep up with societal trends.

Mutual trust also helped the McClearn couple tremendously in those early years. Billie and he trusted each other enough to know that they were in agreement regarding where they wanted to take their marriage and their family. They also trusted each other enough to know that whatever they told each other about their hopes, dreams, desires, or even their whereabouts, was always true. It is ironic how much the element of trust is lacking in relationships today, and how that lack of trust often destroys friendships and marriages that would otherwise have had great potential for success. Billie and Sylvester were fortunate enough to know from early on that trust must be a very crucial element in their marriage. Sylvester thanks God frequently for that early realization, and for giving him a wife who was not only willing to give trust, but was also willing and able to make herself trustworthy.

Only God could have made the McClearn's circumstances possible and only He taught these lessons to two young people who were taking giant steps into an uncertain future. When they got married, Billie was twenty-one years old and he was twenty-two. Yet, they marched into the future with hope and faith in God, believing that He would guide and lead them into a tremendously successful family life for as long as they focused completely on Him.

TEN

CONVERSION TO A NEW LIFE

When Buddy arrived in Newburgh in January 1957, he did not have any grand plans. It was not even his idea to go to Newburgh. Left to him, Newburgh would have been one of the most unlikely places that he would have chosen to go. At the time that he set out from Washington D.C. to Newburgh, New York, all that Buddy knew was that he was coming to live and work in New York. Beyond that, he had no strong demands, desires, wishes, or plans. He trusted the judgment of his brother Thomas, at whose insistence he had taken the step to come to New York. He was as confident as ever that Thomas would never steer him in the wrong direction. Perhaps he had some responsibility to make plans for his future in Newburgh, but he was certainly not in the frame of mind to take on such a task at that time. He was young and comfortable just going with the flow - probably not much different from most teenagers and young adults then and now.

Whereas short-term, day-to-day planning concerns most teenagers, long-term planning is not usually their strongest suit. In fact, most young people rarely make serious plans for their lives. That task requires a sense of purpose and responsibility that very few people have when they are young. Young people need adults to help them plan their lives, and it is very rarely that they forget any adult who steps up and helps them do that. Thomas stepped up and took on that responsibility in his brother's life. For that, and for everything else that he stood for, Sylvester will never forget him.

In 1957, Sylvester did not have any idea how long he would stay in Newburgh, or what else he would be doing besides working. Of course, now he is old and wise enough to know that this situation is not uncommon with young people in their teen or early adult years. Often, young people think only of the present time and have no worries regarding the future. The fact is that most adults are not much different. They want things to happen quickly and they want quick gains. Very often, adults want security, which they expect to receive in the form of a guarantee of what the future holds. The truth, however, is that no human being on earth truly knows what the future holds except God reveals it to him. That was the case with Sylvester when he relocated from Washington D.C. to Newburgh.

Although he was a young man at the time, Buddy's life experiences up until that time made him feel older than his actual chronological age. The reason, of course, is that his difficult life had taught him a lot more about life by the time he was even twelve years old than he would naturally have known by the time he was an adult. So, although he was physically a young man at the time, a strong case could be made that he was mentally an adult.

Sylvester knew that his coming to New York would be a strong determinant to the way his entire future would turn out. At least, Thomas had indirectly instilled that in his head. But the future was actually, of course, in God's hands. As it turned out, waiting for Buddy in New York was a religious experience that would change his life forever. The way that experience occurred remains a mystery to him until this day, but the reason it occurred is one that he has come to understand clearly as the years have gone by.

When Buddy got to Newburgh, he found that his brother Randy was a devout Christian who attended church without fail. So too were his wife and the rest of his family. While living with them in their home, Sylvester became very conscious of their religious life and he participated with them in the religious practices that they engaged in. For example, he would read the Bible and pray with them daily. He even went to church with them regularly. This was all very different from the way he had been spending his time during the last few years which he spent living in the Washington D.C. area. Even in this new religion thing, Sylvester was just going with the flow at his brother's home but, for reasons he could not explain, it all seemed worth doing.

Although Sylvester attended a Baptist church in Washington, D.C. he had no real reason for doing so. He did so only because he needed a way to fill his Sundays and this gave him something to do on a Sunday morning. He did not do it out of any serious desire for holiness. Attending church in Newburgh, however, was different. He realized that people actually dressed up to go to church, and they seemed to take it quite seriously. On a Sunday morning, Randy and his family, accompanied by Sylvester, would get up and go through the entire serious routine of getting ready for church. There was always a strong feeling in the air that, for this family, going to church was much more than a ritual. If you were in that home on a Sunday morning, you definitely got the feeling that they all believed by going to church that they were actually going to the temple in which the presence of God resided. After getting dressed as immaculately as possible, the entire family, including Sylvester, would step out of the house together and go together to the church.

Sylvester realized at this time that this Newburgh church was quite like the Pentecostal church to which his mother would take him and her other children when they were young children growing up. In this church, people seemed to shout at the top of their voices as they sang praises to God in worship. They also danced in the spirit and spoke freely in what he understood to be the "tongues" that have been historically associated with the Pentecostal movement since the days of the Apostles.

The nature of the services in this church was always the same and quite predictable. Going to church on a Sunday morning, one could always expect that Holy Spirit-filled preachers would preach for one and one-half or even two hours. Without a doubt, some church services would already have commenced and ended in the length of time that a sermon spanned. Yet in this church, a two-hour sermon was never long enough to bore the congregation. After such sermons, the congregation would still be sitting, willing, and ready to receive.

Many people believe that they are Christians just because they attend church and some people expect that a person who attends church should have no skeleton in his cupboard. This is not always the case. Although Sylvester went to church with his brother and his brother's family, he never participated whole-heartedly with them in their religious activities. The outward demonstration was always there but God requires more from us. Church attendance did not stop Sylvester from continuing some of the negative behaviors that had become habitual for him. For example, he continued to smoke despite the fact that he attended church, prayed, and read the Bible with his brother and his family. Nothing really changed. On occasion, he would even leave church while service was still going on and would go to the bar.

In addition to cigarette smoking, Buddy had a serious gambling habit when he came to Newburgh from Washington, D.C. He also drank alcohol frequently, and ran with women. Again, this was Buddy's display of what Velt described in his conversation with me as the "pieces of Daddy in all of us".

Randy and his wife never put any pressure on Buddy to do or change anything, although Sylvester is sure that they prayed for him in the privacy of their thoughts and space. They trusted God to change his habits, which he is convinced they considered sinful. His brother and sister in-law were in fact great examples of how evangelism ought to be carried out. They were nonjudgmental and relied only on God to change him. Regardless of what Buddy did, they loved him unconditionally and never gave up on him. They were also a very faithful couple who trusted God and believed in His ability to change even the vilest of sinners.

THE UNFORGETTABLE ENCOUNTER

Buddy's entire life took a completely different turn one day in July 1957 as he played pool with some friends in a poolroom located at that time on Water Street in Newburgh. Water Street runs parallel to the Hudson River and stretches through a very beautiful part of Newburgh, with the River providing a remarkable view. It is also remarkable for the kinds of entertainment and recreational opportunities that it offered in those days to anyone who wished to have fun in Newburgh. It is also a place that has, after decades of neglect, benefited from revitalization efforts carried out in Newburgh. In those days, it boasted of bars, affordable restaurants, and places for young people to just "hang out" with their male peers and drink or meet young ladies. Today, Water Street has regained its beauty and boasts now of expensive restaurants which are the products of remarkable architecture and class.

Beauty is not what Sylvester thinks of when he thinks of Water Street. Instead, he thinks of that street as the spot where his "Saul experience" occurred. Again, he was in the pool room playing with his friends. Suddenly a woman he had never seen before walked into the room to distribute tracts to every one of them who was in the room at the time. She was a simple, dark-skinned quite modestly dressed woman. There was something about this woman that Sylvester could not place. Perhaps it was the peace that seemed to surround her, or the calm demeanor that she presented, or the change in the atmosphere when she stepped into the room. Whatever it was, Sylvester is not sure that he will ever know, nor will anyone except God.

Once she entered the room, the unexpected visitor began to distribute tracts and talk about God to the patrons in the poolroom. She began to speak to them about the reasons why it was important for people in the poolroom to open their hearts and allow God to change their lives. As Reverend McClearn recalls the incident, everything else stopped once she walked into the poolroom and they all listened to the strange woman that had just suddenly shown up in their midst. The unclean language and even the game stopped. Neither Buddy nor anyone else in the room ever said a word to the visitor initially. They probably just hoped that she would leave the room as quickly as she had come in so they would resume their game.

In due course, one of Buddy's peers in the poolroom inadvertently made a comment that was by no means uncomplimentary toward the female, preaching visitor. She heard the young man's comment, stopped, and proceeded to speak directly and sharply to the group about the Word of God. Sylvester does not recall exactly what was said, but he knows that his life changed instantly. As this strange woman walked out of the room, so did the taste of cigarettes and alcohol in the life of Sylvester. His gambling and flirtatious habits also completely left him at that instant.

For an intense moment, Buddy felt as though the room had just been visited by the presence of God. Instantly, he felt like he had just become a new creature. He could no longer remain in the room once the woman left. Instead, he walked out of the room shortly after she did and he never returned. He left as a changed person. Since that time, his life has not been the same. From that point until he got married, Sylvester never even had a sexual experience. The flesh, with its sinful desires, died in him and, like Paul, he began to live completely for Christ.

As has been stated, Sylvester had never seen that woman who was the vessel that God used for this encounter - until her visit to that poolroom. The point should also be added that he has never again seen her since that day. One would imagine that in a town as small as Newburgh, people like that would be easy to run into on a regular basis. That was not the case with this experience.

Several times in his life, Sylvester has wished that he

would see that woman again, if only to thank her for bringing the gospel on that day and bringing him into a personal relationship with his Lord and Savior, Jesus Christ. She probably never knew the change that she caused to happen in anybody's life on that day, let alone in his life. It is even possible that, afterwards, she felt bad about coming into that room and getting insulted the way she did, but he hopes that this was not the case.

Reverend McClearn still sometimes wishes for an opportunity to see her just one time, so he can hold her hand and thank her for what she did. But he is sure that will never occur here in this world, since he doesn't even know who the woman was. However, he does know that God had a plan for his life and He inspired a stranger to execute that plan at a time when he needed Him in his life without knowing how much he truly did.

When one experiences a life-changing encounter like the one Sylvester had in that poolroom, he can tend to push it aside as a religious experience that was probably just meant to occur sooner or later. That may have been true even in his case, but Sylvester will say that his experience was a culmination of events that had been in motion even before it happened. He believes that his brother and his sister in-law had been praying very hard and consistently for God to intervene in his life. There is also no doubt that his mother, who was a preacher, also committed her children into the hands of God. He is convinced that those prayers, coupled with the strong presence of God in their home where he lived, were largely responsible for the change that would later occur in his life.

Sometimes, people are able to point to specific times at which their entire life took a different turn. We go through many experiences daily, but sometimes we are able to point to one or more experiences from which our lives took a new turn. Sylvester cannot point to a series of different experiences, but to only one experience as the catalyst for change in his life. He is convinced that what he has become as a person today is the outcome of the religious experience that he had on that July evening in that poolroom at Water Street in Newburgh, New York. However, he is also conscious of the fact that, even prior to his birth on a North Carolina farm, God knew that that day would come, and that everything that happened would happen exactly as it did. Incidentally, his life has unfolded since that time in a manner that surprises him less now than it would have if he didn't know the Lord. Fortunately, he knows his God, and he is willing to be a vessel in God's hands for as long as he lives.

Once the change occurred in his life, he suddenly wanted to do something for others. He got involved in Sunday school and became very active in church activities. Very soon, he also began to get actively involved in activities to benefit young people. To this day, this urge to do more for people and society remains a very strong part of his life.

The Reverend has learned many things from what he now calls my religious experience. The touch of God is gentle and His hand is uplifting. An encounter with God is usually of such great magnitude that its life-changing impact is one that is unparalleled by any experience ever known to man. Sylvester can say this because it is exactly the way he feels about his life, from the day he had his encounter with Him in that poolroom in Newburgh. As he has read the Bible, he has also had the great privilege of learning about some great men of God whose encounters with God changed their lives and begin a process that would lead them to great heights never before reached by men before them. He is referring to great men like Moses, Jacob, Samuel, Saul, David, and Paul, whose encounters with God heralded the roles they eventually played and the positions that they would later occupy in the Word of God.

Sylvester believes that God does not place us in positions to experience such spiritual encounters, unless He wants to use them for His purpose. Having experienced such an encounter, it becomes the responsibility of the recipient to serve God, seek His will, stand up and do that for which he has been blessed with a new life. Later, the way that Sylvester responded to this spiritual encounter will be discussed in greater detail.

Not everyone is supposed to respond in the same way that Buddy responded to his conversion. After all our encounters with God do not always follow the same pattern, nor do they happen to all of us at the same time. Therefore, it is proper to suggest that every such encounter comes with a message specifically for the individual that experiences it. In other words, the nature and message of Sylvester's own religious encounter will be different from the experience of someone else. Consequently, it is up to each of us to find the message that's in it for us, and to follow the path of obedience. In Reverend McClearn's own life, he likes to hope that he has done exactly that.

The Family Of Randolph And Martha McClearn

Sylvester, Ella, 1909, Girtha, 1956, Joe, Lizzie, Roosevelt, Leroy, Jesse, Estelle, Alice, Cleo, Thomas, Randolph Jr, Father Randolph 1898-1964

The McClearn family with the exception of Mr. Randolph McClearn (the father) who, as always, is absent.

Beautiful Mrs. Martha McClearn

Young Sylvester McClearn, Atlantic City, 1955

Mr. Thomas McClearn. He was like a father to Rev. Sylvester McClearn and took him to stay with him in Virginia.

Rev. Sylvester McClearn, about 20 years old,
shortly after he arrived in Newburgh, NY

The young McClearn couple— Sylvester and Billie

Sylvester and Billie McClearn on their wedding day

Rev. and Mrs. McClearn during their entrepreneural years

Mr. Randolph McClearn, Jr., who is Rev. McClearn's older brother, named after his father

Young Richard McClearn

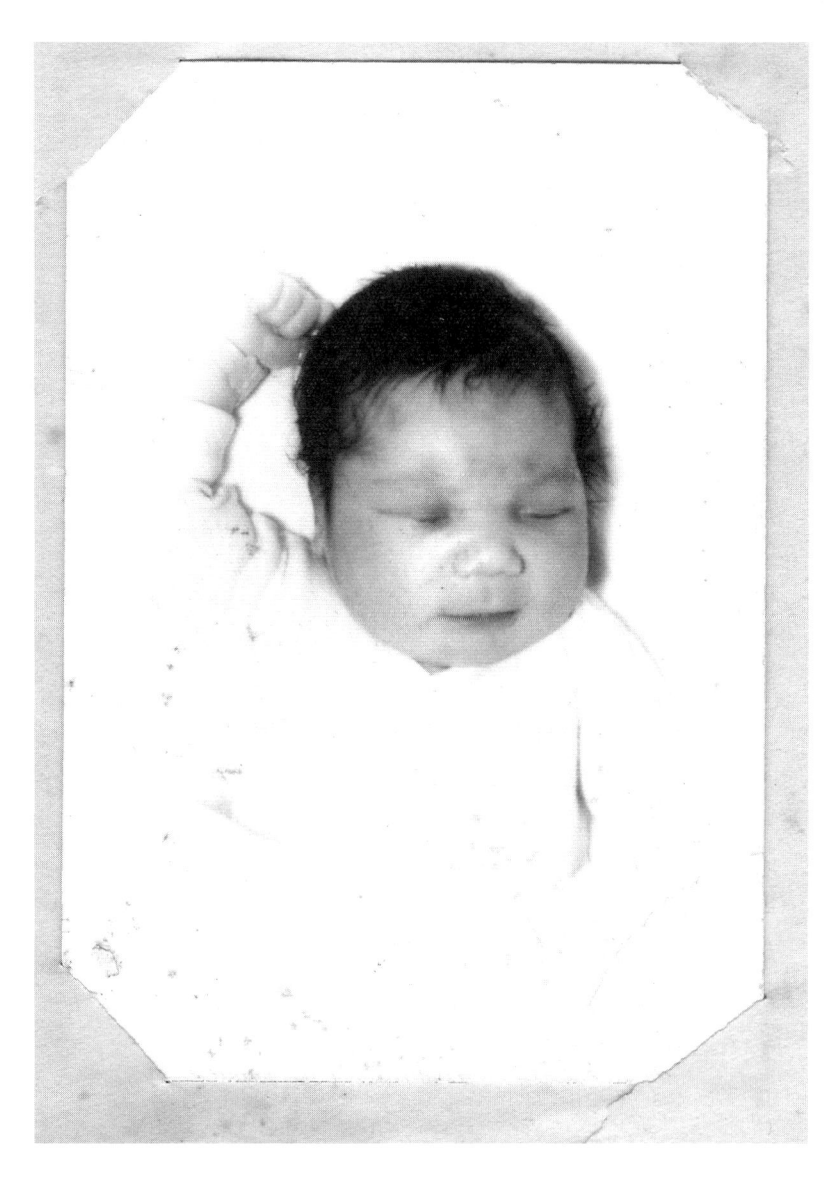

Baby Michael McClearn

Darnell and Billy on their first celebrated birthday at four years old. They were born on February 29th, so their birthday comes around every four years.

Aunt B (Ruby Nichols), Mrs. McClearn's aunt,
who she came to meet in Newburgh.

Jeannie McClearn

Alex carrying his younger cousin

Richard's graduation from Valley Central High School in Montgomery, NY

Darnell as a member of the Fordham Rams (Fordham University Football Team). He obtained his Masters from Fordham.

Richard as a member of the Valley Central H.S. basketball team

Alex at SUNY, Albany— football team

Michael's graduation from Valley Central High School in Montgomery, NY

Michael on High School Graduation Day

Darnell (left) and Billy (right) on High School Graduation Day

Darnell graduation from Fordham University

Alex graduating from Newburgh Free Academy

Michael as a football player at Temple University

NO. 8

Mike McClearn is the biggest of a 'big' family

MIKE McCLEARN

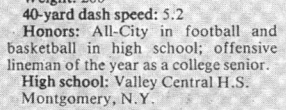

Round drafted: 8th
College: Temple
Height: 6-4
Weight: 280
40-yard dash speed: 5.2
Honors: All-City in football and basketball in high school; offensive lineman of the year as a college senior.
High school: Valley Central H.S. Montgomery, N.Y.

"Mike McClearn is a good drive blocker and has a chance to come in and challenge on the offensive line. Although Mike has always played tackle, Howard Mudd (Browns offensive line coach) feels he is best-suited for guard as a pro. He has been timed at 5.2 in the 40-yard dash every time."
-- Bill Davis

They grow them big in Newburgh, N.Y., near West Point, especially in the McClearn family. Mike McClearn, drafted in the eighth round by the Browns, is the heaviest of five boys at 280 pounds, but none of the others are far behind. All but one stands 6-4 and the exception is 6-5.

"I come from a big family," said Mike and there was no arguing the fact.

Somewhat surprisingly, only one of the brothers besides Mike has been a football player. Darnell McClearn currently is a freshman outside linebacker at Fordham University.

The Browns zeroed in on Mike as more potential offensive line help, an area that needs general beefing up for 1983 and the years to come. Although he spent most of his collegiate playing time at tackle, the Browns believe he will fit in better as a guard.

"I THINK I can adapt to the change without much trouble," McClearn said. "We did a lot of pulling and trapping at Temple and my speed is very good. It's mostly a matter of blocking inside instead of being the last man out."

Few athletes come out of college with strong blocking ability, but McClearn appears to be among those who have it.

"We had sort of a smorgasbord setup on offense," he said. "We threw a lot and pass protection seemed to come natural for me. In fact, it seemed the easiest thing for me to do. I've always had good feet. When I came out of high school, American University offered me a basketball scholarship.

"I consider myself a good run blocker, too, but I can be better. I really had nobody to work with me on run blocking in college."

Temple head coach Wayne Hardin describes McClearn as "big, strong, fast and an excellent pass protector. He has all the tools."

McCLEARN BROKE in with the Owls as a defensive end four years ago and started one game. He was switched to the offensive line the following spring.

McClearn thought he might be picked in one of the middle rounds and took the No. 8 selection in stride.

He had been on the protection list of the Philadelphia Stars and did some talking with the United States Football League team.

"I told them I was going to wait for the NFL draft, though," he said. "When I was a kid growing up, the NFL was the only league to strive for and I told the Stars I was going to shoot for the NFL first."

WEDNESDAY, MARCH 13, 1985

sports

Redskins beef up line from Baltimore — again

REDSKINS, from 1E

The Stars figured they had the option of re-signing him, but he signed a two-year pact with the Redskins.

McClearn more than doubled his Stars salary of $36,000 a year ago as he signed for $100,000 this year and $125,000 next year plus a signing bonus of more than $50,000.

Stars coach Jim Mora said the team was worried about McClearn's knees.

"They [the doctors] told us he'd miss four to five weeks," Mora said. "They also said us the knee was deteriorating with an arthritis problem and his future in pro football was somewhat threatened by this."

Redskins general manager Bobby Beathard, however, said his team feels McClearn's knees are in good shape and he is unlikely to have knee problems with the Redskins.

The Redskins were eager to get McClearn because they are worried about the depth in their offensive line. Tackle George Starke may retire, and center Jeff Bostic and Huff are coming back from serious injuries.

"He can play both tackle and guard, and he gives us versatility and can compete for a starting job," Beathard said yesterday.

The lack of depth in its offensive line played a key role in the team's first-round playoff loss to the Chicago Bears last December. When Huff went out with a broken leg in that game to join Starke and Bostic on the sidelines, the Redskins were left with only four first-rate linemen — Russ Grimm, Joe Jacoby, Mark May and Rick Donnalley. That's one short, and they had to rush veteran Mo Towns into the lineup for the first time this season, and he wasn't ready to handle the assignment. The line lost its cohesiveness and the Redskins had problems running the ball, and when Joe Theismann tried to pass, he never had time to throw.

Since Bostic, who went out with a serious knee injury in St. Louis, and Huff are rehabilitating their injuries, McClearn will give the Redskins some insurance. Huff is in a walking cast and Agnone insists he'll be making it all the way back.

Agnone said McClearn will make the same kind of contribution to the Redskins that Huff made the last two years. "I told Bobby to take a look at the films of him," Agnone said. "I put my neck on the line on this one, and I told him that I'd done that just one other time when Huff was available. After he checked him out, he couldn't get back to me fast enough."

McClearn, who played at Temple, was originally drafted by the Cleveland Browns in the eighth round in 1983 before being cut. He then signed with the Stars for their 1984 spring season. He spent the first two weeks on the developmental squad and was activated when Brad Oates went down with knee surgery in the second week of the season. He spent four of the next five games on the developmental squad and missed

Redskins tap line to Stars

Injured tackle joins ex-Colt Huff in D.C.

By Vito Stellino
Sun Staff Correspondent

PHOENIX — When the Washington Redskins are looking for ways to bolster their offensive line, they're making it a habit to look toward Baltimore.

Two years ago, the Redskins signed guard Ken Huff after he was cut by the Colts, and Huff immediately became the top backup and eventually worked his way into the starting lineup last season.

The Redskins think they found another valuable lineman in Baltimore yesterday when they signed Mike McClearn, who was the starting left tackle for the Baltimore then Philadelphia — Stars in the United States Football League playoffs last season.

"It's Ken Huff all over again," said Baltimore agent Tony Agnone, who represents both Huff and McClearn.

McClearn, who started 10 games for the Stars last season, was sidelined the two playoff games, was sidelined in training camp with bone spurs on his knee. Since the USFL doesn't have an injured reserve list, the Stars waived him at the start of the year and he became a free agent.

MIKE McCLEARN
Insurance for the Redskins

two games with a knee injury before returning to the starting lineup against Washington in the 17th game. He then finished out the season as the starter.

McClearn's injury in camp and Oates's retirement have been one of the reasons the Stars' offense has had problems this year. Joe Conwell had struggled while trying to fit in that left tackle spot.

Beathard said that McClearn has improved in the two years since he was cut by Cleveland. "He was a good prospect in college physically, but he really developed," Beathard said.

McClearn's signing with the Redskins is expected to be the start of a trend. With the USFL in shaky condition, many players whose USFL contracts expire at the end of this season are talking contract with NFL teams. Some have already signed and are just waiting to make the announcement at the end of the season.

ounty Free Press, Tuesday, March 21, 1972

McClearn's Moves To New Location

Mr. and Mrs. McClearn

NEWBURGH: McClearn's House of Fashion recently moved to a new location at 174-176 Broadway, Newburgh. The move to the larger store was made to enable McClearn's to accomodate a much wider selection of clothing. In addition to clothing, McClearn's will now handle a number of other items. Shoes, hats, purses, and uniforms are among the items that the store will now handle. McClearn's will at the same time, continue to specialize in large sizes for men and women, carrying up to size 66 for men and 60 for women.

McClearn's House of Fashion is owned by Sylvester McClearn and Billie McClearn. They have been in the clothing business for the past three years and were in the beauty business for ten years prior to this. Their clientele currently reaches out all the way to Poughkeepsie, Kingston, Middletown, Port Jervis, and Haverstraw. The McClearn's have five children, Richard, 12, Michael, 10, Darnell, 8, Kathell, 8, and Alex, 1 1/2.

Each day is the only one of its kind—plan to live it well.

HIGHLAND Art Cinema
95 Vineyard Ave., 691-7782
March 22-28
Benny Bungles It
PLUS
Masked Ball
COMING WED.
2 First Run Adult Features

MAKING IT

Fashion in Upstate New York

Some five years ago, Sylvestdr McClearn and his wife *(below)* were running a beauty parlor and small clothing store in Newburgh, N.Y., and wondering if they were in the right business. Many of their customers kept telling them they ought to go into full-time fashion retailing. In November 1968, they made the break and opened McClearn's House of Fashions. To finance the switch, they relied entirely on $8,000 they had saved up, a strategy that helped them get credit later on, the McClearns say, when they were ready to expand their new business. The store's multiracial clientele is drawn from an area that is just beyond easy commuting distance from New York City. "It's a very exciting business," says Sylvester McClearn. "As fashion-conscious blacks we think we have a good idea what others like in clothes, and we try to meet the demand." The McClearn's recently opened a second store in Poughkeepsie, N.Y., and last year ran up $230,000 in sales. This year they aim for $300,000; their ultimate goal is a department store carrying the McClearn name.

The McClearn's home in the Newburgh suburbs to which Sylvester moved his family several years ago. He and Billie are spending their retirement there.

(From left) Billy Cathell, Richard, Michael, Darnell, and Little Alex

Darnell's wedding reception in New York (the wedding took place in Jamaica). (Fron left) Richard, Alex, Darnell, Billy and Michael

Mrs. Billie McClearn with her parents, Ida and Charlie Smith

Young Billie Marie Smith with her parents

Rev. and Mrs. McClearn with their children, Michael, Darnell, Alex (Rev and Mrs. McClearn), Richard and Billy Cathell

Richard and his family, wife Karen, daughter Michelle, and grandson.

Billy and family— Bernadette and daughter Kendall

Michael, his wife Kate, and their son Marcus

Darnell and his family— wife Kathy, and children Alison and Miles

Alex and his wife, Andrea

Jeannie, Otis, and daughters, Tiana Janiece and Nyimah Iman

The McClearn grandchildren

The McClearn siblings, Darnell, Michael, Alex, Jeannie, Richard and Billy

The McClearn family at Richard's 40th birthday party

Billie Marie Smith as a teenager

Billie Marie Smith as a school girl

Newburgh pastor: Let's build bridges

Record photo by Darlene Drabik
The black church must "keep people's consciousness focused," says Sylvester McClearn.

Two reasons why the Valley Central Basketball Team is on top are the McClearn Twins — Darnell and Billy.

The United Methodist Church, Newburgh, New York

ELEVEN

"BE FRUITFUL AND MULTIPLY," SAID THE LORD

There is an old saying that we ought to be careful what we ask or wish for, because we just might get it. In a way, that is exactly what happened to Sylvester and Billie. When they were courting, Billie asked Sylvester how many children he would like to have. Without thinking much about what to say in response to Billie, Sylvester stated: "Five boys; I like to have five boys". Then he smiled and added, "Five boys". Think about this: five boys, all running around the house and doing what boys do - being where they shouldn't be, disturbing the quiet of the home, by talking or arguing at the top of their voices, disagreeing over which sports team is better, and throwing balls without thinking of where the ball might land. What a thought!

Since boys are generally considered to be so energetic and aggressive that they tend to keep parents on their toes, the thought of having five of them under one roof might sound scary and crazy to some people. But Sylvester had his reasons for wanting that. The reason he desired to have only boys for his children was because he was scared. This may sound uncharacteristically cowardly to people who know this giant of a man now. But Sylvester knew himself well enough to expect that he could not possibly be a good father to a girl. He thought it would be easier to parent boys.

Sylvester's reasons were simple: he was certain that he would be over-protective of a daughter if he had to parent one and he felt that, if this occurred, the consequences might be too great to handle. He was almost certain that he would have great difficulty trusting his daughter and trusting boys around her. Having once been a boy himself, Sylvester knew that he would be afraid of boys coming close to his daughter and she would somehow be unfairly victimized by his fear. He imagined that his fear of boys would negatively influence his perception of his daughter and consequently his approach to parenting her. Finally, he believed that he understood boys better than he could ever understand a girl the way he would a boy. Sylvester was also confident that he could talk to a boy if he had to. He did not feel he could be equally confident about a relationship with a daughter.

Although he had known for some time that he did not wish to have a daughter, Sylvester had never really given a thought to the exact number of children that he would like to have - until that very moment prior to their marriage when Billie asked him the question. He had not thought about it prior to that discussion. In fact, he had never thought about having children until Billie came into his life. He never even came close to thinking about marriage, let alone having children! Yet, when Sylvester told her that he would like to have five sons, God must have heard him and must have taken note of his statement, because that is exactly what happened.

In the fall of 1958, Billie became pregnant with the couple's first child. From the time they found out about Billie's pregnancy until the day their child was born, Sylvester maintained a level of excitement difficult to describe. It was certainly immeasurable. His excitement never once waned throughout the duration of Billie's pregnancy, and he was determined to do whatever he could to make it a smooth pregnancy for her. So he prayed a lot and offered her as much help as he thought she might need in getting things done. But Billie was always a strong woman and was able to continue to perform most of her tasks with remarkable effectiveness well into her pregnancy.

Although he would have been happy with whatever gender of child it pleased God to bless them with, it never occurred to Sylvester while Billie was pregnant that she might have a girl. Instead, he expected without any doubt that she would have a boy. On July 30, 1959, their first son was born and they named him Richard Kyle. In those days, prospective fathers were not allowed into delivery rooms when their spouses were giving birth. Instead, they were required to remain in the hospital lobby until the delivery had occurred. Then they would get news of the delivery from the hospital staff, usually a midwife, who stepped out into the lobby and informed the father of the successful delivery, the gender of the child, and the condition of the child and mother.

Sylvester clearly recalls that moment when the nurse approached him in the lobby at St. Luke's Hospital in Newburgh and told him that his wife had just delivered a healthy baby boy, and both mother and son were doing well. Instantly, he felt like the proudest, most blessed man in the world. As Reverend McClearn told me this story, his face changed and a glow became quite visible on his face. People who know him well would later tell me about seeing that same kind of glow on his face each time he speaks of his family. I would, myself, see it over and over again in the course of interviewing him for this book. Sylvester has always believed that the birth of a child, from conception to delivery, is one of the greatest of God's miracles. If anyone thinks he walks like a peacock, the explanation for that observation can be found in God's great blessing in his life - his family. It pleased God to allow this miracle to happen in his life four more times.

In January 1961, the couple's second son was born, and they named him Michael Anthony. Billie's pregnancy with Michael went quite smoothly, except at the end, when Sylvester was expected to track the time of his wife's contractions. This was a great and welcome role for him, since he wanted to be very involved and helpful. The only problem was that in his great desire to have everything go right, Buddy began to panic a great deal. Rather than stay calm and calculated as was probably expected of him, he panicked on one occasion and rushed Billie to the hospital. This occurred a few times before Billie's actual due date. Only mothers should have a right to laugh when they read this revelation, since many men would probably do what he did if they found themselves in the same situation. As a matter of fact, many men, including those that are laughing now, wouldn't even know what to do if they were given that same responsibility to track the contractions of their pregnant wives.

Over the years, Billie and Sylvester have had many laughs about this experience, which was not funny at the time. Sometimes, Sylvester laughs because it reminds him of the story of the boy who cried wolf. At other times, he laughs because it reminds him of how inept he once was in these matters. Needless to say, this experience helped turn his pathetic and laughable state of incompetence around. In time, he became the expert male on matters of childbirth. His competence and alertness increased greatly the older he got and the more pregnancies Billie had.

Stories like these keep memories of childbirth alive, fresh and healthy, even decades after one has retired from the enviable task of making new babies. One wonders what it would be like if a group of men sat down and shared their experiences regarding their wives' pregnancies. Such a discussion would probably produce more respect from men toward their spouses. Indeed, there would also be many stories of near-disaster but, thank God, they can laugh after the fact.

People have asked Reverend and Mrs. McClearn if Richard immediately accepted the arrival of a younger brother or if he had difficulty adjusting to Michael's birth. I also asked them this question. They answered that with their children, they were very fortunate indeed. They never had to worry about adjustment difficulties either with Richard or with Michael and him. Richard seemed to have a big room in his heart for a sibling and as it turned out, this tended to be the pattern for each one of the McClearn children that came later. For

Reverend McClearn, parenting two young children did not produce any significant challenges that he recalls. Even when the number of their children increased, the experience was still very pleasant and exciting.

Thanks to their children who provided them the wonderful opportunity to experience the beginnings and development of positive sibling relationships, it was a very long time before Sylvester learned what sibling rivalries meant. Of course, in his family of origin, the interests of his siblings and he were diverse and they disagreed frequently, especially when his mother was not home. However, they remained very close as siblings, and their disagreements were nothing compared with what he has seen in many families that he has observed over the years.

It is possible to make the case that, without knowing it at the time, the way Richard welcomed and accepted his baby brother set the stage for how all of the other siblings, when they came, would receive and treat each other. It may have been something that Billie and Sylvester did that made Richard so receptive to his new sibling. Or maybe he was just born endowed with compassion and grace. He is not certain exactly why, but he has to say that the foundation laid with Richard became one on which his children have continued to build.

Sylvester and Billie were catapulted to a new level of excitement when, on February 29, 1964, she gave birth to twin boys who they named Billy Cathell and Sylvester Darnell. The births of their twins surprised them because it had never occurred to them while Billie was pregnant that she was carrying twins. Of course, these days it's quite possible to know those things in advance. Now, it is even possible to know the gender of a child before he or she is born, but at the time of the birth of Billy and Sylvester, the now-widely-used technology of sonograms was as yet unavailable. Considering the fact that 1964 was not such a long time ago, this means that we as a society have come a long way very quickly.

Suddenly, the McClearn family went from a family of four to a family of six with the birth of Billy Cathell and

Sylvester Darnell. Every baby item now had to come in twos because of the twins. And besides that, they were born on February 29 in a leap year, which meant that they would celebrate their birthdays only once every four years.

As is common with twins, Billy and Sylvester were almost always together while growing up, and they did most things together until they were old enough to go to college. Then they separated and went to different colleges. To this day, they maintain the kind of closeness that is perhaps best understood by people who shared the same womb for nine months and came into the world together.

After having four children, the McClearn's did not think they were done. Even if they had, God was not done with them. Sylvester had spoken years earlier and God had heard his request. So in 1971, the fifth son of Billie and Sylvester was born and they named him Alex Bernard. Like his brothers before him, Alex came into the world in good health and very good size. In other words, he was big and long. Unlike his brothers, however, even as a child, Alex was a calm, soft-spoken child who rarely found himself at the receiving end of anyone's anger. Naturally, everyone in the family treated him as a darling, since he was the youngest child in their home. He was also the calmest. In a way, there seemed to be an unspoken consensus that Alex could do no wrong - and he rarely did. To this day, he remains the family's Alex and his mother's "baby."

Although Billie and Sylvester never had a daughter of their own, they were blessed with one that they ended up raising and loving as their biological child—Jeanie. Jeanie had been adopted as a baby by Billie's aunt. When Billie's aunt died, the responsibility of parenting Jeanie became theirs. They were grateful, knowing without a doubt that it was a blessing that God was conferring on them. The responsibility was easy to carry out because they and their sons accepted Jeanie as their own. Jeanie became a daughter to Billie and Sylvester and a sister to their sons. Therefore, when Billie and Sylvester speak of their children today, they are indeed referring to their five sons and their daughter, Jeanie. When the boys speak of their sister, they mean exactly that - their sister, Jeanie.

Over the years, Reverend McClearn has watched Alex, Jeanie, Darnell (which is what they called Sylvester), Cathell (which is what they called Billy), Michael, and Richard grow into adulthood and it has been interesting to see them take into adulthood the same qualities that Billie and he saw in them when they were children. They all remain very close-knit, caring, loving, compassionate, jovial, hardworking and religious, and some are highly sociable.

Sylvester believes that childbirth is one of the greatest miracles that occur daily in our world. It is a miracle that comes directly from God who makes it possible for children to be born every day, formed in His own perfect image. To him, a child comes complete with perfection and innocence, and it represents a blessing that cannot be equaled even by the greatest technology that man can ever develop.

Billie and Sylvester had the great blessing of experiencing this miracle in their lives as many times as it pleased God to allow them to do so. There is neither pregnancy nor childbirth unless God determines it. It is all in His hands, and His power ensures that a child is formed, protected in the womb, and eventually born to the earthly parents that God has chosen for such a child. This blessing that God confers upon His children is one for which we should be forever grateful, and one we must never abuse. When God chooses us to become parents to a newborn, He does it for a purpose. As parents, we have a responsibility to fulfill God's purpose for us by doing the will of God in our interactions with our children from birth through adulthood.

The Bible encourages us to bring up our children in the knowledge of God. Before Samuel was born, his mother promised to have him dedicated to the service of God, and that was exactly what she did. She recognized that her pregnancy and the birth of her child came directly from God. She understood that Samuel was a gift from God and she was willing to commit him completely to God, the giver of life. It was important for

Sylvester and Billie to take their lessons from such powerful men and women of God in the Bible who accepted God's gifts and gave back to Him what was due Him. So Billie and he accepted God's gifts of their children and were determined to raise them in the way of the Lord.

TWELVE

WHEN PARENTS AND CHILDREN GROW TOGETHER

Most people believe that every child is different, even if they are twins. Having been parents for several decades, Sylvester and Billie are among those who believe this to be true. They have observed significant differences in their own children as they have seen them grow. Although the common threads of compassion, love, care, hard work and other positive characteristics can be seen with every one of the McClearn children, each is unique and complete in his or her own way. That uniqueness is often obvious to both Billie and Sylvester. Usually, it is also obvious to people who have known the McClearn family closely over the years.

Considering the differences that children bring with them, one of the big challenges for parents is often to be able to fashion all of those differences into a potent and functional family system of which they can be proud and confident. Sylvester and Billie were no exceptions, but the approach that they adopted in working through their parenting challenges is one that requires some discussion.

Sylvester and Billie do not deny that they spoiled their children but they have no regrets that they did. They are aware that parents generally tend to spoil children, and they do not think that this is necessarily a bad thing. What some people may perceive to be a spoiling of children was really, for Sylvester and Billie, a demonstration of their love for the children. It never extended to the point of excusing any of the children from acts that were inappropriate, but the couple certainly ensured that their children would know no suffering. Sylvester and Billie never condoned acts of irresponsibility in their household, but this does not mean that their children never stretched the limits of what was acceptable in the family. In fact, some of the McClearn children engaged in vices - though this was more of an exception than a rule. Besides, it is a fact of life that some children will test parental and societal limits in the process of growing up, regardless of who their parents are. To that extent, the McClearn family was not an exception.

While some people may suggest that it is impossible to love all of one's children equally, Sylvester fully and unreservedly disagrees. He believes that this suggestion is, in his words, "a cop out" that has been made popular by people looking for an excuse to justify what may be the inability of some parents to actually express practical love to their children. On his part, Sylvester has no problem making the claim that he and Billie loved and still love their children equally, and very dearly. It is impossible to measure exactly what that means, since love is both an emotional and personal thing that exists in hearts that we cannot see and cannot read. Our only way of knowing the truth about how much anyone loves is through the actions of that person.

The claim that Sylvester makes about his and Billie's equal amount of love toward their children is not entirely shared by all of the McClearn children. For example, one of them said to me in an interview: "I don't buy that! It does not apply to me. When my brother and I graduated from high school at the same time, my parents bought my brother a new car and they bought me a beat-up bike. To me, that is not equal love. But that's the way it has always been throughout my entire life. They treat me as an inferior child and they wonder why I have made all the mistakes I have made in my life. Only my mother knows and understands my pain." Suddenly, he stopped as if the next point he was going to make would be the most important of our conversation. Then he continued, "But make no mistake! I love my family very much and would die for my parents or any one of my brothers. They have done a lot for me and they are my life. I am torn between telling you the truth, which is what I have just done, and keeping my mouth shut so I don't get misunderstood – because I do not mean any harm. I love my family too much to want to cause any trouble."

The contents of this conversation with one of the McClearn children brings out a very clear difficulty in writing a biography of any family that is indeed a giant among families. Does dissent from a position held by most in the family mean rebellion and irresponsibility on the part of the dissenter? Does such dissent diminish the image of the family or does it make the family appear imperfect and human – which is really how we all are? What happens when what one member of a cohesive family says has the potential of making an impact that could ripple even for a short time? All of these are possible side effects of writing a book about life and it by no means ought to tarnish the subject of the book or the source of the information.

Reverend McClearn was himself conscious of the possibility of conflicts in perceptions when he said in an interview with me: "Children have their own views of how they were raised and what kind of parents their mama and papa were. Whatever I tell you will be my view. I'll be curious to know what my children think – what they have to say about their upbringing."

While his children were growing up, Sylvester had a very good relationship with all of them. They were always at home and they enjoyed each other's company very much. Adults now, the McClearn children live in different places — some very far from home. Yet, to every observer, they continue to maintain the close relationships that they grew up with. There is nobody who cherishes the closeness that he observes in his children more than Sylvester. He willingly confesses that every time he thinks of the quality of his relationship with his wife and children, he is convinced that he could not ask for a better relationship with anyone. According to the Reverend, "I can stand on the mountain top and proclaim without holding back that I am madly in love with my wife, my children, my church, and everything around me. This is the reason I can tell you that I am truly blessed."

Although he had dropped out of school in sixth grade, education acquired great meaning and importance to Sylvester in adulthood. He was conscious of the negative impact that such limited amount of education was having on his life. He believed that more education might have given him a much better life. Therefore, as a parent, Sylvester wanted his children to have a better life than he did. For them to accomplish the kind of life that he had in mind, he expected all of his children to graduate from high school and receive college education.

Anyone who has ever raised as many as six children understands that such a task presents very difficult challenges, and there is always the potential possibility of losing one or two of them on the way. In their case, Billie and Sylvester didn't just have six children; five of them were boys. Considering what that means in terms of peer pressure and all of the potential challenges that attend the lives of young men, the educational expectations that Billie and Buddy had for their children were bound to be difficult goals to accomplish. Therefore, it became important that they develop a strategy to direct and encourage their children to stay on the right track. For them, that meant developing high moral character in their children and emphasizing their staying in school, graduating from college, and leading productive lives after that.

Sylvester and Billie constantly pushed into their children's heads that they would have no opportunities for high-paying employment unless they had college education. They chose not to reward their children's high school graduations with any kind of celebration because Buddy feared that this might make them feel like they had accomplished enough to change their minds about attending college. They decided that they would celebrate no graduation in their home unless it was a college graduation.

To attain their educational goals for their children, Sylvester took the lead in ensuring that their children did what was required of them, and Billie was right there supporting the effort. In his effort to get the children to do his bidding for their own good, Sylvester adopted well thought-out means, some of which have since struck him as somewhat amusing. None is funnier now than the deliberate decision to do what he himself describes as "putting my heart out there and offering them some feeling of guilt" in case they might be thinking that they did not wish to go to college. He would say to his children, "You will break my heart if you drop out of school, or if you decide not to go to college." None of his children wanted to be responsible for breaking their father's heart, so they took him very seriously. Although he cannot categorically state that the guilt-trip approach that he adopted was what got his children to comply, there is little doubt that *something* had a major impact on his children with respect to their education. But this was only one of the many methods that Sylvester used to push his children. He and Billie believe that it was indeed the combination of all of those efforts that produced the great results that they are now enjoying.

Eventually, all of their children went to college. The parents taught their children to have a sense of responsibility that was defined and pushed by their parents. Sylvester and Billie were determined to drum into the heads of their children that "free-loading" was not acceptable in the family. The children always responded by following the values and guidelines established by their parents, and they complied as faithfully as both parents expected and required of them.

Once each of the McClearn children graduated from college, he or she left the family home and went to live on his or her own. They were neither told nor forced to leave the family home, but they were aware of the values that their parents had been trying to teach them, and going away to college seemed to enhance their sense of independence. This increased independence never clashed with the values that their parents had labored to instill in them. The evidence for this was to be found in the way the children continued to respond to the expectations that their parents had placed on them through their years of growing up. For example, even when they became adults and left home, Richard, Michael, Darnell, Cathell and Alex knew that they were not allowed to return home with girls. If they did, they stayed in separate rooms. The only exception was if they came home with their wives after they got married.

As parents raising young children, Billie and Sylvester were great examples for most people who knew them. They were not parents who acted impulsively in the hope that they would some day stumble on the right course of action to take in raising their children. On the contrary, they lived by example, even for their children. They did not attempt to instill any values in their children which they did not themselves possess, and they did not give any instructions without having to work to ensure their implementation. They also sacrificed a lot in the process. In other words, they did not attain great things without doing the work that cause great things to happen. This was of course appropriate and is to be expected of any couple that desires to accomplish great things for their children and themselves. Since nothing great comes easy, we must never lie on our backs and expect magic to occur for us. The McClearns certainly did not.

CHURCH AND FAMILY

Prior to becoming parents, Billie and Sylvester had become born again Christians. Consequently, they were very conscious of the importance of raising their children in the way of the Lord. As devout Christians, they knew some of the instructions in the Bible regarding parenting, and they were especially conscious of the admonition in Proverbs 22, verse

6: *"Train up a child in the way he should go: and when he is old, he will not depart from it."* They wanted their children to be educated and, by the grace of God, they all received college education. However, it was also important for them to bring up the children with the fear and knowledge of God. Behind closed doors, Sylvester and Billie would share their common hope and desire to have their children grow up and live productive Christian lives.

For starters, Sylvester had an idea that has proven to be greatly effective in determining the kind of Christians that people grow up to become. He thought that a great step in the direction of raising Christian children was for the family to always attend church together as a family. Never were he and his wife going to give any of their children the right to remain at home while their parents and some of the other children were in church. That wasn't going to be.

This is not a practice that Sylvester invented. He knew that it was a method that had consistently worked, and he was willing to adopt it in his home. Unfortunately, there seems to have been some departure from that age-old practice in many households. As a pastor, one of the things that has grieved the heart of Reverend McClearn over the years has been seeing one or both parents increasingly going to church while their children remain at home. Engage the Reverend in a discussion of this subject and you will see how passionate he can be about what he believes to be the responsibility of parents in shaping the faith of their children.

Perhaps because of his very deep love for children, the Reverend hardly ever misses the sight of children in church by themselves while their parents remain at home. Sometimes, one parent attends church alone, while the other parent does not want to be bothered with church. So, he or she (usually he) stays at home while his or her family is worshipping God in church and returning home afterwards with blessings for the entire family. There is hardly a doubt that such actions do not provide good examples for children. Sooner or later, children follow the example of the parent who stays at home and they begin to stay home as well rather than go to church.

Due to Sylvester and Billie's philosophy, church attendance was made mandatory for their children. Both parents knew that it was sometimes a challenge for their children to attend church every Sunday as was required of them, but they were happy that it was a challenge that their children accepted and complied with. They are also happy that, even after they left home and now as they live their lives as adults, their children have continued to practice this important lesson that started out as (perhaps) a "boring" rule.

In his own family of origin, Sylvester's mother was the one who went to church and took her children with her. His father was the one who stayed away from church, although he did not deny his wife. He must have known that there was something in it for him! In fact, most of the brothers of Randolph II did not attend church either, but their spouses did. Consequently, a strong Christian tradition developed and lives on in the extended McClearn family to this day. It was all due to the work that the women did.

Once he got to know and accept the Lord Jesus as his Savior, Buddy knew that he wanted to have a different life from the one he had growing up. That also meant that he began to look forward to going to church with his wife and children — all of them together. The first rock on that foundation was the quality of wife that he was blessed with. With two people possessing a Godly heart as they both did, the desire to get their children to attend church with them turned out to be a forgone conclusion. Sylvester and Billie are grateful to God for making that possible, exactly as they had dreamed and hoped.

THE BALANCING ACT

One of the greatest challenges parents often face has to do with striking a balance between providing a reasonable structure and showing love to their children. Often, parents struggle with the need to make demands on their children and the need to discipline them when they do something that is not acceptable. The struggle usually comes from the feeling of guilt parents tend to have in these circumstances. Usually, the guilt feeling comes from the fear that if one requires the children to follow a certain level of structure and discipline, including punishment for noncompliance, then one cannot truly be showing love to those children.

Some parents feel that their children will perceive themselves as not being loved by their parents if they are punished for wrongdoing. The fact is, however, that parents do their children a great disservice when they allow acts of misbehavior to slip because they assume that their children will develop this misperception. It is always possible to parent children with structure and discipline and show them love at the same time. Many parents know this from experience because they do it every day.

Child development experts now tell us what the old people always knew: that children are better off and grow into responsible, healthy adults when they are raised with love and structure going hand-in-hand. The point can in fact be made that parents who truly love their children and want them to prosper will teach them to respect and work within appropriate rules. Actually, children not only need rules; they often subconsciously want the adults in their lives to help them structure their lives.

As Sylvester and Billie worked together to attain their goals for their children, a pattern emerged that soon became second nature them, and subsequently to their entire family. Some mornings, Billie would get up and go to work while Sylvester stayed home and got their children ready for school before he went to work. Also, whenever Billie was busy, he took care of the children. Both engulfed themselves in the lives of their children and they demonstrated their love to them in many ways, chief among which was to maintain a consistent presence in their lives.

THOSE COLLEGE YEARS!

As their children got older, the desire of Sylvester and Billie to provide moral support for them kept them on the road most of the time. At one time, most of their children were attending college in different cities. For example, Richard was studying at the State University of New York in Buffalo and Michael was at Temple University in Philadelphia on a full football scholarship. At the same time, Cathell was at Ramapo College in New Jersey, Darnell was at Fordham University in New York, and Jeanie and Alex were in high school.

All of the boys had the typical McClearn body size which is unmistakable. Even at very young ages, they were quite big and tall, and they used their sizes for a remarkable degree of good for themselves. Except Michael who played football, all of the McClearn sons played basketball, and their parents made it a point to attend their children's games regularly. Consequently, they traveled frequently from one college campus to the other, so they could be there for every one of their sons. Eventually, their traveling was made easier by their purchase of a mobile home in which they then began to do their very extensive traveling.

Michael was very dedicated to football, his chosen sport. It was obvious that he wanted to make a career out of playing football. He worked very hard to get a football scholarship to go to college, and the family was very happy for him when he accomplished his desire. As it turned out, playing football at Temple University was not the limit to Michael's football career aspirations. It never was. His dream was always to play professional football, and college was the road to the National Football League (NFL). While he was waiting and doing what he needed to do to get to the NFL, Michael tended to neglect his academic responsibilities. He became more interested in attaining a professional football career than he was in going to college.

As things often tend to happen with dreams if pursued through hard work, Michael's dream of playing in the NFL paid off eventually. The Cleveland Browns drafted him into the NFL and he played for Washington Redskins. Although he was now a big man in the professional league, he was still a McClearn, and his parents made every effort to get to his games. We are never too old to be appreciated by our parents.

Going to the big NFL games was quite an adventure in itself. The thrill, energy and fanfare that surrounded those athletes were always so exciting that, as parents, it was sometimes hard for Billie and Sylvester to contain their excitement. For Billie, life was just good. For Sylvester, life was not only good, but he was constantly reminded that the road from Angel Highway, North Carolina was a long one but through his son, he was now in the big league. That realization was well worth his time.

Visiting their children on their college campuses always gave Billie and Sylvester a feeling of accomplishment and satisfaction. Considering where he had come from, to see his children now in the process of finding their own ways through life, and to see how academic endeavors were becoming an integral part of their lives, was always quite an emotional experience for Buddy. It reminded him that his dream to have his children experience a life different from the one he had experienced was indeed realizable. It was refreshing for him to be able to see a future in which his children would not be denied privileges for lack of education — something that he had to endure over and over again in his own life. It was his dream that his children would experience a much better life than he had, and he was indeed happy that he was able to see them begin to do so in his own life time. That is progress.

Most parents with children in college ought to understand and accept that it is impossible to know exactly what their children do when they are out of sight from mom and dad and away at school. One should probably hope that the children are living their college lives according to the values engrained in them at home.

Whenever they were visiting with their children in college, Billie and Sylvester knew that the children were putting up their best behavior. They also knew that, after the children left home, they would do their best to abide by the values of the family from which they came. Every time they visited their children in any of their campuses, they had the opportunity to meet their friends as well. They never expected perfection, even in their selection of friends, but they expected their children to be sensible in whatever they did. And they were indeed quite sensible.

Sylvester and Billie would be inaccurate if they claim that they approved of all their children's friends when they were young. They did not. For the most part, they were happy with their children's choices of friends, but certainly not in every case. However, they were very careful not to pass any negative judgments, so they would not inadvertently turn their children into rebellious kids. Instead, they chose not to make any conscious effort to develop any criteria for their children to employ in choosing their friends. They tried to present that they trusted their children to see and negotiate their social life by themselves, figuring things out along the way. Also, Sylvester and Billie expected that their children would make friends who had similar values to the ones with which they were raised. Clearly, such an expectation comes with some risks, and the McClearns had to struggle with some of those risks as all of their children did not always choose friends that had the same moral values that were predominant in the McClearn household.

Perhaps one can expect that some of the McClearn children were imperfect and made some mistakes in their social lives, but the exact mistakes are unclear because the family generally does not discuss errors by family members. Some might say that this is due to the family members' human desire to present themselves as a rosy family, and others might say that it only makes sense not to wash one's dirty linen in public. What is clear, however, is that this fact is partly due to the highly religious state of this family. In a state like that, people often tend to avoid discussions of negativity and focus instead on their victories because the former is perceived as giving glory to the devil instead of giving God the glory for triumphs. To that extent, Reverend McClearn would like to focus on the fact that everywhere he and his wife went, on and off campus, people spoke very well of their children, and they were proud to be introduced as their parents.

LESSONS ABOUND

One of the interesting experiences Buddy has had as a parent has been watching his children negotiate and fit into their places and roles in the family. If this process has been a struggle, they have definitely been handled very well. Buddy loves his children as much now as he ever did and he knows that they always want to give much more materially than he is willing to accept from them. His desire is for them to enjoy their lives and everything that God has blessed them with. He wants them to worry less about him and focus more on their own lives.

Now, he is trying to figure out where his place should be in his own family. Specifically, he wonders how to be a man among the men who were once kids - his kids. On one hand, he wants to be able to continue to see them as his children, which is what they are. On the other hand, he realizes that they are all grown up now and are not kids anymore. Sometimes, he wishes that they would see and accept him as one of the boys. But, at the same time, he is not sure that that would be appropriate. On the contrary, Billie seems to be in no conflict whatsoever regarding her role. Nobody in the family disputes this. Everyone acknowledges that, better than Sylvester, Billie is always able to assert herself to her adult children and has no problem saying to them, "Keep quiet! I am your mother."

When asked if there was something he would change if he had the opportunity to raise his children all over again, Sylvester had obvious difficulty answering the question. At first, he explained his difficulty with this question as follows: "I hardly ever wonder about the past. To me, that would be engaging in a process that can result in developing a list of regrets from which nobody benefits. What is done is done and I believe that everything that happened in my life happened for a purpose." After a long pause, the Reverend stated: "If I must answer that question, I would have to say that one thing I would do, which I didn't do to my satisfaction, would be to teach them the value and power of economics. I would teach them how to manage money when they earn it, and how important it is to save for the rainy days. Being only human, none of us truly knows what lies ahead for us tomorrow." What a powerful lesson for every young parent!

Reverend McClearn acknowledged that he would also teach his children how to manage emotions "because emotions can easily get the better of you." In addition, he said he would engage his children in learning important lessons in the power of friendships and what impact friends could have on the lives of people. Although he now thinks that he did not spend as much time on these important concepts as he now believes he should have done, he is encouraged that his children have all done well applying to their total lives the values that he and Billie taught them.

Billie has a very practical but unexpected answer to what she would wish to do over of she had the opportunity to do it all over. According to her, "If I could do it again, I would not allow Michael or any of my children to play professional sports." Billie is a very modest woman with a great sense of right and wrong, and an understanding of the less glamorous aspects of professional sports which only family members of professional aspects understand very well. When television cameras are turned off, the people who get to deal with the challenges and emotional pain that accompany professional sports are usually the families of those aspects. Some may wonder if the solution is to discourage one's children from engaging in professional sports, or to do a better job of preparing that child for the realities of life in professional athletics. This point is debatable but Billie knows exactly what she is talking about and neither her experience nor her conclusion is debatable in her mind.

ON A MORE PERSONAL NOTE...

Requested to reflect and send a message to his family, Reverend McClearn got emotional as he once again proclaimed his love for his wife and children. He wants his children and all who read about his family to know that there is no greater privilege than to know God, love one's family and self, and to treat others appropriately. The Reverend does not say what he doesn't practice in his own life. His life is replete with lessons that it is important to live a life that God will be pleased with, and to be a good man.

But for the presence and guidance of God in their home and the blessing of a remarkable wife in Billie, the task of parenting would certainly have been a tremendously difficult challenge for Sylvester. For one thing, he had no prior experience to draw upon. Unlike his wife who had a close-knit family led by a strong father who was both physically and emotionally available, Buddy never saw his father actually play the role of a father. His father was a good example of a man who was a father only in name. As has been discussed elsewhere in this book, Randolph II was the father of fourteen children who never had a close relationship with any, and never provided positive examples either in his words or in his deeds. Physically, he was a very strong man but emotionally, he was absolutely unavailable to his family. His physique was of little or no help to his family. In contrast, the man Buddy put his strong physical physique to work for the benefit of his family. And he was not only strong physically, but emotionally as well.

Considering the type of father that he had, Sylvester is

himself amazed that he was able to develop as much love for his family as he has. He has stopped trying to understand what happened. Instead, he has resigned himself to a simple explanation: that what he has for his family is truly the love of God that is made possible only by His grace. The love of God transcends all, and cannot be reasonably compared with even the greatest love that any man is capable of. All that the man Sylvester has always wanted to do as a husband and parent has been to allow God to teach him to love his family and others in the world with God's love, which is the only true and complete love. Indeed, the Reverend McClearn has allowed God to teach him and he has not only been a great student but also a great adherent to the lessons taught and learned.

THIRTEEN

FROM RAGS TO BUSINESS SUCCESS

After a life of poverty on a North Carolina farm off Angel Highway, and later in Smithfield, and then in Washington D.C., Buddy became an adult in Newburgh, New York, living with his own family. That family was made up of his loving wife Billie and their children whom they both cherished very much. As they progressed in their family life and in their relationship with God, Sylvester must have begun to feel that he could do anything that he chose to do. His new attitude, defined by unparalleled self-confidence, was very consistent with what Paul wrote in Philippians 4, verse 13, when he asserted, "I can do all things through Christ which strengtheneth me." At some point, he decided to become a businessman, and he did very well at it.

The decision to go into business was jointly made by Billie and Sylvester but it was really a natural extension of something that had already begun to develop. Billie already had a beauty salon that was flourishing. In addition, she was designing and making hats that she was selling both from home and from her beauty parlor. While this was going on, the couple's keen eyes recognized that there was a huge fashion void in Newburgh. They noticed that no clothing stores in the community catered to people that were too big for the generally small and slim-fit outfits sold everywhere.

After a series of discussions and analyses in their bedroom, at their dining table and in their car, Billie and Sylvester set out to open a store to sell "big and tall" clothing. At no point did they disagree on the need to fill Newburgh's fashion void, or on what was needed to fill that void. Their discussion focused mainly on the logistics. They recognized that this would be no easy task and they wanted to get it right. Once they made up their minds and were confident of their decision to handle the undertaking, the enterprising couple proceeded to carry out a feasibility study as best they knew how. In the process, they became even more convinced that the opportunity for this type of business was wide open in their community and surrounding towns. So, they took advantage of this vacuum and made their move, backed with prayers and with the confidence that they believed was made possible only by the Holy Spirit of God.

For the McClearns, the decision to go into full-time business was major. Enormous tasks and uncertainty loomed. Yet, in his characteristic manner, Sylvester chose to focus on the tasks rather than the uncertainty because he believed very strongly that there was no uncertainty with God. The next major tasks in their undertaking were to select a location for their store, develop an inventory, purchase materials, then set up the store and begin business. They already had some merchandise in their home, which they continued to sell while they tried to tackle the necessary tasks to get their store started. Since they could not think of a ready storefront to rent that was suitable for the purposes that they had in mind, the McClearns bought a building and modified it to exactly what they wanted their business to look like. Once everything about the store was set and they were ready to go, the budding entrepreneurs took the merchandise that they had in their home and set them up in the store.

Sylvester the new entrepreneur resigned from his employment, effective the same day that their first store opened for business. This type of move takes remarkable courage because it represents a risky willingness to give up a safety net known as a "job" for a blank uncertainty called "business." This is the kind of risk that often tends to separate those who succeed in business, as in life, from those who do not. Many people who don't succeed in a venture dream of success without taking the risk that is needed to enable success to occur. Those who succeed also dream, but then they wake up and execute the dream. Sylvester was in the latter group, and time would begin to tell if his gains were worth the risk.

The main business focus of the McClearns was women's clothing and, as has already been indicated, their goal became to develop stores to sell "big and tall" clothing for women. They began with one store and saw the business grow more rapidly than had been imagined. Very soon, the business extended from one store that focused exclusively on hats and clothing for big and tall women to six stores that were much more expansive in terms of the products that they sold and the customers that they served. Although exciting, the expansion did not occur overnight, or without sweat. A lot of time, energy, and hard work went into starting the business, and that much or even more energy went into the process of expanding the business.

All his life, he had mostly done physical labor but running a modern business was a different ball game. Having to call on his mental faculties, as he now had to do, was new to him and it required all of what he had in him to be able to make his new tasks and goals into successful realities. The transition from working with his muscles to having to work with his brain was quite challenging for Sylvester and his ability, or inability, to meet that challenge would have tremendous impact on the business and his life in subsequent years.

For one thing, he knew how to rest physically but had no idea how to rest mentally. And although he knew that relaxation was the appropriate response to physical exhaustion, it was sometimes difficult for Sylvester to make the time to actually rest his body in the midst of everything he was doing. In the circumstances, his mental exhaustion sometimes got worse than it should have. Quite commonly, he would keep going for as long as he was able to get up and walk, even when he was indeed mentally exhausted. Sometimes, he could feel the difference between mental and physical exhaustion, but he did not know how to respond to the former.

In addition, McClearn found himself suddenly thrust into an arena of customer relations for which he had never been formally trained and he was ill-equipped. His only recourse was his natural ability to maintain a friendly attitude even in the face of stress and pressure. Even when he was exhausted, he remained determined to be the best at what he did. He became the embodiment of punctuality, drive, organization, determination, and every positive thing that went into the successful operation of a business. He was determined to push himself over physical limits, but he had to pay a high price for success. To the public, he was doing great. But he knew that he was struggling as a person.

The immense hard work that was measurable in terms of very long hours sometimes drove Buddy to the edge of his human limitations. For example, on several occasions, he fell asleep at the wheel while driving, and doubtless it was only by the grace of God that he got to his destinations alive. He also received frequent speeding tickets as he shuttled between his stores and the places where he filled his inventory.

There was perhaps no more stressful time than the Easter and Christmas seasons every year. Anyone who has ever owned or worked in retail business knows exactly what this means, and the family members of such individuals know it too. Just managing to get through these seasons was always a major challenge. The inventory that had to be filled and refilled, the sales that had to be made, and the records that had to be kept always combined to make this period very stressful, exciting, pressured, and of course, highly profitable in monetary terms. This is perhaps even more so today, considering that these Christian celebratory seasons have become increasingly commercialized over the years.

Although he lacked the kind of knowledge that formal education provides in terms of running a business of this magnitude, Sylvester was blessed with the ability to recognize God's guidance. Clearly, that was sufficient to lead him as a person and as a business man to greater heights than anyone could have imagined. In the process, he learned a lot more than he ever thought he had the capacity to learn – but that was largely possible because he was willing to learn.

Without a willingness to learn, it is difficult for even the greatest potential learner to absorb the simplest of principles. In his case, no business principles were too basic. He tried to absorb and implement everything he could to make his business as prosperous as he desired. His biggest enemy was his illiteracy, but that was also sometimes his major strength. Since he could neither read nor write, Sylvester McClearn was greatly handicapped in his management abilities. But, since he could neither read nor write, he was very conscious of his limitations and felt the need to work harder than he would otherwise have done.

Like anything in life, the business had high and low points, all of which served to enhance the learning experience for Buddy. For example, race riots frequently plagued Newburgh in those days and his business was not immune from the consequences of those riots. Whenever one of those riots occurred, business slowed down because many people stayed away. That was indeed a time in Newburgh during which people from different racial and socioeconomic backgrounds were trying to learn to live together regardless of their differences. The riots were not pleasant, but they did serve as a signal to Sylvester that he had a role to play in improving the lives of people and the community of Newburgh that he now called home. This realization jolted him into actions that produced contributions in Newburgh that were so immense that they left indelible marks in the history of the town and in the hearts of its people.

As a businessman watching his country and his community evolve through crisis and uncertainty, Sylvester McClearn saw the need for involvement in his community, and he did not wait for an official invitation to get involved. First, he moved to sponsor what became the first African American parade in Newburgh. In a city where race riots had become somewhat frequent, and employment opportunities were minimal, his goal was to give black people something to celebrate. He was not a politician or self-proclaimed civil rights activist with altruistic needs to fulfill. Instead, he saw himself as a truly blessed man with a responsibility to give something to his community and people. To this end, he was determined to contribute to the spiritual and emotional uplifting of the black people in Newburgh.

Very soon, the parade that started out as an idea for one celebration became an annual event. Despite the negative emotions prevalent in Newburgh at the time, the city administration always cooperated with and supported Sylvester's efforts to contribute to the community by sponsoring a black parade. Always, about ninety percent of the performers, floats and music bands in the parades were black or black-owned. Since it was always his approach and attitude to be the best at whatever he did, he always felt it necessary to make the parades very elaborate. And they were widely received by the city's inhabitants regardless of race or ethnicity.

For five years, he organized this black people's parade and it just got bigger every year. In a great sense, the yearly parade day became a celebratory holiday as people – individuals and groups – marched up and down the city of Newburgh, toward the Hudson River and back, and people celebrated with food and parties as they would with any major holiday. After five years, it had become too big to be put together by one small group like the McClearns. To continue to execute the project alone had become a massive endeavor both physically and emotionally. So Sylvester made a conscious decision to open up the planning and organization of the parade to other businesses and community agencies in Newburgh. Once that was done, the parade ended.

The reasons for this are not hard to imagine. When the administration of otherwise simple things for simple human benefit are extended to more than a few people, artificial competition and self-interests come to the forefront at the expense of original thought and ideals. In the process, unnecessary bureaucracy takes root and considerations of the common good of humanity and society are all but killed. Although this is not the way Reverend Sylvester McClearn would like to characterize what happened with the parade, there is little doubt that much of what led to the end of such a remarkable idea was grounded in developments similar to what has been described here.

Over the years, Sylvester has sometimes wondered about the circumstances that led to the demise of the parade, and he has wondered about how much more the parade could have done for the community, had the concept lived on in practice. However, he does so without lament or regret because he believes with all his heart that he did the right thing. At a time when his fellow African Americans in Newburgh and across the United States needed the opportunity to have their dignity accepted and respected, it was right for him to play his part in his community by doing something what would remind society of the dignity of his people.

It was also right for Sylvester to have recognized that the parade had become bigger than one man, and to bring others into the organizational tent. If we would all play our part to improve the quality of life in any society or situation that we are blessed enough to be part of, we would all certainly leave this world a much better place than the way we met it.

Many people may wonder how he was able to achieve the degree of business success that Sylvester attained in those days, considering the fact that his illiteracy and other factors constituted such obvious limitations for him. After all, he did not have any extensive formal education and he had no prior experience running a business. He did not even come from a wealthy family, which also meant that he did not have the opportunity to obtain any start-up capital from rich family members or friends in high places. This is crucial considering that today's financial and business analysts often recommend that potential business people should borrow or request gifts from family members and friends. Whether solicited or not, the fact is that people who succeed in business these days usually have start-up capital from family and friends. But Buddy did not have a wealthy family or a rich group of friends who could have assisted him with any money to go into business. Despite that, he delved in and triumphed.

His experience as a businessman is one that he will always remember fondly. It was an exciting point in his and his family's life. The challenges of owning and running his own business on a daily basis created a great feeling of excitement as well as a driving desire to tackle and overcome the challenges. His low level of education did not deter him from attempting to accomplish the goals he knew he could achieve. In fact, it made him feel that he had to work harder than he might otherwise have done if he had gone into business with a much higher degree of education.

Owning and running his own business also brought his family remarkable financial blessings. With their improved finances came a great degree of flexibility, evidenced by great improvement in their ability to meet their needs, and even do more. In those days, Sylvester had many things going for him, despite the fact that he had the limitations that have already been described. To be an accomplished businessman, he realized that it was important to put a lot of effort into his endeavors. He always had very high standards for himself, and these determined the quality of the expectations that he placed on his family and himself. In whatever they did, he wanted them to be the best that they could. Therefore, he approached business in the same way. He wanted his business to be the best in town - both in terms of the quality of items they sold, and in terms of the quality of service they offered to people.

At the time he was developing and managing their "big & tall" clothing stores, Billie continued to own and manage her beauty parlor. In both businesses, his wife and he did the best they could to ensure that very high standards were maintained. When they developed Billie's beauty parlor, it was very important to Sylvester that it should be developed as a showcase for all similar businesses in the area. They accomplished that to the best of their ability.

Interestingly, nothing in Sylvester's attitude had anything to do with a competitive spirit or desire hidden somewhere in his psyche. Instead, his decisions were based simply on a strong desire to use his God-given talents and blessings to achieve the best attainable purpose or goals for them. The only way he knew to pursue his goals was to work very hard and make a difference in the process.

Also, a major driving force for Sylvester was to him to ensure that nothing in his life, and in whatever Billie and he did, would conform to the offensive stereotypes of what a black business was supposed to be like. Many adults in this country have certainly heard that businesses run by blacks have low expectations, poor standards and weak reputations. They have also heard the stereotypes of what the nature and character of a black person is supposed to be like - such as incompetent, cannot keep to proper schedules, unprofitable, disrespectful to customers, poor management skills... the generalizations go on and on. Quite conscious of the stereotypes, Sylvester was determined to ensure that his business was run with a high standard of efficiency and respectability that was anything but conforming to the stereotypes. In retrospect, Sylvester is thankful to God that he was able to do that.

TIPS FOR STARTING A BUSINESS

As someone who has "been there and done that," Sylvester McClearn strongly suggests the following rules for anyone who may be considering going into business:

First, do not go into business looking for people to help you. You must be prepared to go in with an understanding that you may receive no assistance from anybody. Go into business ready, knowledgeable, and determined.

Second, go into business with the goal of providing a service. Profit should never be the only reason for going into business. If that is your motivation for going into business, you could be very disappointed the first time you count your money and realize that you may be operating at a loss.

Third, you should definitely go into business with a first-class attitude and priorities, rather than a second or third-rate attitude that can only be self-defeating.

Fourth, you must be aware that any business worth doing may take some time before it begins to bring you any notable rewards. It is therefore essential to plan very carefully before plunging into business. In case of the McClearns, the move into the business world took a remarkable degree of planning and calculation that spanned a period of one and half years before they launched the business. Although they were always sure of what they wanted, they were very careful not to rush because they were conscious of the potential consequences of doing so. in the end, their patience paid off tremendously.

REFLECTIONS ON SUCCESS

The McClearn family reaped tremendous blessings from the businesses that they owned. The blessings, in turn, made life much easier for them. For one thing, they did not have to think too hard and long about where and how to get money when a need arose. The money was there to do what they wanted. Yet, his wife and he were determined to maintain humility and to teach their children the same.

Buddy came from the old school, so he didn't say much to his children regarding their socioeconomic status. The logic on which he operated was simple: If you want your children to stay in school, you don't go telling them, "I got all of this with a sixth grade education." He believed that this type of conversation might make them think that they could do the same. He did not want any of them to harbor the thought that they could drop out of school and still become successful. So he avoided any actions or statements that could have led them in that direction of thinking. Instead, Billie and he focused extensively on their children's education and character development.

The family's blessings through the business were immense indeed! In addition to the number of stores that rose out of one start-up store, Sylvester and Billie were also able to own five apartment buildings. While running their business, they bought a house in the suburbs and moved the family out of the City of Newburgh. This had nothing to do with disdain for a city that was obviously quite beautiful and had been home to them for decades. Instead, it was just a choice that they made because Billie and he wanted something different for their children. What they wanted was a place that was removed from the trappings of city life, with a school district that could afford their children an efficient leaning environment and opportunities to attain their interests and dreams. As it turned out, this move turned out to have a tremendous impact on their children.

Even as he looks back on his life as a businessman, Sylvester recognizes that the successes that he attained are capable of clouding the limitations and agonies that he definitely had. In other words, it is possible for him to think and write only of the successes that he accomplished and ignore any mention of the internal struggles and external challenges with which he had to contend. However, he chooses to remember both the good and the bad because he believes that it is by being so honest with one's self and others that one learns to understand and appreciate life.

FOURTEEN

WHEN DISASTER STRIKES WITHOUT WARNING

Lack of formal education presented Buddy with a huge obstacle in his life, leading him to take steps that he might otherwise not have taken. Although it is unclear how, it is safe to expect that he was somewhat conscious, perhaps sometimes too conscious, of the shortcomings brought upon him by his near-illiteracy. This is a suggestion that the Reverend disputes, although he acknowledges that he purposely worked harder than he might have, had he the level of education that could have propelled him to greater heights with greater ease. Although there is no way now to tell what might have been, one thing is certain: the fact that he envisaged his business as a trailblazing venture propelled him into a determined state where he wanted and tried very hard to leave nothing undone. Nor was he ever going to leave anything to chance. Undoubtedly, his personal qualities and desires largely influenced his business-related thoughts and actions.

Sylvester McClearn was, and remains, a person who likes to have complete control over his life and finances. He strives to maintain accountability in all that he does, and he expects the same from people who work with him. He tends to trust people deeply - until they give him .reason not to. He is always very open to providing help and support to family members, friends, and others who might be in need of assistance at any give time. In the course of running his business, all of these characteristics came into play. Sometimes, the experience turned out to be quite bad for him.

The business expansion from one to six stores spanned between eight and ten years, during which Sylvester was stretched to the limit. As good as it appeared, the expansion meant that the business now naturally moved from one small mom and pop store to a chain of stores. That leap required the building of a management style and business environment that fit a business of that magnitude. It also meant that he had to trust other people to open and close store branches at the designated opening and closing times, since he could not be in all of the stores at the same time.

Unless one has a sophisticated management or organizational structure, which this business didn't have, there is some danger in entrusting such crucial aspects of one's business to other people that one may not know very well. In the absence of that structure, McClearn had to start depending on people to count his money and take care of things that he would normally not have entrusted to them. Naturally, this opened the business up to a degree of vulnerability that was both real and disturbing.

Since he had very little education, McClearn lacked the business acumen or technical know-how to do his own bookkeeping for the business. To make up for this deficiency, he employed people to handle the responsibility of his business accounting. He also employed people to work on the floor of his six stores. Some of his employees were family members who needed employment and he brought them into his business because he wanted to do what he believed was the right thing for them. While that may have been the right thing to do, the fact that his employees had unfettered access to the store registers was not such a great thing.

It is uncertain why this was really the case. From what is known of Sylvester the businessman, however, two things are clear in this regard. First, it was important to him that he be of help to as many people as possible by providing employment to those that had such a need. So he almost never said no, and did not develop a process to screen his potential employees. If they came with a need, they got what they wanted, and they had access to everything in the store. What Sylvester expected of them was hard work and trustworthiness. That wasn't a difficult thing to expect from one's employees but it was sometimes a difficult thing for many to comply with, especially when the overall boss wasn't looking. But the boss couldn't always look. He was busy running six stores and could not humanly be in more than one place at the same time.

Secondly, Sylvester wanted very much to be a caring employer and looked upon his staff as though they were all his family, deserving of love, respect and nurturing. That would not have been a bad thing had all of his employees reciprocated in kind. Unfortunately, some did not. Yet, today's Reverend Sylvester McClearn has no regrets. He is just happy that he was able to treat his employees very well and harbors no ill feelings for whatever treatment he may have received from any of them in return.

Since he had been in the labor force for nearly all of his life, Buddy knew how he wished to be treated as an employee. He attempted to bring that knowledge into the running of his own business and allowed it to shape the way that he treated his own employees. Buddy should know, considering that, as an employee, he organized and led his colleagues in the first known labor movement against unfair labor practices by his then employer in Newburgh in the fifties.

Several people trace the history of the improvement in labor relations in Newburgh to that movement that was led by McClearn. But McClearn never gives himself that much, or any, credit for that and other historically significant actions that he was responsible for. As he sees it, he saw that several wrongs were occurring and the victims were the working poor Blacks who were paid low wages for long hours of work, received no benefits, and were treated as dispensable garbage by their employers. At a time when Blacks were expected to take such treatment and go to work daily, as though they were receiving exactly the kind of treatment that they deserved, Sylvester who was in fact in much better economic shape than most employees decided that he had seen enough. So he organized his colleagues and led them to a strike and peaceful demonstrations against their employers.

By doing that, McClearn had four goals: to make their employers realize through first-hand experience that they would have no business without the "little guys" that worked for them. Secondly, he wanted to empower his colleagues by giving them a voice, and thirdly, he wanted his peers and himself to be respected by their employers. Fourth, he wanted people who had devoted so much of their lives to the company to be given some opportunity for advancement, despite their skin color. McClearn and all of his peers accomplished their goals beyond what they had imagined would occur prior to the start of the strike. The demonstrations and strike hit the employers in their pocket books. As a result, and they caved in and began to for the first time in Newburgh, to treat black employees as employees deserving of consideration, respect and promotion rather than as objects to be seen and not heard.

When he became an employer, Sylvester believed that it was important to trust his employees, and he expected them to handle their responsibilities effectively, and to be dependable and accountable to him in their tasks.

Information or implications regarding some of Sylvester's not-so-honest employees are included in this book, not to cast aspersion on the character of anyone who worked for him. Instead, they are here to show how much he was affected by his lack of education, and how his inclination to trust has not always served him well. Be that as it may, the point must be made that there is great value in Reverend McClearn's continued belief that there is a great deal of goodness in mankind. He believes that he benefited from the goodness that defined the hard work and dedication of many of the people who worked for him.

MISFORTUNE OR LESSONS?

As the old adage goes "When it rains, it pours". Sometimes, misfortune rains either to test our character or to make us stronger. Having said that, there are people who believe that the only purpose of their misfortune is to destroy them. Sometimes, this may in fact be the case.

Sylvester's experience with misfortune was huge and decisive, and it came unexpectedly. In the late seventies, thieves hit his business immensely. Over the years, this had actually become a frequent occurrence at his stores. But the burglary that broke Sylvester and destroyed any chances of the business continuing to exist occurred at his main store. Every single item in the store was stolen. This very tragic experience created strong feelings of violation and unfairness in him. It was not just the act against him that was heartbreaking, but the unimaginably hard times and anger that it produced.

Just imagine going through the city and seeing items from your store strewn all over the streets! Imagine getting frequent calls from the police informing you that one of your stores had just been burglarized again! Imagine getting a final call informing you that yet another burglary has occurred, and you realize that this could mean the termination of your main means of livelihood! Imagine all of these happening in a city to which you have been highly dedicated and have made immense contributions in terms of money, time and energy! There are really no words to adequately describe the extent of the pain.

To this day, Sylvester can neither understand, nor can he explain, why anyone would have chosen to do that to him. The first questions that come to mind when one hears or reads this are: "What about insurance? Didn't he have any? Of course he did. But, although he had business insurance, the exercise of filing insurance claims was absolutely futile. To insurance companies in those days, you had to prove that every single item that was lost was indeed lost, and show that it actually came from your business. That was certainly a

Herculean task. Besides, due to the frequency of burglaries to the McClearn and similar stores in Newburgh at the time, no insurance policy was adequate to cover the dangers to which the business was exposed.

Suddenly, business became slow, and Sylvester did not have enough money to jump-start the business in the manner that was called for. It would have meant starting afresh, but financially, he could not afford to do so. One by one, he lost all of his stores, and consequently the entire business. His money was gone, his businesses were all lost, and McClearn also began to watch his popularity in the community slip away.

Most people in Newburgh knew what had happened to Sylvester, and there were even clear indications that many people knew who were responsible for the burglaries and theft that killed his business. Most people who knew the facts chose not to step forward to help the police investigation, or to help Sylvester recover his stolen belongings. However, some parents went to him now and again to report that their children had participated in the crimes. Then they would return the stolen items and beg Sylvester not to have their children prosecuted for fear that they would be incarcerated.

Sometimes, it was better that he did not know who had participated in the robberies because the information tended to produce hurtful feelings. The last time his store was burglarized, a known criminal in the city was implicated. That was the burglary that led to the end of the McClearn business. Some men who felt deeply about the crime and knew Sylvester's pain came forward and offered to help him get his things back from the criminal. Sylvester obliged and went with them to the man's home with a loaded gun. That was the closest that Sylvester ever came to doing something he never imagined he could do - shooting somebody.

The visit led to an argument that became quite personal. Suddenly, Buddy's entire life flashed in front of his face and he knew exactly what he needed to do. Rather than use his gun, he turned around and walked away because his family was more important. He was not going to spend a day in jail, away from his family, because of a common criminal. Imagine what the story line would have been! How about this for an example: **"A SUCCESSFUL, CHRISTIAN BUSINESS FALLS FOR THE GHOSTS OF HIS FATHER'S PAST!"** That same night, Sylvester went back home, lay awake in bed for much of the night, thought about everything that was happening to him, and made the decision to close down the business.

Unless one has been through an experience like Sylvester's, it is almost impossible to accurately picture exactly how this happens, or to feel what an individual feels who has had so much, and then loses all or much of what he had labored very hard for. Having been through it, Sylvester can present a clear picture of what happens to such an individual, although he is still not sure that he completely understands why or how these things happen.

Based on his experience, he is convinced that everyone who has had such a terrible thing happen may not have the same emotional feelings or react to the occurrence in the same way (since people are different and react differently to similar experiences). The feelings of loss and frustration associated with such a traumatic experience, however, can be quite profound for anyone.

Nothing had happened to warn Sylvester or Billie that they were about to lose the business and the money that they had worked very hard to acquire and to keep. It is easy to claim that Sylvester maintained hope and confidence when he experienced the losses that he did, but that will not be exactly accurate, since he is only human. Being a Christian, he was certain that God would watch over his family and him. He was also aware that it was very important for him to take steps to provide for his family, whether or not the business was still there to help them maintain the living standards to which they had become accustomed.

For him at this time, the realities were clear: (1) the business was gone, but his family was still with him, and they were all in good health. For that, he had God to thank. (2) His family and he still had a roof over their heads, in spite of the loss of the businesses. (3) He recognized that it was very important to find ways to continue to earn some consistent income. The potential dangers of doing nothing were quite obvious. All of this meant that he had to act very fast. It also meant that, if he was going to do something to earn income, then he could not afford to lie down, fold his hands and feel sorry for himself, or wallow in guilt, anger, helplessness, or hopelessness. He only had time to jump into something else quickly and hope that whatever he did would be enough to protect whatever he had left. Otherwise, he and his family could lose their home and many other things that Billie and he had worked very hard to acquire.

Some of the things that Sylvester decided to do may have been humiliating to other people in similar circumstances, especially for a person like him who had not only worked hard but had experienced a tremendous degree of business success. For Sylvester, however, it was time to maintain humility rather than worry about humiliation. But how do you go through the highs that he and Billie experienced and seemingly crash to the low point at which they now found themselves? How do you go from having so much to a point where everything suddenly becomes a luxury because your purchasing ability has been very badly hit? These are all very realistic questions, and at the time, Sylvester had several thoughts along these lines. However, he was often reminded that such thoughts could become stumbling blocks in the way of progress for his family and himself.

In his desire and effort to maintain his home and sustain hope, Sylvester accepted a job as a janitor at a local trucking business. His son, Michael, who had been working in one of the store before it was burglarized, also worked at the same truck stop. In an interview with Michael, he spoke about how sad and difficult this felt to watch his father perform such humiliating tasks everyday. In Michael's heart, a high degree of anger built up toward the people who had destroyed his father's business and hurt him so greatly. Even more annoying to him was the fact that some of those people were family members who his father had employed out of the kindness of his heart.

In Sylvester's mind, taking on menial jobs was just something that he had to do in the circumstances, and he remains glad that he did so. He believes that, as a parent, it is important to do whatever can do within the confines of legality to give stability to one's self and one's family. That's exactly what he tried to do in this case. He was just a man driven by a strong desire to give his family his best and to sustain them through the most difficult of times, even if that meant doing jobs that were not glamorous but menial.

People who know what happened to Sylvester as a businessman wonder how he could have moved on freely, and without revenge or prolonged anger, after his businesses were practically destroyed by people who clearly meant harm toward me. The truth is, not only did he move on from that point to this point in his life, he can also say with great confidence that he harbors no anger toward anyone who participated in causing the destruction that his businesses encountered. At the same time, he harbors no anger toward the accomplices and accessories to the crime, some of who like the perpetrators may in fact still reside in Newburgh.

Forgiveness is a powerful force in the human spirit and existence, which is why our Lord Jesus Christ spoke extensively about its significance. Over the years, Reverend McClearn has been able to forgive the people who tried to destroy him by taking away the things that he had. It is difficult for people who do not have Christ in their lives to understand how anyone could forgive another person who tried to destroy him. Even for those who claim to be the best Christians there are, the ability to forgive completely is scarce to come by. In the Reverend's case, it certainly did not occur under his own power. Instead, God made it possible for him to forgive those people and move on. In the process, Billie and Sylvester believe that God has restored them completely, and has blessed them with even more than they had in those days. For that, they are forever thankful to God, but they are also greatly thankful for the lessons that they learned through that sad but remarkable ordeal.

FIFTEEN

WHEN YOU ARE CALLED, YOU ARE CALLED

Although he is a pastor now and has been for decades, Reverend Sylvester McClearn does not recall making a conscious plan or decision to go into the ministry. Christians know that when you give your life to the Lord and completely submit yourself and your will to His Holy Spirit, you never know where He will lead you. He leads you where He pleases, and your responsibility is to just obey Him. McClearn believes that is exactly what happened to him. God's Holy Spirit led him into the ministry and, as a servant of God he obeyed. This was really the only thing he knew how to do as a Christian. It is still the only way he lives his life.

Regarding what made him become a minister, there are many people even his own family who do not understand what happened to him and how it happened. He is not even sure that he can completely explain it himself, other than the fact that the move was a direct extension of his relationship with God.

Most people who know Sylvester well have pondered numerous questions. For example, how does one transfer the aggressive character required in the business world that is driven by material profit to a minister's world presumably defined by meekness, patience, submission, humility, and spirituality? How does one just move on from good and bad business experiences such as Sylvester had had from running his own business – especially the sad experiences that ended the business? How does one take all of those memories and continue to work as hard to improve his community as Sylvester has continued to do to this day? Remember that this is the same community in which he suffered his unforgettable experiences.

The answers, as well as the strength to live those answers, cannot be found within any human. It is impossible to get anyone to recall any time when Sylvester sat down and tried to plot a way out of his difficulties. What everyone recalls, including Sylvester himself is that he continued his life as though he had placed his situation in the hands of someone else. Indeed he had. He placed the situation entirely in the hands of God and, with God occupying such a prime place in his heart, he felt guilty every time it occurred to him that he was on the verge of developing a grudge against his detractors.

To this day, he holds very strongly to the motto: "Love everyone, including your enemies". He believes that he cannot afford to hold any grudges because of his circumstances. When he speaks of love and forgiveness, the preacher truly comes out of this man who is truly blessed and is, truly, a man of God. Here are his own words in response to a question: "I refuse to live in the past when I can live a fulfilled and happy life with God now and forever. Besides, God has taught us how to live. He desires every Christian to have a forgiving spirit and to forgive even the people that have been the most hateful toward us. This is not an option that we exercise; it is a command with which we must comply."

He continues after what is barely a pause: "People who have never experienced the presence and power of God in their lives may not understand how this can be, and how you can forgive people who have hurt you very badly. But we can, and as Christians we must. In my case, I did, and I can confidently say, like David, that "… I never saw the righteous forsaken." Today, with my whole heart I can sincerely say that my family and I have more now than we did when we owned a prosperous business. For one thing, we definitely have peace of mind. Although we lost a lot when I lost the business, I have no doubt that we gained a lot more than we can count."

The statement, as presented in Reverend McClearn's own words, typifies the kind of man that he is. When he speaks of gaining more than he lost, he cannot be talking about material gains. Undoubtedly, he had a very prosperous business that went down, along with most of the fortunes that he had earned. Later, he became a minister in a traditional church where the life of a minister is not marked by wealth and glamour, but by humility and compassion. Therefore, he couldn't really have regained the money and material that he lost.

Looked at in this way, it becomes obvious that the gains about which Reverend McClearn speaks have largely to do with the ultimate kind of happiness that all men should strive for. He is a man who, despite his material losses, has found a place in which he has been able bring his life to the ultimate point of unison between mind, body, and soul. Therefore, he is a happy and satisfied man whose life is at rest, and who wants for nothing because he has it all in Christ. One remarkable thing about this is that his wife Billie sees their situation in exactly the same way as her husband does. She is very convinced that, as they have served the Lord, they have gained much more as a couple and a family than they ever had before the demise of their business.

SYLVESTER AND CHURCH

Buddy's mother, who was a very religious woman, attended a Pentecostal church when Buddy was young, and she took her children with her. The church that Randy was attending with his family when Buddy came to live with them in Newburgh was also a Pentecostal church. As has already been discussed elsewhere in this book the wedding between Sylvester and Billie also occurred in a Pentecostal church. They remained members of that church for several years after their wedding.

While in that church, Sylvester participated actively in various ministries within the church. As he did so, he became increasingly aware that the Lord was calling him into the ministry – to do more for Him. He did not know what to expect or how to respond, but he knew that he did not want to be a stumbling block in God's way of fulfilling His will in his life. Sylvester was in no doubt that his submission to God would have to be absolute, just as it had been on the day he made the commitment to give his life to Christ. He was not about to restrict the move of God's power in him, since he knew Jonah's story very well and knew what could happen to anyone who tries to run away from obeying God's command.

As a Christian and active church member, he had seen many other people get called into the ministry and he was not sure if they knew what the ministry meant prior to the call. In fact, he still wonders now how many people would go into active ministry if they knew the responsibilities involved and what they would have to do. It's probably better not to know the outcome before responding to the call. Over and over again, we learn of people who had no knowledge of what the ministry entailed before they heeded the call to get in. Always, God shows His will and His way to anyone that He has truly called.

Reverend McClearn has since learned that there is hardly an appropriate time or an adequate way to prepare for the ministry unless we know what awaits us in the future. Since we are only human, it is impossible to know even that basic reality. In his experience in the church, Sylvester had watched the church just turn people loose who had been called into the ministry before he was. Once it was determined that they had been called to devote their lives to the service of God, the church often allowed the individuals to find their own way. They were given the opportunity to discover themselves and to independently learn what aspects of the ministry they might be best suited for. Once they made those discoveries, they were given room to develop.

When Sylvester realized that he was getting called into the ministry, he expected the same sequence to occur that he had seen occur with others before him. Therefore, he was able to go into the ministry with an attitude that was similar to the one with which he generally approached his tasks. He wanted to be the best minister of God's gospel that anyone had ever met, and he was confident that the church would allow him the opportunity to develop. His goal was never to please anyone, but to glorify God. Therefore, he studied the word of God relentlessly and practiced everything that he possibly could to make him a better person in his personal life as well as in his work for God.

At the time that he was developing his determination and zeal to be a minister, Sylvester was unaware that such a task would cause him some difficulty in the church. Why would he think that? He expected the church to welcome and support ministers who desired to engage in the ministry exactly as the Bible requires. He expected that this would be consistent not only with the philosophy of any church, but also with the dictates of Jesus Christ who commanded us to spread His gospel to all nations and all creatures. In addition, Christ taught us over and over again to ensure that the underprivileged among us received our attention.

Armed with a strong knowledge of the word of God, Sylvester hoped that stepping up into the position of a minister would afford him the opportunity and platform to continue to do for his community the work that he had already begun to do as a businessman. Unfortunately, this desire and motivation caused him great problems. It had never occurred to Sylvester that the church could restrict him from pursuing hopes, dreams and aspirations — all of which he believed were firmly rooted in the gospel. Therefore, Sylvester prepared only for the work of God as a minister, but he neglected to prepare himself for the kind of seemingly non-caring politics that he did not even know existed in the church prior to that time.

Although he loved the Pentecostal church in which he had been a very active member for several years, and was now a minister, Sylvester grew increasingly uncomfortable with several positions that were taken by the church leadership. For example, he received criticisms in the church for sponsoring the parades that he had sponsored for years as a businessman in Newburgh. Yet, those parades, as has already been discussed, were meant to achieve exactly what they accomplished, which was to strengthen the spirit of the African American community in Newburgh at a time when there was so little going for Africa Americans as a people. Quite commonly, he was also criticized for going to visit his children on their college campuses rather than attend impromptu church meetings.

As if all of that were not enough, Buddy desired very strongly to march in support of the civil rights movement one time during the civil rights struggle. This desire was grounded in the simple fact that he believed very strongly, as he still does, that God created man in His own image and sees us all as equal in His sight, regardless of race. He also believes that we are all made as a demonstration of God's beauty and completeness, a quality that ought to be honored rather than despised.

Sylvester is still not sure if the leadership of his church believed differently than he did about equality, but he knows that the church did not perceive of the civil rights struggle as a cause in which they ought to engage. Yet, this was a black church. This is an important point for the same reason that it is important to state that this was certainly not unique to the church in which Sylvester was a member and minister at the time. Simply, it had nothing to do with race. In fact, most Pentecostal churches in the United States at the time were opposed to the civil rights movement. In fact many Pentecostal Christians even considered Dr. Martin Luther King a devil – until he died. After he was murdered, it became common to hear some of the same black Pentecostal Christians who had vilified King along with their white counterparts make statements like: "Brother Martin was killed trying to do the right thing for us black folks". Is that hypocrisy? You bet.

Generally, Pentecostal Christians and churches perceived of the civil rights movement as a rebellious action that was intent only on attacking a system that they considered as the established will of God. Indeed, the civil rights movements were aimed at buckling a system of injustice that several so-called Christians in this country probably perceived as God's establishment. This is indeed a position that Pentecostal Christians and their church leaders held and still hold quite commonly.

These facts are presented here at the risk of being considered an attacker of the Pentecostal movement in the United States. Such a characterization of me will not be accurate for one good reason. I am a writer and a Christian who believes that every Christian who gives his life to Christ, and is saved, sanctified and filled with the Holy Spirit is indeed a fulfillment of the promise of Pentecost that Christ made before He left our world in His human form. In that sense, I am myself a product of Pentecost.

However, the point here is that most Pentecostal churches in the United States have always tended to emphasize only what they consider as the "spiritual" while almost completely neglecting social and other issues that they consider to be "worldly." Therefore, although a Pentecostal pastor may preach against social problems from the pulpit – if he does at all – he will completely avoid any active participation in efforts to alleviate those social problems, unless of course there is a television camera there to capture his "goodwill". Yet, God has called His people to be the salt of the earth, which we can only be when we see ourselves not only as citizens of heaven, but also as citizens of the earth that we currently inhabit.

To a large degree, Rev. McClearn himself was both victimized and blessed by this same thinking. His efforts to get himself involved in something as basic as participating in a march to support the civil rights movement were consistently rebuffed by the leadership of his Pentecostal church. It was just not something that they did! Unfortunately, it is still something that most Pentecostal churches and their ministers do not do. To them, that is not a spiritual act. No wonder the churches and Christian leaders that maintained active participation in civil rights struggles in this and other countries, including

South Africa, were not from Pentecostal churches. Instead, they were from the so-called traditional churches – Anglican (Episcopal), Baptist, Methodist, Catholic to some extent, and non-Christians.

Often, one wonders what Jesus Christ would say or do in response to this reality. One thing that is for sure is that the wealth of a church should never be determined by its ability to keep everything that God blesses it with. Instead, as Reverend McClearn himself preaches, the richness of a church should be determined both by its ability and its willingness to give of itself to those in need. That is how God makes good stewards of us, as individuals and as a group or an institution. According to the Reverend, "God blesses us, His children, not so that we become attached to what He gives us, but so that we can become blessings to others as God Himself has blessed us. Job was a very wealthy man but he never got attached to what he had. We must all learn to be like that." Amen!

It was against the backdrop that has been presented that Sylvester received an invitation early in 1981 to meet with a minister from the United Methodist Church, also in Newburgh. Sylvester did not know what to expect. On that day, he made the twenty-minute drive from his home to the church at Grand Street, got out of his car and walked into the warm handshake of Reverend Frank Wettestein, an older white man who seemed genuinely happy to see McClearn. Rev. Wettstein was at that time the pastor of the church. Soon after Sylvester took the seat to which he was ushered, Reverend Wettstein, who had also sat down, spoke very solidly: "Brother McClearn", he began, "I want you to become the Associate Pastor of this church. I believe that God has led us to you and I know that there is no better man to fill this position at this time." Reverened Wettstein paused, and then continued: "What do you say?" Without waiting for a response, he added: "I know it may be a little difficult for you to give me an answer at this time. So, please, you don't have to give me one right now. You go home, talk with Sister McClearn, and get back to me at your convenience."

Sylvester didn't know what had just happened to him.

He was stunned. But what had in fact happened was that God had sought him out and was placing a call to him. Without any prompting from Sylvester, the Reverend Wettestein told him that he wanted Sylvester to be the best pastor that he could aspire to being. He also told Sylvester that it was always the desire of his church leadership that their pastors should be educated all the way through college.

Even for a man like Sylvester who did not have a high school diploma, or even a full elementary school education, the entire discussion with Wettstein sounded like music to his ears. Suddenly, he acquired a strong motivation to go to school. Yet, he felt that it was important to lean on God for direction. Consequently, he committed the offer to God in prayers. In no time, it became clear to Billie and him that this was all part of God's leading, and he knew that, once again, he would have to obey God and leave the Pentecostal church he had been attending. Again, that was a church where he got married, had his children, and began his ministry.

Although he was uncomfortable with some things because of the leadership of the Pentecostal church that had become his home church for many years now, he had no resentment toward anyone, including the church leaders. Besides, he was not seeking an opportunity to leave the Pentecostal church when he got the call from Reverend Wettestein. Such a thought was indeed very far from his mind. At the same time, he was cognizant of his responsibility to allow himself to be led by God. He let God lead and he followed the lead.

ASSOCIATE PASTOR MCCLEARN STEPS INTO THE UNITED METHODIST CHURCH

Before giving his word to Reverend Wettestein, Sylvester read up on the United Methodist Church and learned a lot that pleased him greatly. He was impressed by the traditions and foundations of The United Methodist Church, a church that was founded in the 18th Century by John Wesley, an

Anglican priest from England. From its beginning, the United Methodist Church had the interests of the poor at heart, and based all of its teachings and practices on the Holy Bible. In Newburgh, where Sylvester lived, the United Methodist Church was active in extensive efforts to improve the community through a program that it called "community outreach." The church sponsored outreach activities aimed at helping the poor and needy in the community, as well as improving the quality of life in the area. Considering that this kind of effort was one that Sylvester himself cherished and desired for himself and the church of which he had been part for several years, there was no way for him not to be impressed by what the Methodist Church was doing.

Once he transferred to the United Methodist Church, Sylvester enrolled in school right away, studied for and passed the General Equivalence Diploma (GED) examinations and decided to use the opportunities that the Methodist church was offering to his advantage. Lest anyone is left with the impression that going through the GED process was as easy for Sylvester as ABC, truth be told that it was by no means so. The story of the process is a remarkable one that deserves to be told.

In March of 1981, Mrs. Thompson, a Caucasian teacher in the Town of Newburgh received a call from a very polite African American gentleman who said to her: "Ma'am, I need help with my reading and writing skills. I am wondering if you would be able to take me on and teach me". That telephone call was the beginning of a relationship between Mrs. Thompson and the McClearn family that remains very strong to this day. Taken by the gentleness and humility of this man that was on the phone with her, Mrs. Thompson invited him over to her home for an evaluation to help her determine how much help he might need. Mrs. Thompson was a teacher in one of the local schools but she also had her own private school where she taught children on the ground floor of her home.

In his customary way of obedience, the African American man, who was Sylvester, showed up in the home of Mrs.

Thompson at the appointed time. From the testing, Mrs. Thompson determined that Sylvester's reading skills, though not where they should be, were better than his writing skills, which were severely lacking. In fact, his writing skills were at third grade level. Mrs. Thompson realized that she and Sylvester would have to work very hard to bring him up to the level where he needed to be, and she saw that he was ready and determined to do the work. They started out with spelling. They would tape-record the lessons and Sylvester would play the tape over and over in his car daily.

Sylvester had a very full life – between family, business, and the church where he was very active. On occasion, he felt very discouraged and would not show up for his lesson. Mrs. Thompson would call the house, ask him to come over, and he would comply. Then he would inform Mrs. Johnson that he did not get his assignments done. Mrs. Thompson would always request of Sylvester to show up anyway "for continuity" even when his work was undone. Armed with determination and desire, with great support from Billie and Mrs. Thompson, Sylvester soon sat for the GED examination and passed. Then he took courses at the Orange Community College in Newburgh where he proceeded to obtain an Associates Degree.

Mrs. Thompson has very fond memories of the time when Sylvester was her student. She carries with her memories of a physically big man who was always willing to stoop down and learn even the most basic of academic tasks. Even after his GED and Associates Degrees, Sylvester continued to contact Mrs. Thompson for guidance with his college work. Sylvester had an unparalleled love for learning, and Mrs. Thompson knew not to suggest that he take a break. He wanted to go to the top and she was going to remain supportive to him for as long as he was willing to do it.

In her effort to work with Sylvester, Mrs. Thompson always had Billie on her side. Sometimes, it was Billie who would let her know when things were emotionally hard for Sylvester. Billie didn't even have to say anything when Mr. Thompson called; the tone of her voice was always sufficient hint for Mrs. Thompson that Sylvester wasn't doing very well. For example, when the McClearns' business was burglarized one time, Mrs. Thompson called the McClearn home and requested Billie to have Sylvester come over. When he did, they talked. Mrs. Thompson looked straight at Sylvester and said: "Did it ever occur to you that God was sending you a message?" Sylvester responded: "Yes and no". They went on to talk in detail about the emotional and spiritual implications of the tragic occurrence.

Shortly after that conversation, the McClearns' business was robbed again. This time, the business was completely stripped. Sylvester knew that the business was completely gone this time, and he was distraught. Again, Mrs. Thompson was able to get Billie to arrange a meeting between her and Sylvester. When the two met, Mrs. Thompson was direct in her usual way: "Sylvester, God has hit you over the head with a two by four", she said, "When will you get the message?" Sylvester did in fact get the message and the rest is history.

Once he responded to the call of God, Sylvester was determined to do whatever it took to be a great servant of the Master. He enjoyed his education under the guidance of Mrs. Thompson. Mrs. Thompson recalls Sylvester's love for American History and the challenges that two courses, "Women in History" and "Feminism" posed for him. His greatest difficulty was with college Algebra, but he got through it with determination, a willingness to learn, and a humble attitude. His character provided Mrs. Thompson all the encouragement that was necessary to continue to work with Sylvester toward his eventual success. As it turned out, the degree of success that Sylvester attained was largely unparalleled considering his life's journey up until that time. When he started to work with Mrs. Thompson, the only person in his life that could actually read and understand his writing was Billie. To learn as he did and to change his life through education, Sylvester chose to go to a woman who did not look or speak like him for assistance. He listened to Mrs. Thompson as she worked with him and he kept his eyes on the prize. It worked.

Within two years, Sylvester was writing fluently.

After attaining his high school equivalence diploma, Sylvester became highly motivated to learn more. Not long afterwards, a man like himself who had lived much of his life without ever imagining himself in college found himself enrolled as a student in Wesley Theological Seminary in Washington, D.C. When he arrived at the Seminary on his first day, Sylvester felt as though he was in dreamland. He look around at the big beautiful buildings on the campus, thought of the cotton fields of his youth in North Carolina, and was reminded that he had indeed traveled a long, hard road. Then he began to think of some famous theologians and ministers who attended Wesley and walked on the same grounds where he would be threading for the next few years.

Sylvester did not have the luxury of celebrating this accomplishment for a long time because no sooner had he been admitted than he got introduced to the challenging tasks that all college students must encounter. He had a permanent smile on his public face during his first week as a student of Wesley, but his times alone were replete with reflections and a mix of emotions.

Sylvester was very excited about the opportunity to learn, especially about the walks of other Christians before his time. As he sat in his first class at Wesley, he hardly paid as great attention as he could to the instruction, because he could not stop wondering who of Wesley's alumni might have sat atone time or another on the seat that he was sitting on. He was happy to learn about the voice of God as He speaks and acts through people. Also, spending time with his college professors was a very special experience. Sylvester's hope and faith increased with each step, as he saw himself accomplishing things that he had never imagined that he could do.

Many parents often tell their children that they were "A" students when they were in school. It is never certain why they do that. Perhaps they do it to encourage their children to do well, or because they want to look infallible to their children. This is a problem that Reverend McClearn does not have to worry about. He knows that his wife and children are very proud of him, and always will. His was a "B" student in college and he remains very proud that God made this possible. In about nine or ten years, he had gone from a fourth grade academic level to earning a Bachelor's degree in his name. This is truly a remarkable man. Over time the working relationship between Sylvester's family and Mrs. Thompson developed into a very good friendship that continues to this day.

Although his academic success remains very important to, one of the things that Reverend McClearn seems to be most proud of is an experience that he describes as "one of the biggest sources of joy that I experienced when I made the transfer from the Pentecostal Church." Shortly after he arrived in the United Methodist Church, the Bishop instructed all ministers to go and demonstrate in New York City in support of Mr. Nelson Mandela who was in a South African jail for daring to fight for equal rights for his fellow black people in his country. This was indeed a situation to which Sylvester could relate.

Although he never participated in the civil rights movements of the fifties and sixties, Sylvester had developed a very inquisitive mind that made him question many things, even when he wasn't saying much. He was quite conscious of his race and the plight of black people around the world – whether it was in America or in far away lands. He knew that black people were always at the door but could never get into the party because their race constituted a barrier. Growing up, he thought that this was a problem that was unique to the United States and, although he was so young and was struggling for his own survival, he knew that he could contribute in his own little ways to his own self-perception as a black boy.

Without the power and intellect worthy of a civil rights campaigner in the fifties, Buddy elected to do his own campaign by supporting those blacks who did his people proud by excelling at what they did. Therefore, he became a great fan of boxers like Joe Lewis and Sugar Ray Robinson, and baseball players like Roy Campanella, Willie Mays, and Johnny

Rosebury, Jr. His favorite sports were baseball and boxing, and he would stay home to watch boxing on his small black and white television set at nine o'clock every Saturday night. As a child, Buddy always heard his parents say: "If you want to succeed, you have to be twice as good as the white man". Buddy saw his favorite black athletes as better by at least two times than their white counterparts. Therefore, he considered them as worthy representatives and great ambassadors of the black race. He knew that any black person at the level that those young men were in had to be highly legit to be there. He also knew that there were many white people who wanted those black men to fail, so he wished them very well and rooted for them every time any of them stepped into the boxing ring or stepped up to the mound.

When he found out about Nelson Mandela's imprisonment for fighting for equality for the black people of South Africa, Sylvester knew that Mr. Mandela must have been good enough at what he did for the white people of his country to have been so bothered by him. What he had also known when he became a Christian was that God wanted His children to be on the side of the oppressed. It was against this background of knowledge, principles and beliefs that he jumped at the opportunity to match in support of Mandela and in protest of his incarceration. There is really no way to describe exactly how refreshing Sylvester found the instruction of his Bishop and the opportunity to actually take the side of the oppressed people of South Africa, symbolized by Nelson Mandela.

To have a Bishop and a church that understood the importance of both the sacred and the social, and accepted the responsibility to honor and work on both was a thriller for Reverend McClearn. It was perhaps even more exciting that the Bishop instructed his clergy to take this on and be ready to be arrested in the process. Sylvester obeyed the instruction from the bottom of his heart and, to this day, he holds that experience as a badge of honor.

Sylvester and Billie did not anticipate the changes that would occur in their lives when he made the decision to switch from a Pentecostal to the United Methodist Church. As it turned out, the church put him through a process that was both unexpected and curious. To become a minister in the United Methodist Church, he had to undergo a battery of tests, including psychological tests to determine his emotional stability and his understanding of, and readiness for the responsibilities associated with his calling. Every prospective minister of the United Methodist Church went through this same process.

Undoubtedly, there are facts about Reverend McClearn's ministry that his children will learn for the first time when they read this book. For example, they have for years wondered about the transition that their father made from their familiar upbeat, predominantly black Pentecostal church to the slow-paced, predominantly white United Methodist Church where everything was different. Even worse is the fact that, after Sylvester became the pastor of the United Methodist church, he had to contend with a remarkable degree of opposition and rejection, which most people close to him have attributed to racial prejudice.

In due course, the United Methodist Church that was once all-white became a mostly black church, as most white members of the congregation left the church in protest. In Sylvester's opinion, the fears were really not due to the fact that the white members of the church did not want a black pastor. Instead, according to his interpretation, they were afraid that if he became the pastor of the church, eventually the complexion and style of the church would eventually change. That caused the discomfort. In 1985, he became the Pastor of the United Methodist Church in Newburgh, a position that he held until his retirement in June 2002.

TAKING STOCK

As he looks back on his life and work as a pastor, he considers it a great honor to have had this remarkable opportunity to serve God. To look around and be able to say that God chose him to do this difficult job is amazing. I am not sure why God chooses a person like Sylvester McClearn, nor does Sylvester himself know. He would certainly like an answer to that question. One analogy to this aspect of his life is that which is written in the Bible about Moses. Moses also wondered why God would choose a man like him to do the job that He sent Moses out to do. But nobody knows the heart of God. He will do what pleases Him, even if it means picking the most unlikely person to do His most important task.

If asked to advise young people going into the ministry, Reverend McClearn knows exactly what he would tell them. He believes that the most important thing he would say to them is that they leave themselves completely open and willing to be used by God as He sees fit. They must consider the ministry as a service to God rather than an opportunity to pursue their own happiness. God must always be first; and we must always be last.

Nobody who knew Buddy decades ago would have said that Sylvester McClearn would become Reverend McClearn, and that he would become the first African American pastor of the all-white United Methodist Church in Newburgh, New York. Yet, that is exactly what God chose to do with his life. Sylvester became a willing tool in God's hand, to wield as He saw fit for the purpose of bringing glory to Himself.

A STRONG WOMAN TAKES HER PLACE

SIXTEEN

BILLIE STEPS FORWARD

By now, it is clear that Billie is the wife of Sylvester "Buddy" McClearn and the mother of his children. There is nothing ordinary about the McClearn couple. Instead, they are an extraordinary pair. More than just a regular married couple, the two have been partners for over forty years. The opinions that they express about one another reveals a tremendous amount of genuine love, mutual respect and understanding. For example, Billie says of Sylvester: "I could never have asked for a stronger, gentler, kinder, more intelligent, more exciting, and more humane partner than I have in Sylvester. He is the man whose life story makes mine more complete." Of Billie, Sylvester says as follows: "God brought her into my life and it is impossible to measure what she means to me. She is the best woman in the world and I love her with all my heart."

Billie was born on August 6, 1937, in a small Texas town known as Cushing, in Rush County. Cushing was one of those little places that you could actually miss if you fell asleep briefly while traveling through. It was a great town where almost everyone literarily knew one another and you could cover the entire length of the town on foot without even breaking a sweat or breathing heavily. But, although out-of-town folks from the city would have had difficulty understanding why anyone would want to live in Cushing, the inhabitants loved their town because it was unspoiled by the hustle and bustle of city life. Besides, they could always lay claim to the idea that people cared for one another.

At birth, Mrs. McClearn's name was Billie Marie Smith.

Billie's parents were Ida and Charles (Charlie) Smith, both born and raised in Texas. She grew up as an only child on a farm owned by her father. Billie had a multicultural background, which seemed to influence the way she was raised – with a remarkable degree of open-mindedness. Her daddy Charlie had one white parent and came from a big family. As a result, most of his relatives were light-skinned with long and straight black hair. They never used hot combs and never needed a perm. His parents had seven children, which meant that Charlie had three sisters and three brothers.

At birth, Billie was dark-skinned because her mother had black skin that was as smooth as butter. Like the man he married, Ida's mother came from a family that was also multicultural in its composition. Her mother had a cultural background that included Indian heritage while here father's cultural background included African heritage.

When Billie was born, her father's family wanted to have nothing to do with her because of her very dark skin. It was even common for family members to openly make statements casting doubt on the fact that Billie was indeed her father's child. This is by no means a unique situation. In marriages that involve more than one race, there are almost always family members who lack the ability to see beyond skin color and embrace the beauty of nature. That has always been the case, and it is uncertain if it will ever change. Unfortunately, among the people who always get hurt in the process are innocent children who never asked to come to the world. The perpetrators of the hurt are often the adult family members who have difficulty restraining themselves from making reckless comments within hearing range of the children.

Billie's father and his three brothers had a very close relationship with one another and they worked very hard together. As very young men, they bought farms of their own next to one another so they could see each other and spend time together daily. To this day, some of their family members still live on the land that they purchased in Texas.

Growing up, Billie often wondered what it might have

been like to come from such a big family as her dad's. Being raised as an only child was a very lonely experience for her. She coped well with her situation by learning to play by herself, which was really the only choice she had most of the time. She sometimes thinks that this negatively impacted her in more ways than one. For one, Billie believes that being an only child growing up with two adult parents made her a selfish little girl and affected her social skills, such that she could not relate very well with people.

Regardless of whatever negative experiences Billie may have had as a child, she is very happy about her childhood, about which she claims to have very great memories. It is the otherwise simple things in life that shape much of the memories that Billie had. For example, she remembers sitting by the fireplace and receiving heat from the burning wood while she did her homework. This was really the only source of heat that the family had in their old, wooden three-bedroom home at the time. Like many houses in those days, the bathroom in the Smith home was outside of the family home rather than indoors. They got their drinking water from a well, using a bucket to draw it. Then they would heat the water on the stove to bath, wash dishes, or clean anything.

That time was sophisticated without the people knowing it. Charlie and Ida Smith raised their own vegetables, cows, chickens and hogs for their own meat. For example, they had a very effective method for preserving their meat in a smokehouse. As Billie recalls it, some of the meat was sugar curried while some was prepared with salt, making it possible to preserve the meat from one year to the next. Otherwise, maggots would attack the meat. Whenever this happened, Billie's mother would pick the maggots out of the meat. With a little bit of preparation afterwards, the meat was ready to be eaten. This was always all done in compliance with Ida's usual spirit of preserving rather than throwing out food.

The family ate chicken necks and feet, gizzards, liver, and other parts of a chicken that are not widely eaten today. They also ate pigs' feet, ears, tails, liver, intestine, shoulders, ribs, heads, brains, and anything else one can imagine. This was the way many people ate in those days. Creativity was alive in the kitchen in black households, and mothers knew how to make a cool meal from anything. That is an art that seems almost lost on their children and grandchildren who are now many of today's African American mothers. We strongly need a return to old times.

When she was growing up, Billie's family was poor, although not as poor as the families from which many of Billie's friends came. Her parents always ensured that the family had a lot of food in their home and had a roof over their heads. Charlie also had an unforgettably beautiful and very decent truck and a tractor that he used on his farm, on which he cultivated cotton and watermelon on his farms. The farm products were sold in the market in the local area and beyond. As a child, Billie was the one that would drive the tractor at harvest time, while the adults picked the watermelon and loaded them on the big tractor-trailers that would come in from other states. These tractors carried the watermelons to the market for sale. The tomatoes that were grown on her father's farm were also in great demand and were sold in most of the same markets as the ones in which the watermelons were sold.

Billie often worked side by side with her father on the farm because he liked to brag about her and she knew it. Of course, children like to hear their parents commend them, and Billie was no different. Her father's frequent praise often made her work even harder to impress him. Subconsciously, Billie was also aware of the stereotypes regarding male and women's physical strength. So, she often felt a need to show her father that she could work just as hard as her male cousin that was of the same age as she.

The Smith family was very hard working indeed. Their work was never just limited to their Cushing abode. In fact, they would sometimes travel to West Texas to pick cotton. When they did, they would sleep in wooden shimmies or on the floor. It was quite common for family members in those days to wear one another's clothing, and that's what the Smiths did. For Billie, the highlight of their trips to West Texas was always the food truck that came at lunchtime with peas, sweets, and other goodies. Thanks to that truck, the family often tended to spend much of their money on food.

One experience remains very vivid in Billie's mind, and it is one that still has many unanswered questions. She recalls her father and one of his brothers once taking their families down by the Red River to pick cotton in Louisiana. At some point during the trip, they all lost any awareness of their bearings, or their whereabouts. Therefore, they were unaware that they were going into a plantation. When they got into the plantation, they were escorted through a large gate, past a big white mansion, and into some old, dilapidated shacks. Then they were ordered to remain there and warned that there would be severe consequences to pay if they went off the grounds. They had to purchase their food and other needs from a store that was located there on the plantation grounds.

Suddenly, Charlie and his brother realized that they had just made a terrible mistake. They could not hide their shock and fear and, once the strong and bold adult men showed that they were scared, everyone in the party became very scared. While there, they met a black man who told them that he had been on the plantation for his entire life and had never exited what he described as "the big gate." It is uncertain how long the Smith family spent on this plantation, but much of the time was spent by Charlie and his brother trying to plot an escape. Eventually, Papa Charlie was able to trick their captor into letting them go by promising to come back with several men to help with the work on the plantation. One night, they escaped without harm to anyone in the party. To this day, Billie shivers at the memory of this experience, and the thought of what might have happened.

In addition to everything else that he did very well, daddy was also a very good hunter and fisherman who would hunt for game and would also fish regularly. Often, he would skin the hides of the animals that he caught and would sell the fur in the market for very good money. Needless to say that Papa Charlie would not be much endeared to the hearts of animal rights activists today. Yet, it would certainly not be fair to characterize Papa Charlie as an animal hater. By no means was he one. Before it was hip to treat animals with respect and nurturing, Charlie ensured that the animals in his home were well fed and could all be accounted for at the end of the day. If one was missing, he went out to search for it and to bring the animal back to the safety and security of the Smith home.

As if it happened yesterday, Billie recalls a day that he came home from his fishing outing with an alligator. That was quite memorable for the fact that the entire community came to the Smith home to congratulate him and to participate in an alligator feast. This was a very rare feat befitting of great adulation, and the community was very proud of its hero and was willing to put everything on hold to celebrate his accomplishment. In those days, such accomplishment by one member of the community was considered an accomplishment of the entire community.

Charlie was a multi-talented man who never gave up an opportunity to use his talent. In that way, Sylvester was like his father in-law. To be able to do all that he did, Charlie had a greatly supportive wife in Ida, his very dear wife – just like Sylvester does in Billie. Like Sylvester, who had a religious mother, Billie's mother was also a religious woman. Historically, African American women have always been very religious, much more so than the men. This remains a fact to this day. There was one difference, however, between the McClearn family and the Smith family. Although Randolph II was not religious, Charlie Smith was. He was in fact a deacon in the church that he attended with his family. To this day, that church continues to spot a cornerstone erected in honor of Deacon Charlie Smith. Charlie and Ida raised Billie in church, which means that they attended church regularly and they took her along. This is in fact interesting, considering the fact that neither of them had religious parents. In fact, Ida's grandfather was an alcoholic. Her mother died very young, leaving Ida to be raised by her alcoholic father. What a stressor that must have been! The consequences of alcoholism are well documented and quite extensive indeed.

Due to the stressful circumstances of being raised by an alcoholic father, Ida wanted very badly to get out of her home, and she saw marriage as her ticket to accomplish this desire. So, at a young age, she married Charles Smith, a much older man than she was. When the couple got married, they were almost forty years apart in age. Ida was Charlie's third wife, and she had stepchildren who were older than she was. By the time of their marriage, Charlie already had seven sons from his first marriage. Billie's stepsiblings and Billie maintain regular contact with one another.

Billie's upbringing by her parents was very strict. The structure in their home was replete with rules and regulations, which included church on Sunday and during the week. Even as a teenager, she was not allowed to attend ball games unless with an adult escort – usually one of her uncles. They were always careful not to make themselves conspicuous on those outings, but she knew they were there, and they never kept their eyes off Billie. In retrospect, Billie despised them for playing that role, but that was the way it was done in those days, and this practice kept the young women in line. Despite the regimentation to which Billie considered her life subjected by her parents, they and she maintained a very close relationship. When her father died in 1985, he was 107 years old. By that time, Billie had had numerous opportunities to interact with him as an adult, and he knew and loved Sylvester and all of Billie and Sylvester's children very dearly. To them, he will always be "Grandpa Charlie".

Billie's mother's father was Henry Bowen, a very gentle man by all standards. He came from a close-knit family, a value that he passed on to his own children. Henry had three siblings, L.V. Bowens, Ida Bowens (after whom Billie's mother was named), and Velma Bowen. At a young age, Billie's grandfather met and married Ella Melton, a beautiful woman from a great family who also had three siblings—Jack Melton, Will

Melton, and a sister named Ruby Lee Melton.

Henry Bowen was a farmer who worked very hard for white people, but never earned enough money at the end of the year to pay off his debts to his white employer. It was never clear what those "debts" were but, then again, no black sharecropper was ever sure why he had to remain with his white master from year to year to pay a debt that he didn't owe. That was just like most of the African American men that were abused by their white masters for whom they worked as sharecroppers. Needless to say that the sharecropping system was replete with abuses, the victims were always the black farmers.

Billie's mother and her brother (Billie's uncle) had also worked on farms owned by white people, along with their father. Even for these children, the working conditions were equally bad. In fact, Billie's mother started working on the farms when she was 7 years old and her brother started working when he was 6 years old. The ram-shackled hut in which they lived on the farm was not fit for a white man's dog. But it was home for Ida's family, and considered fit for a black man's family. When it rained, water would often sip through the roof into the family's abode until Ida's father somehow found a way to patch the roof. On the other hand, the white master and his family lived in what was comparatively a mansion. The closest that the black farmer got to the home of the master was when they talked with other blacks who worked as house keepers at the white man's home.

Neither Ida nor anyone in her immediate family ever saw the white man's house from the inside. She and her brother were fed dinner on tin pans that were passed to them on benches. Dinner for Ida's family was whatever was left over after the white man's dog ate. Although this was often humiliating and painful for Billie's grandfather to endure, he was never in a position to complain. This is not to say that he never complained. Whenever he did, the white man whipped him. After several years of such physical assaults on him, most probably meant to break his spirit, he became a quiet, defenseless man.

As a young girl, Ida and other black kids had to walk as many as three miles to school because they were black – and it did not matter if the weather was hot or cold. There was a different rule for white children. Unlike black kids, white children were transported to school on school buses. Billie's generation had it a little better. Unlike her mother's time, she had the opportunity to ride a school bus to school.

It is ironic, however, that although she came along many years later, Billie's school was also segregated – just as her mother's had been several years earlier. Unlike white schools, Billie's schools had outdoor bathrooms, a brush field basketball court, and only black teachers. Also unlike the white schools, these black schools had no gymnasiums. Lunch was not provided at school, so the kids took their lunches to school in syrup buckets, often with biscuits and syrup. At the time, people did not think much of the discriminatory practices of the day. Since all black people were treated in the same way, it was just a way of life for them.

When Billie was growing up, racial prejudice was extensively practiced in Texas, and racism seemed to permeate every institution and sphere of life in that part of the country at that time. I have already written about the quality of black schools, in which we had no access to indoor gymnasiums, equipped libraries, and sophisticated sports grounds and equipment – unlike the white schools. This fact is just one example of the long list of inequalities that defined life in America in those days. Actually, one wonders how equipped predominantly black schools are, even today.

It may be difficult to imagine this in today's world, but the reference here to "white schools" and "black schools" is really as specific as it sounds. Only white children attended white schools, compared with those that were specifically for black children. Black and white children did not attend the same schools in those days. All through her elementary and high school years, Billie never had the opportunity to attend an integrated school. She went to school only with black children, like herself, and all of her teachers were black.

One thing that Billie remembers very clearly is that the teachers always received and treated the kids as their own children, and they became part of the children's families. Clearly, they were more than just teachers to the children that they taught. The teachers went to the extent of ensuring that school children were properly groomed. If the children were not properly groomed, the teachers did not send them back home and did not call parents to tell them that there was a problem. Instead, they would wash the faces and comb the hair of children who did not appear to be well groomed. They were even allowed to cane the kids for any inappropriate behaviors, or for poor academic performance, though they resorted to the cane only as a last step. Whenever a child was caned at school, his or her parents for behaving inappropriately at school also caned the child at home. Parents and teachers worked together as a team. They had one goal in mind: to raise educated, well-developed African American children.

Every morning at school, all of the children were assembled for prayer, singing, and recitation of the Pledge of Allegiance, which they all had to learn. It was considered very important that they proclaim their allegiance to the United States of America despite the fact that this was a country whose established institutions seemed to perceive such children as unworthy Americans deserving of neglect. But the loyalty of African Americans to this nation has historically been without question – at least in the hearts and minds of African Americans themselves.

One wonders what emotions went through the minds of Billie, her mother and other Blacks as they were made to struggle and suffer ignominiously. We know that they endured with their heads held high, and we know that they were all innocent children and families on the game boards of racist oppressors. But what did those African Americans think when they became adults? Certainly, the sentiments are different for each person. But, as terrible as the injustices suffered by Billie's generation may have been her mother's generation of African Americans and others before them suffered much more than we did. There is no doubt that her mother did not ask to be born black, but she was. She did not ask to be born and raised in the United States at a time when blacks hardly had a right to claim or expect any dignity, but she was. For every African American and his or her forebears, the historical significance of the experience is immeasurable.

For Billie, aspects of the memory of the black experience is very sad for several reasons, not the least of which is that her mother and her family are really not certain of their identity. Her grandfather told Billie's father that he had to take up the name of his slave master. In this way, the family lost its original name, and therefore its identity. There is no doubt that this is a common African American story. Yet, until her mother's death in her sleep on June 10th, 2001, she maintained a constant smile on her face and harbored no animosity toward anyone for the life to which she was subjected. Instead, she thanked God always for what she considered to be a life of blessings. For that, she will always be loved and seen her as Billie's number one example.

SEVENTEEN

SYLVESTER AND BILLIE: PARTNERS FOR LIFE

Some people believe that great partnerships can only occur between couples that come from similar backgrounds and lead similar lives. The story of Billie and Sylvester McClearn reveals the inaccuracy of this suggestion at the same time as it validates one fact: for people who believe and put their loves in God's hands, God builds and fashions lives and relationships in His own way, and He is capable of merging different worlds that may seem far apart to us as human beings.

Buddy and Billie came from different backgrounds and were brought up differently. Billie was her parents' only child and, although her family was poor, their poverty was relative. Her father, Charlie Smith, owned his own farm, as well as the home that he and his family lived in. In the area where the Smith family lived in Texas, most people were pretty much on the same socioeconomic level. This may have been one reason why it never occurred to young Billie that her family was poor. Charlie was a great husband to Ida - his wife and Billie's mother. He was also a great father to Billie and his other children. As the great provider that he was, Charlie ensured that his wife and children were not only very well cared for, but he also made himself available to them as well.

It is interesting that the story of Billie and Sylvester McClearn starts from two different states in the country and brings together two people from two different worlds. But several questions are relevant. For example, how different, really, had their worlds been prior to meeting and marrying? To the extent that they both came from the Southern United States, their world was really not very different. They were both descendants of slaves whose families had been stripped of their culture and, even, their names. They were both subjected to the injustices of institutionalized racism from a very early age – evidenced by Sylvester's family's struggles on the farms and Billie's experience in segregated schools. They were also two people who had grown up quickly, although Sylvester was more so because of the harsh realities of his family system and upbringing. They were also both young people who were blessed with a remarkable degree of wisdom and loving family members. Each knew not to take life foregranted, and neither was the kind to sacrifice his or sense of dignity or pride for the pleasure of anyone.

From a socioeconomic perspective, however, Billie and Sylvester came from two different worlds. One came from an obviously poor family and the other did not. Billie came from an intact family and Sylvester did not. One had a father that was available to his family both physically and emotionally, and the other did not. One came from a family where education was encouraged and the other did not. One had a high school diploma by the time they met, and the other did not. One had two religious parents and the other did not. One had been on his own for years and his experience equipped him to take on the world, and the other had lived a largely sheltered life.

So, what are the chances that a young person from North Carolina and a sheltered young person from Texas would meet in New York and together begin a life journey whose destiny they had no knowledge of? What are the chances that two people from two very different backgrounds would meet and enter into a union, such as the one that Sylvester and Billie entered into? What are the chances that you would find a life partner when you are not even looking? Billie certainly wasn't looking, and neither was Sylvester. But they found each other and, together, they wove a brilliantly beautiful story of love that continues to evolve decades after their first meeting. Their actions rather than their words tell the story of what they have fashioned together.

Ask Billie these questions, and her answer is both humble and thought-provoking. "I don't know", she responds, and then continues "But I can tell you now from my life and my husband's, that only God has the answers to these and other questions like that. God alone knew what would happen with us when we were born, even when Sylvester was working on farms and raking leaves in North Carolina, and I was living in the comfort of my parents' home in Texas. God is truly awesome. Isn't He?" Who would argue with that?

Largely because of Billie's home situation, her schoolteachers and her parents, who were always there to encourage her education, she was able to attend school regularly, graduate from high school, and receive a college education. When she completed her education, Billie chose to attend a trade school known as Sweats Beauty College in Tyler, Texas, where she studied to become a beautician. Upon graduation, Billie took up a job as a beautician, still in Texas. That was what she was doing when her aunt, who was at that time residing in Newburgh, New York, arrived in Texas to visit Billie's family.

Like Billie's mother, this aunt was a very pleasant woman who reminded Billie of the incredible amount of love in her family. It took a short time before Billie fell in love with her and she with Sylvester. From her, Billie learned a lot about New York and became convinced that she wanted to leave Texas and return with her aunt to New York. The attraction for Billie was the opportunity she believed that such a move would provide her to earn more money than she was earning at that time in Texas. Billie discussed her desire with her aunt who wasted no time asking Billie's parents for their permission to have Billie join her in New York. Charlie and Ida gave their consent, and Billie left their home for the first and last time.

Think of this! Your only daughter, who you have cherished from birth, comes to you at a time when she and you are supposed to be enjoying one another's company greatly as you watch her grow into adulthood. Then she tells you that she wishes to leave your home for a far away land. You know that this is probably a good move for her, but you also know that it could be several years before you see her again – and you may never have another opportunity to know what is going on with her on a daily basis. Although her parents agreed to let Billie go, it was certainly not an easy decision. Instead, it was one over which they agonized, but they also knew that Billie would be in good hands with her aunt and with God. To this day, one image that has never left Billie's mind is that of her father crying like a baby on the day she left Texas.

The night before Billie left for Newburgh, dad was in a very somber mood. Then on the morning of her departure, the tears were flowing freely on his face. As she sat in her seat as the bus pulled away, Billie looked out and saw her father crying. Billie also began to cry and wonder if she was doing the right thing. More than that, she was upset that she was hurting her father by leaving her parents. To see a strong, grown man cry is not a pretty sight, let alone one as strong as Papa Charlie.

Billie had no idea what awaited her. All she knew was that she was armed with a desire to come to New York to make money. As she would learn later, this was just a first major step toward the plans that God had for her life away from home. When she got to Newburgh, she worked very hard at various jobs, sometimes maintaining as many as two jobs at one time. She would work in a pocketbook factory during the day and in a hair salon in the evening. Later, she was employed at a beauty shop. Due to her life-long desire to always please her parents, Billie made sure that she sent money home to them on a regular basis, even when it was obvious that they didn't need the money. She just felt a need to give back to parents that had done much more for her than she could ever thank them for.

It was very soon after she arrived in Newburgh that Billie met Sylvester McClearn through a member of his brother's quartet, who was also a friend of Billie's aunt and uncle. Billie is very honest about her first impressions of Sylvester. She thought nothing of him that first time, except that he was just a big guy who came to visit with a family friend. Although she thought Sylvester seemed like a good person, she had no desire to be with him. As a result, she tried to gently push him on to her girlfriend. When, for their first outing, he invited Billie out to a movie, she agreed only because she wanted to be polite to him. Let's call that sympathy date! To make it even more interesting, Billie invited her friend to go with them, and she had that friend sit between Sylvester and herself. After a series of such actions that were meant to rebuff Sylvester, Billie began to feel guilty about what she was doing to someone who had now clearly shown himself to be a good man. Eventually, she agreed to become involved with Sylvester and the rest is history. Sometimes, Billie and her girlfriend still recall those days. When they do, she tells Billie that she should have taken Sylvester at the time, to which Billie responds: "It's too late now, girlfriend."

When Mitchell Elliot, the mutual family friend, introduced Sylvester and Billie to one another, Billie was dating someone else and had no desire to be with another man. She would never date two people at the same time, or began a new relationship while she was still with someone else. To this day, Billie believes very strongly that this is a wrong thing to do. That was a very interesting situation. Billie was the only person in her home who did not like Sylvester. Her aunt and uncle were completely in love with him because they could see exactly the kind of person he was. One day, Billie did what she calls "a very stupid thing". Sylvester was visiting and the other young man came by. Billie left with him to see a movie, leaving Sylvester at the house. What happened later is better described in Billie's words: "Would you know?" she asks, "This did not go over well with my folks. They were truly upset with me. But Sylvester still came back to visit often, despite the bad ways that I treated him, and we began to hang out. I told him I was sorry for my actions and he accepted my apology. Very soon, I lost interest in Noel and Sly became my guy".

The courtship period between Billie and Sylvester was very stormy but, to them, it was also exciting. On one occasion after they were engaged, Sylvester and Billie argued so intensely that he requested and got back the engagement ring he had given her. Considering how stormy their courtship had been, it would have been unfathomable to the human mind that their marriage would last for as long as it has. In retrospect, they both believe very strongly that their meeting and the relationship that evolved were entirely orchestrated by God. Growing up together in their marriage has been very special and there are no words, even for a poet, to completely describe how wonderful this marriage has been.

Considering how close Billie was to her parents, it is appropriate to wonder how either or both parents accepted news of their daughter's relationship with Sylvester. Her father had no problems at all with the news. In fact, he took it in great strides. Her mother on the other hand was devastated when she first heard about the relationship because she didn't know what kind of man Sylvester was. When Sylvester asked Billie to marry him, he wrote a letter to her mother and asked her permission for him to marry her daughter. He enclosed a photograph of himself in that letter. According to Ida in an interview with me several years later, something certainly happened to her when she read that letter. She was not sure exactly what happened, but she knew instantly that Sylvester was a good man and that her daughter was in good hands. Mrs. Ida Smith actually kept that letter for the rest of her life.

Sylvester and Billie had a very beautiful wedding. It is generally assumed that women never forget wedding days. Even if she could, Billie is unwilling to speak for every woman, but she knows that the day of her wedding to Sylvester is one that she will always remember as though it happened only minutes ago. Everything about the wedding points to the fact that Sylvester can indeed be rightly referred to as a romantic. Prior to the wedding, he took care to do some little things, which were very important to Billie. For example, he had an apartment, which he renovated, and would not let her see until the day they got married. When she eventually saw the apartment, she was moved with appreciation, amazement, and excitement because of how it looked and the extent to which he had gone to get the apartment that way for her sake.

Within twenty-four hours after their wedding, something happened, which angered Billie greatly, although she laughs about it now. Anyone who reads this will get even a clearer picture of the kind of man that Sylvester is. Again, this is one of those stories better told in Billie's words. Now, read on:

"Our wedding had occurred on a Saturday. It was a very special day for me. On the next day, which was Sunday, I thought that Sylvester would take me away on a honeymoon. Was I wrong! That morning, Sylvester woke up and requested that we get ready for church. I couldn't believe what I was hearing. I was stunned and I let him know exactly how I felt. Rather than attend to my emotions on this matter, he got dressed, left me in the apartment, and went to church. Needless to say, I felt very hurt at the time. But after I thought about what had happened, I realized that through this action Sylvester had just demonstrated that, just as Paul stated in *I Corinthians chapter 11, verse 3*, he was a man who was willing to allow Christ to be Lord over him. This was a good thing. I believe that we need more men like that in our world, who know their place, and more women who are willing to take their place. If we each take our place and we allow God to be the overall head of our homes, then we have nothing to fear, and no regrets.

The new McClearn couple never had a real honeymoon, in the actual sense of the word, but they more than made up for that with their children as they traveled extensively and enjoyed immeasurable amounts of time with them. The birth of each of their sons was very special and they enjoyed every stage of their development as they watched them grow. Each graduation gave these parents a great feeling of pride and accomplishment, and every sports event in which they participated was a special delight for Billie.

To engage Billie in an exercise of counting her blessings

would be futile because she recognizes that the blessings are so numerous that she would never be able to count even a tenth of them. However, she is willing to let anyone know that finding and getting married to a mate that complements her is a blessing that many people only dream of. For her, it is a reality because God was in her relationship with Sylvester from the start. She believes that God found Sylvester and her and brought them together to begin a relationship that is now decades old, but which remains fresh every day.

Billie went into her marriage armed with the values with which she had been raised in Texas. She had been taught that marriage was for life. So she went into it with the expectation that she was in it for life. As far as Billie knows, that is exactly the way it should be. This is not an indictment on people who get married and get divorced but it is, instead, a celebration of, and an emphasis on commitment in marriage. Two ingredients that stir a good marriage are genuine love and mutual understanding. The presence or absence of these ingredients can mean the difference between a successful marriage and a failed one. In the marriage of Sylvester and Billie, both ingredients are alive and well, and the marriage is as healthy and strong as ever.

Billie acknowledges that it is a great blessing to be married to someone like Sylvester, with whom she has consistently been able to laugh and enjoy life. Together, they have raised their family in church and church has remained a very large part of their marriage and family life. Often, Billie hears that people begin to look, speak, and think alike after they have been married for several years. That has indeed become the case for Sylvester and her. As they raised their children, Sylvester and Billie actually seemed to have the same ideas most of the time. This actually made the task of parenting much easier for Billie, and it has made life a lot of fun.

Billie maintains a close relationship with her children but she does not interfere in their lives, especially in their relationships with their mates. This is a rule that she developed for herself and has always followed. The reason is because she believes that husbands and wives are supposed to be one, just as the Bible tells us. That is also what she desires for her children and their spouses – that they would be one always. She does not want to lose her children, which could easily happen if she chose to interfere in their relationships. As she puts it: "If I interfere in their relationships, I could lose my daughter or son in-law and lose my child. I have no desire to let that happen. Therefore, I stay in my place rather than getting into their lives to influence their relationships. I keep it all together by keeping things separate". How wise!

Asked what she would do differently if she had to parent her children all over again, Billie's response is quick and deep – as though it is something she has thought about for a long time. According to her, "There is only one thing I would really change: I would not want any of my children to play professional sports. That is without doubt a glamorous life that is difficult to go through without physical and emotional bruises. It is an exciting life but certainly not worth the liabilities". Billie should know. Her son, Michael, played professional sports with the National Football League where he played for Washington Redskins. That experience left Michael with very deep emotional and physical bruises that challenged the McClearn family tremendously.

BUSINESS EXPERIENCE:

Running a business with Sylvester was a very exciting experience for Billie as an individual and for them as a couple. Billie's favorite term for describing the business experience is "a whirlwind" because of the excitement that it generated for the couple's lives. Being entrepreneurs completely changed their lives and they reaped immense financial rewards. In addition to the businesses that her husband developed and ran, Billie also had a beauty shop that she ran effectively.

She had the kind of aggressiveness that was needed to run a successful business, and she applied that to her business activities. That business aggressiveness obviously came from her father whose independent nature helped him to carve out a successful life for himself, despite the degree of racial oppression prevalent in Texas at the time. Besides owning his home and farm, Billie's father also owned cars and tractors, all of which were clear evidence of his success. On the other hand, Billie's mother was a calm, laid-back individual who was, like her husband, very loving and caring. In addition, she was great at teaching how to live and how to mold one's character into one of repute.

MINISTRY

When Sylvester decided to go into business, the couple reached that decision together and went into business together. When it was time to get out, they went out together. When he was called into parish ministry, they also made the move together. The way they left business and went into full-time parish ministry remains a marvel for even to Billie who saw it all unfold. All she knows is that the hand of God was clearly over the decision and move.

For several years before Sylvester actually went into the ministry, it was quite obvious that God was calling him to get out of business and into the ministry. In fact, six years before actually going into the ministry, he bought a brand new ministerial robe, just because he thought it was beautiful. He hung it in the closet for those six years and never wore it. He had no desire to enter the ministry. Of course they were having a great time in business, and Sylvester had never been to Bible school. Therefore, he would not answer the call. Then God took every material thing they had as they lost all of the investment that they had built over the years. But for that, it will always be left to wonder if Sylvester would ever have heeded the call of God. Clearly, God has His way of forcing obedience.

A THOUGHT FOR PROSPECTIVE MINISTERS:

Very often, Billie sees young and not-so-young people who are stepping into the ministry and they remind her of Sylvester and herself several years ago. If she could just speak to them about this huge step, she would tell them to be sure that God has really called them and they are really heeding His call. It is not an easy road to travel, which is why Billie recommends that anyone going into the ministry should first seek counseling to prepare themselves for the challenges that the ministry throws at all who genuinely get involved.

From Billie, we know that once you go into the ministry in a whole-hearted manner you lose your privacy to a large extent. The ministry actually moves into your house, as your work does not end in the church building. If you are married, your spouse becomes everybody's person. For this reason, it is always important to have a very good relationship with your spouse, and to be willing to remain supportive at all times. Otherwise, the stressful circumstances that develop can envelope the couple and become a hindrance to them from doing the will of God. The minister must know his place before God and his congregation, and the spouse must know and be willing to take her place and be supportive toward her husband as she does the will of God.

FROM MOM WITH LOVE

Given the opportunity to speak to her children through this book, Billie had the following to say: "I know that you are all adults now, but there are things I think I can still say. To each one of you I say the following: you must always keep God in your life and at the center of everything you do. Regardless of where you find yourself, you must never think more highly of yourself than you should. God is the source of your life, and you owe it all to Him. We often forget the prayers that come from other sources on our behalf. You must never forget that your father and I are praying for you. We love you".

EIGHTEEN

GROWING TOGETHER

Perhaps the best people to ask about anyone are his or her children. However, this is not always the best thing to do because children may not always say the "down and dirty" stuff about their parents. This is of course the reason why family members are rarely considered good character witnesses in court. Instead of saying it like it is, they often attempt to gloss over whatever weaknesses they may see in their parents and paint a very rosy picture instead. The McClearn children are no different. Asked to discuss their parents, most of them reeled out the words: "great, strong, tough, loving" and other words like these. In other words the McClearn children for the most part did what most children would do – present their parents as angelic saints.

Again, since family members are not always the best character witnesses, it would be easy to dismiss what the McClearn children have to say about their parents, but for one fact. That fact is that the information they offer and what they say about their parents are exactly what everyone else says about Billie and Sylvester McClearn. They are overwhelmingly described as God-fearing very hard workers, and great achievers. Most people, including his wife and children, perceive Sylvester as a best friend, a man of abundant wisdom, one who understands life to the utmost, a visionary, and a highly moralistic man. He is also considered a great listener, civil rights and community activist, a very upstanding man, a man whose heart is filled with great love for his family, his people, and the church.

Like any good teachers, Sylvester and Billie knew that

their home must be their first teaching platform. Therefore, they ensured that the rules that they established in their home were very strict. It is uncertain if they implemented their home rules with equal zeal as they got older and had more children. To this, the couple and most of their children would yes, but their oldest son Richard begs to differ. "Since I am their oldest child", he offers, "I consider myself their test baby, on whom they tried everything before extending it to my siblings. I would not be telling the truth if I said that I was always an angel, complying with every rule in our home. Like most children, I rebelled a few times but I was very cautious not to incur my father's wrath because I didn't want to have to answer to a belt and switch. My father did not believe in "sparing the rod", so he would often react to our misbehavior by using corporal punishment. Dad was tough".

Sylvester is the kind of man who has always taken the Bible literally. He never spends any time attempting to analyze the Bible. He believes in complete obedience and he teaches that to everyone in his family, his congregation, and his community. When the Bible says: "Do this", he does it without any questions. In the same way, he seemed to take literally the Biblical injunction that if you spared the rod you would spoil the child. This is also not unlike most African American parents in those days that believed in the importance of teaching values to their children by any means, including using "the rod". For Sylvester, that was not an extremely difficult thing to do, though he would prefer to have had no cause to use his belt to teach the lessons that he knew he had to teach to five sons and one daughter.

Cathell has his own stories to tell about his father's whip. Without mincing words, he states "My father would whip us without reservation. When he was done, the evidence of his work on us was very often left on our bodies in the form of blood and swelling. To this day, I have never felt as much pain as I did when he beat me one day. After that beating, I stayed in my room crying, and my mother came over to my room and said to me: "Your father is in the room doing the same thing".

Learning that my father was also crying was a very profound discovery as I suddenly realized that I had caused my father great pain".

This is a discovery that Richard also echoes. According to him, he can clearly recall several times when he would see his mother crying after her husband had beaten any of the children, though she never challenged his authority to do so. She knew he was just doing his job as a father. Richard only found out from his mother while this book was being written that his father would always go into his room and weep after he spanked his children. Of course that information was not general knowledge at the time, but nobody could have imagined that a strong man like Sylvester would do something as humiliating as that - cry.

Cathell has another story that is funny now but was not when it occurred. He had met a girl during a visit to New York City and ran his father's telephone bill for that month up to six hundred dollars. When daddy got the bill, Sylvester went home and beat Cathell senseless. As if he did not learn enough from that experience, Cathell went out of control once he really discovered sex, alcohol, and drugs. One night, he stayed past curfew time in a girl's home and his father sent Michael look for him. Michael found him at the girl's apartment one hour later. Before going to the girl's home that day, Cathell had bought some clothes from his father's store and dressed himself up to impress. On the way home, Michael wasn't saying much, so Cathell asked Michael if he knew what he might be in for. Michael's response was short but said it all: "It ain't gonna be pretty bro," he told Cathell. Instantly, Cathell knew he was in hot water. Upon getting home, his father said very sternly: "Take my clothes off. I am not going to beat my clothes on you." Cathell obeyed, and his father proceeded to beat him real hard. This is an experience he will never forget, and a behavior he never repeated.

Sylvester has always been a no-nonsense, firm man with an unparalleled amount of integrity, strength and commitment to family and community. He was extremely diligent in work and family responsibilities, rough, blunt, challenging and demanding at the same time, and possessed no fear, except the fear of God. He built a business empire on nothing but integrity. In the process, his life taught his children from an early age that wealth does not always have to come in money, but rather in spiritual and emotional strengths, and through a healthy trust-building endeavor.

His achievements notwithstanding, many people very close to the McClearns, including their children, are convinced that Sylvester would be only half the man he is today without his wife. Billie has always been his backbone as well as that of the family. In fact, one of the McClearn children described his parents' marriage and successes in this way: "I think my mother had the ideas, and my father was the working man who put the ideas into great action and achieved tremendous success by so doing".

Raising five sons and coping with her husband (another male) must not have been easy for Billie. But if anyone could have done a great job at it, it was certainly she. As she did that job, the rest of the family basked in it without any strong realization of what it meant to handle all of those responsibilities as effectively as she did.

If there was any pain in the family, the McClearn children didn't know it because they didn't feel it. This was because Billie and Sylvester were able to protect their children from information regarding any pain that might have been present at anytime, especially following the loss of the family's business. Following that loss, the family experienced some financial difficulties that they never discussed with their children. Now, the children are able to imagine it only because they are all adults now and realize that it is not a cake walk to raise as many children as their parents raised without experiencing some occasional financial bumps.

Billie and Sylvester maintained an open home in which every family member, however distant the relationship, was guaranteed a highly comfortable welcome. Consequently, several family members lived in the McClearn home and were raised by Sylvester and Billie as their children. Among these were Sylvester's brothers Roosevelt (Velt) and Jesse, and his sister Alice. So also did the Reverend's niece Phyllis, who is the daughter of Sister (that is, Cleo Sanders). These family members lived with Sylvester and Billie, sometimes for as many as three years, and became as siblings to Richard and his brothers. Each of them remembers with great fondness the time that he or she spent in the home of the Reverend. They all acknowledge that he influenced them tremendously and have great appreciation for the role that he and Billie played in their lives.

The circumstances under which each family member came to live with the Reverend and his family were different. For Jesse and Alice, it was tragedy that led to their address change. Jesse was nine years old when his mother passed, so he went to live with his older sister Estelle. Six years later, Estelle also died. When the family met to decide what to do, the Reverend offered to take Jesse into his home. Alice who had also been living with Estelle came later. In 1965, Jesse graduated from the Newburgh Free Academy and went on to a brilliant career in the United States Army. Alice graduated from the same high school two years later. When he returned from the military, Jesse lived with Sylvester and Billie for another year before moving on.

As evidence of the closeness that they feel with Jesse, some of the McClearn children see him as a very close brother, though they recognize and respect him as an uncle. Like Jesse, the McClearn boys all became great athletes and, like his brother Sylvester, his mother and maternal grandfather Jesse is also a preacher, though his denomination is different from his brother's. He is a Baptist preacher.

Every one of the McClearn children points to two events in their life as the thing that had perhaps the greatest influence on them. One is the business that their father ran. That business provided not only a reference point for them, but also was a classroom in which some work ethics, economic and social responsibilities were learned. For example, it remains very important to Richard to follow the work ethics that he saw his father exemplify. He cannot recall his father ever calling to work sick; neither can he recall his mother staying home from work – unless when she was pregnant. No wonder, Richard suggests that the attitude that he and his siblings bring to work does have a lot to do with the mark that his parents set. In addition, most of the customers at the McClearn business were white and Sylvester attended to them with the same spirit of love and genuine friendliness with which he attended to everyone else. This was a great lesson to his children – to treat everyone with respect, regardless of their race.

When Richard was ten years old, Sylvester moved his family to, Meadow Hill, a part of town that was predominantly white. It remains unclear exactly what he was thinking at the time but that move has since become what every single one of his children point to as the other major influence in their lives. If Reverend McClearn took that action to provide his children with the opportunity to learn how to interact with people across class and race, his goal was certainly achieved. This position is based on this writer's independent opinions of what has since happened in his children's lives as well as their individual assessments of the move. Suddenly, the children were enrolled in a school district where they looked different from most kids and teachers. Suddenly, they had to interact and learn with these other people, despite their obvious differences.

It is uncertain if the Reverend knew what the long-term consequences of that move would be, but his children unanimously agree that that single act by one father was largely responsible for much of the successes they have attained in their professional careers as adults. For one thing, it prepared them to be able to interact confidently with people who might not be like them. That skill, which the McClearn children possess, is invaluable in today's business world and it has served them very well. Of this, Richard and Darnell are very clear.

Being the first or second African American family to

move into that neighborhood did not always make things easy for the McClearn family. Several times, white boys who wanted to beat them up ran the McClearn children home called them derogatory names regularly. They withstood that initial period of difficulty and, eventually, the McClearn boys and the white boys who once harassed them became very good friends.

Beyond the feelings that existed among the people that were already in the neighborhood, there may also have been some sentiments in other quarters regarding this move to the suburbs. Whenever there are racial and/or socioeconomic implications associated with a re-location, the discussion often tends to focus on how the family or individual was accepted or rejected in the new neighborhood. Rarely is there a discussion of the sentiments of people in the neighborhood left behind. For example, it is important to consider what the other family relatives and friends left behind in the Newburgh area felt when they saw one of them move his family to a white suburb. Seeing one family on one side of town, which was the "white side", and seeing another side of the family on "the black side" of town sometimes has the capacity of causing shifts in the larger family interactions.

In the McClearn family case, nobody is certain of what the implications were. Otherwise, it is just one of those things that this family does not discuss. If any negative sentiments existed, such sentiments were definitely softened that may have existed were however softened by the fact that, in some sense, Sylvester and Billie were deeply lacking in pride and ensured that they and their children were able to move between both sides of town (including race and class) as effectively as was humanly possible without rubbing any feathers in the wrong way.

As part of his employment, Darnell lived in London, England for some years. When he did, he took his family with him because of the benefits that he believed they would receive from such a move. He was doing what he believed his father would have done given the same circumstances. His father's decision to move his family to the Newburgh suburbs had made a tremendous impact on Darnell's life, and he hopes that his own decisions regarding his children has also positively impacted their lives. The lessons that Darnell learned during those early years in the Newburgh suburbs have been with him through his life and continue to guide him even now in his current executive position at Citibank.

In any discussion of civil rights advocacy in Newburgh, Reverend McClearn clearly has a place – a unique place. Contrary to many civil rights advocates, who only interact with people from their own racial and/or ethnic backgrounds, Sylvester is one civil rights advocate who maintained close interactions with everyone, regardless of race, ethnicity, age or gender. The attitude that he presents is very consistent with his strong religious belief that we are all children of one God and are therefore brothers and sisters, regardless of how we may appear. "When think about my father's attitude toward people", remarked one of his children, "I am surprised that he has not yet run for political office, because I am certain that he could really make a great difference".

But the Reverend's calling is a much greater one. He is a servant of the living God and, to that end he will do exactly what he believes that God is instructing him to do. At this time, running for election is not one. He may be politically astute but he is definitely not the kind of man that would say or do anything for political reasons. He will tell it as it is at all times without looking for praise from men. This is very much the opposite character of most people who become politicians. Often, they say and do things that, for the most part, are politically expedient rather than morally and spiritually just.

As one who has spent much time with the Reverend, I will be surprised if he ventures into elective politics. Yet, his son and most people who know him are right that he can make a major difference by engaging in politics. Undoubtedly, our society needs people like him in politics, and this may very well be what could eventually get him into politics: recognition that he has a major role to play in it. As far as making a difference, anyway, Reverend McClearn already has, and there is nothing left for him to prove.

This is an assessment that Sylvester may not completely agree with, especially if he perceives it to mean that he should stop working as hard as he is doing to improve the lot of mankind and his community. Fortunately, that is not what is intended. I once sat in on a meeting between the Reverend and his son, Darnell, at which we were discussing an appropriate title for this book. It was very interesting to listen to the Reverend's questions to himself, to his son, and to me, and to hear him express his opinions very strongly in a way that I had never seen him. He presented a very sharp difference with his son's opinions on the subject matter. By so doing, he highlighted what may in the near future become a major issue in the relationship between the African Americans of his time and today's young African Americans – as well as those who are coming behind. Very clearly, Sylvester said to his son and me: "I do not want to be irrelevant. I refuse to be. If you hide my race in the way that you present even the title of this book, you have made me irrelevant. The road has been a long one for black people in this country. I hate to think that we would now think of ourselves as having arrived when there is indeed a very long road yet to travel. If there is still a struggle, I want to be part of it in any way I can".

The Reverend's message to his corporate executive son and me was very clear: "For as long as I live, I will not forget where I come from, and neither should you. If you forget your history and your responsibility to that history and your people, you become irrelevant in the overall scheme of things". On that day, I left the McClearn home with greater appreciation for a man who has achieved enough to turn his back on his struggle, but who will not because he knows that he has a God-given responsibility to uplift the human spirit.

Sometimes, there is a unique conscience that the children of ministers carry, even without realizing it. Each of the McClearn children is quick to state that he or she feels no pressure from being a McClearn or from being a minister's child. Yet, each will also tell you that sometimes, he or she can almost hear the voice of dad or mom admonishing them for even daring to think of doing something wrong. Each also often feels like Richard who claims that he frequently hears himself asking: "Where am I going with this?" "How would my parents deal with this situation?" "What would they say about this?" He knows that this comes directly from the influence of his parents. Each of the McClearn children is very conscious of the fact that what he or she does reflects on their parents. Rather than acknowledge this as pressure, Richard prefers to see it as a responsibility by arguing that: "if that attitude is a burden that one must carry for being a McClearn, it is one that I carry with pride and gratitude to God. If it is a burden, I also carry it as a show of appreciation to my parents who worked very hard to make a name for themselves".

As close as the McClearn children claim to be, some of them have a sense that they are not as close as their father and his siblings were. For example, Darnell laments what he perceives as an unnecessary distance "even in the age of technological development" and he sees this as a shame that must be corrected, at least for the sake of their children. Cathell deplores what he considers as the individualism in some aspects of the family and claims that there haven't been consistent efforts made by some to foster closeness. He believes that one of the reasons for that is the fact that some like him are always viewed by some family members through the prism of the mistakes that he made at various points in his life. As a result, he argues, his efforts have failed to yield even the degree of closeness with his twin brother that most twins are known to have.

But how close are the Reverend and his brothers and sisters – dead or alive. The answer to that question comes in only two words: very close. Richard believes that his father and his siblings were influenced in establishing this closeness by the work that his grandmother did in raising them. Maybe, but that does not completely explain the fact, considering that Billie especially has also worked tremendously to foster closeness among her children. To get the more accurate response, we may need to consider the following facts:

First, with a father who was often physically and emotionally absent from his family, and abusive to them when he was around, the Reverend and his siblings learned to bind together in support of their mother and, in the process, developed their own relationships with one another. Secondly, having such a poor family as Sylvester did meant that survival became the joint responsibility of everyone, but more so of mom and her older siblings, most of who learned not to think only of themselves but also of their younger siblings. Therefore, Sister was playing the role of mom to her siblings when mom was not around, Thomas played the role of dad, Randolph III played his own role, and Buddy was the caretaker who made sure that his younger ones had something to eat when there was no food at home. In such circumstances, the family naturally became much closer to one another than most families can ever be.

In the context of Reverend McClearn's nuclear family, however, all of these situations were absent and his children never had to deal with any such hardships. This is a good thing, but what that has meant is that none of them had caretaking responsibility thrust on him or her to the point where extended closeness would occur to the degree that the Reverend has with his own siblings.

Another factor to consider in finding an explanation to the lack of closeness about which the McClearn children speak is the fact that capitalism has made significant in-roads into the family system – black or white. Therefore, the more successful individuals get, the busier they are and the less time they have to maintain relationships with family. They spend more time with business associates than they do with their siblings, and they spend the only little time left trying to relax by themselves or with their own nuclear families. This is a fact of life in today's world, and it is perhaps a state that white people understand and accept more than blacks do because black people have a difficult time giving up their traditional definitions of the family system, even in the face of these realities.

Again, how close are Sylvester and his siblings, living or

dead? There is never a day that Sylvester does not remember his siblings who have passed on. Their pictures are hung up on walls in his home, as though it is a memorial to them and he is convinced that he will see them again in glory. Do not ever try to persuade him otherwise. In fact, one of the McClearn children is very clear that the only place where he has seen his father cry was at his brother Randy's funeral.

The final burglary that ended his business undoubtedly tore him apart, but none of his children ever saw him cry. It was certainly his brother's death that did it. He and Randy had had a very close relationship, and when Randolph died, the Reverend drove his family all the way to the funeral in Rocky Mountain, North Carolina. When they got there, they went to get something to eat before the funeral, and the Reverend announced between tears "I don't want to be here. I want to go back home." After the family ate, they drove another twelve hours back to Newburgh, NY without saying much. That was a very long trip back home because of the silence that dominated the vehicle.

Although he doesn't speak much about death and dying, the Reverend and his children seem conscious of the fact that men in his family of origin have historically not lived very long. Often, the Reverend acts in ways that suggest that he may be thinking that he could be the next of the McClearn men to go, and this concerns some of his children because they want him around forever. Diabetes, high blood pressure and heart disease have commonly run in his family, and have been responsible for many of the deaths – though alcohol has also played a significant role in the deaths of some of the McClearn men. Joe Lewis was one who, according to a member of the family, "drank himself to death". Alcohol continues to be an active part in the lives of some McClearn men. Some others have had serious problems with alcoholism and are now in recovery. But this is not just a problem for the McClearn family. It is also a problem that is faced by several African Americans and Native Americans in this country. Many people would say that the extent of the problem suggests that members of these groups have resorted to the bottle as a way of escaping the injustices that they have historically faced in this country. While there may be some truth to that suggestion, it is important to add that the generational evidence that is available also suggests that the genetic basis of alcoholism cannot be ignored in any discussion of alcoholism in African American families.

Regarding those who are living, every Fourth of July weekend is the McClearn family reunion period, and Sylvester is always in attendance. It is the time when they all remind themselves and their children of how much the McClearn name means and what their role must be to ensure that the name is protected and maintained with dignity. Therefore, everyone with the McClearn name knows that he or she is somebody, even if the shoes on his or her feet have holes. It may be a product of the magnitude of the pride associated with the McClearn name that Sylvester would not accept even a cent from his children, however successful they become.

It is interesting to watch Sylvester and Billie now as they have approached old age. What one sees is that one huge contrast has arisen in their interactions with their children. Sylvester, who was the strict disciplinarian when they were raising their children, has become the very friendly, playful one. In contrast, Billie has emerged from her very quiet shadows to become the stern one who tells her adult children what she wants them to do and when. On their part, the children know that their only choice when mom speaks is to obey. She is mom and they will always be her kids, however old they become. This is of course the way many parent-child relationships go. Parents are always parents and children are always children, even when they become parents themselves.

The McClearn children obviously have remarkable respect for one another, and for their parents. About their respect toward their parents and each other, Richard put this eloquently when he said, "At my age, you tend to look back often at your childhood and feel the need to thank your parents". Regarding his twin brother, Cathell remarked, "My twin brother is a very successful man who, in my opinion, made all the right moves and is now reaping the benefits of his hard work. I have often wondered what form my life would have taken had I made some right moves myself, instead of so many wrong moves. Of course, I cannot change my past now, and I come from a family that does not let you spend your entire life dwelling on the past".

Regarding his mother, he said: "I always thought that my mother was the buffer between our father and us. She was the ultimate tool in their relationship. My assessment is that she was the person who was able to do to perfection even things that my father was unable to do. A complete Texas country girl, she is the backbone of everything in our family".

Cathell's love and admiration for his twin brother knows no bounds. This probably explains why he believes that the biggest challenge and triumph that his family has faced occurred when he was 16 years old. His twin brother was diagnosed with a lump in his throat and this became a very trying time for the entire family. A doctor took a throat culture and said it would be a few days before they knew what was up. As if it were yesterday, Cathell recalls getting off the school bus on their street one day, looking up toward their beautiful single family home, and seeing their father jumping up and down like a child and shouting "It's benign, it's benign!" Cathell is certain that he will never forget that picture, though he is sure that some members of his family will be surprised that he considers that event his family's greatest triumph.

Sometimes, bad news follows on the heels of good news. That is exactly what happened to the McClearn family during that period. A day or two after Darnell's health was determined to be fine; a telephone call came to the family home, which Cathell. It turned out to be the police calling to inform Sylvester that the alarm at his store was going off. Cathell contacted his father and they went to the store. For a moment that seemed like an eternity, Sylvester stood dumbfounded in front of the store, unable to move or go in. Eventually they raised the door of the store stepped in and found that everything was either stolen or destroyed. Shortly after that incident, the business was over and Sylvester's blood pressure began to be problematic.

It is uncertain what the emotional impact of the demise of the business was on the McClearn children. This is because it has never been fully discussed. Given an opportunity to do so in an interview for this book, one of them gave the following analogy: "The destruction of the business by people who did not mean well toward my father and my family took a big piece out of me. I felt like a dancer on a dance floor when the music stops. Suddenly, the lights were out and I was forced to deal with my own identity. This in itself became a task that was both very difficult and very confusing". It is uncertain who else among the McClearn children felt like this. Hopefully, none other did.

For that McClearn child, the task of dealing with his identity remains a difficult journey but he is waging the battle as best as he can and hoping that he will come out ahead.

NINETEEN

PILLARS OF STRENGTH

By every measure, Sylvester is a pillar of strength. Most people who know him are conscious of this fact. This is also one reason why his son Darnell is very comfortable being called Darnell by most people, rather than Sylvester, which is really his first name. Otherwise, several people in the Newburgh community might have expected Darnell to live up to his father's large name and image. That might have been a really tall order. Regardless of who you are, it would certainly be a highly compelling task to walk and live like a giant like the Reverend McClearn who certainly walks around in very big shoes.

Strangely, all of the McClearn children still look up to their father, despite their ages and professional accomplishments. At the same time that they all see him as a giant, they also all see him as a man – though they acknowledge that he is more endowed in many ways than most men that they know. The fact that the Reverend has been able to maintain that image among his children is a great testament to his humility and his recognition of his responsibility to his family. It also makes things much easier for his children in the sense that they are not intimidated to go to him for any advice or discussion when they feel the need to do so. Undoubtedly, he has done a very good job of ensuring that his children can live their lives without being weighed down by his shadow – and his children are conscious and appreciative of this.

Sylvester is not a man of many words and never blows his own trumpet. Instead, he lets his life and works speak for and about him. As a result, he is in a position that is usually the case with people like him. Like most such people, McClearn is known simply as the generous and gifted pastor whose contributions to his community are beyond compare. While this is true, it is also true that most people do not actually know the real person that he is. Fortunately for his family, they have been blessed with the opportunity of knowing more about this man than most people will ever do. Consequently, they know that he is a man with a history of grassroots beginnings who pulled himself up by his bootstraps and made good for himself and his family.

Since the above characterization of the Reverend is accurate, the point may also be accurately made that he is also somewhat of an enigma. This is because it is very rare in today's world to find a man like the Reverend, who brought himself up from nothing to a position of respectability, and does not judge others in society who cannot do the same for themselves. Instead, he stretches out his hands and helps to lift them up because he believes that he has a responsibility to do so. He does not seem to feel that others should be left to struggle to pick themselves up.

Despite pulling himself up by his bootstraps, Sylvester always prefers to err on the side of helping others. As a result, this Reverend has participated actively in the creation of many community support projects, including food pantries for the needy, and organization known as the Newburgh Ministries. He was also very active in the establishment of a transitional residence known as Project L.I.F.E., established to provide appropriate housing for women and their children who have hit hard times. He is a special man with the rare courage not to be embarrassed, especially when he believes he is doing the right thing.

This is indeed a testimony to this man's will and his strength of purpose, and a major reason that explains his willingness to go to back to school as an adult and learn how to read and write properly. He faces situations head-on, where many others look for exit routes, and he puts everything he has into everything that he does. It is therefore no wonder that he recorded tremendous successes in the business world even before he went back to school to acquire formal education.

Sylvester has a tremendous and enviable ability to win people over who may not wish to interact or do business with him when they meet him for the first time. He does so through his good communication skills and his ever-ready willingness to learn new things, even from the most relegated of people. He is clearly not the most articulate of people but people like him very much because he talks well and possesses very transparent sincerity. Regardless of what people say about how decadent our society and world have become over the years, it is also true that people love people whose sincerity they can count on. Sylvester McClearn is certainly one of such people.

Clearly, Reverend McClearn's personality and image are products of his religious values. He is a man who has perfected the art of making his personal views secondary to the word of God. This is exactly what the Lord Jesus Christ requires of us.

Given the opportunity to assess his father's forays into the business world, his son, Darnell who is the Managing Director of Citibank was at times critical and at times full of praise. He presented his analysis as follows: "I think that the most encompassing way is to describe him simply as "quite an entrepreneur". When my father owned his business, my brothers and I worked for him. In a situation like that, it is very easy for the young individuals in our position to begin to see themselves as sales stars of some sort, but not me. I don't think that we became employees in the store because we were great sales people. More than anything else, I think we were just cheap labor for my father. This, of course, is what every businessperson likes to have".

Then Darnell continued: "My father's entry into the business world and the way in which he prosecuted his business, represented a strong display of originality. The concept that he created was the beginning of the big and tall casual male business in the area. He thought of the concept and executed it as early as the 1970s, before the departmental stores thought of the idea and began to develop it for their own businesses. When blacks everywhere were looking to get jobs, my father decided that he wanted to run his own business because he felt that he wanted to be different. He went for it and did well."

"If I have any critique of my father", continues Darnell, "it is that he is so selfless that he never even developed a hobby for himself. I think he may have considered his community work as a hobby when, in my opinion, it was pain. Another critique that I have is that he takes himself and his life too lightly. He does not seem to recognize his own accomplishments, and therefore tends to take himself too lightly. He is a very modest man. He was a cosmopolitan-renaissance kind of man who gave his family a cosmopolitan-renaissance kind of life. Unlike I, who am tied up with work and family and never have time for community action, my father gave of his time and effort to the community in which he lived. He started what was known as the Black Enterprise of Newburgh. If I am allowed to take a critical look at my father as a businessman, I would say that the level of his understanding of retail business did not seem to be high enough to adequately match the pace of the changes in that kind of business. While changes continued to occur in the clothing business, my father's knowledge of change could not keep up. It was therefore just a question of time before he would have left the business. However, he met his own challenge but his lack of knowledge led to his own demise. But I admire his courage".

Prompted to say more, Darnell set out to provide the following analysis that is both very deep and very honest: "Although my father does not like to talk about this, he began, "my honest opinion regarding the demise of his business is that he trusted members of the black community so much that he let his guards down. People that he trusted were out there taking advantage of him and he either didn't know it or didn't want to believe it. Then we opened the store one day and everything my father had worked very hard for was gone."

"My father", explains Darnell, "could not understand why blacks were more apt to steal from him, despite his years of service to the community that he cherished so much. In many respects, my father was always a very naïve man who has always believed that people can and will change. This opinion is largely grounded in his faith, which fosters his belief that everyone should be given a chance to change. He tends to believe that he has a mission to be part of the process for change. Unfortunately, the reality is that people do not always change".

Anyone in business knows that the balance between work, community, and family responsibilities is very hard to strike. In this, Sylvester has the tremendous respect and admiration of every member of his family. Sylvester struck it all and maintained the remarkable balance with remarkable competence. He was cosmopolitan in the sense that he tried to accomplish much by doing what was unusual in those days – asking his wife to partner with him as a team. That was a very unusual act indeed, and is still unusual for African American men.

It is reasonable to suggest that one of the reasons the marriage of Sylvester and Billie has lasted as long as it has is not just because Sylvester is a good man, but also because he regards his wife as a partner in his journey through life. It is therefore the reason why this book is not just about the Reverend, but also about Billie, without whom the McClearn team would not exist.

It is unclear how their partnership evolved to the point where it is always as if they have the same game plan to everything. One of their children has suggested that it may be that, once they knew each other, his mother went along with the program and allowed his father to succeed without being an obstacle, and, without yearning for the limelight herself. This is a very reasonable suggestion, but the fact that she is almost never in the limelight is the reason why many people may think of her as insecure.

People who know Billie well know that she is anything but that. Instead, she is a woman who seemed to have made up her mind early to take her place in her marriage and be both physical and spiritual support for the man she chose to marry. Such a decision requires a depth of respect and humility that is rare in our world today.

Billie is the silent strength behind the obvious pillar. She is clearly a very great silent leader. For as long as anyone can recall, Billie has always been silent in her role but, all of their children believe that she was probably always the business mind while their father was the doer. One of the children once said, "When they close the door behind them, they probably have a deep discussion and maybe an argument here and there that nobody is ever privy to".

The approach that the McClearns adopted in dealing with their children has been described by one of them as a factor in the formation of what he calls "my conscience". He believes that his conscience was developed from his early years with his parents, such that to this day, he is often concerned that his father would probably be upset if he did something wrong and dad found out. How does he handle that? He does his best to stay on the right path at all times, regardless of the circumstances. He also works very hard to achieve his goals – much the same way I saw his parents do. Fortunately, he and some of his siblings have experienced in their own lives the benefits that could accrue from such hard work.

This is a position that is also echoed by most of the McClearn children, although one of them is willing to point out that his parents did not always succeed in protecting some of their children from a life of drugs, sex and alcohol. That may well be, but what is also true is that they provided the foundation for a conscience, such that any one of their children who engaged in such a behavior was making a choice. The behavior was never a product of a lack of knowledge of right and wrong but a decision to do the wrong thing.

Every one of the McClearn children is quick to point to their efforts at raising their children in a manner that their parents would be proud of. Richard has one daughter and three stepchildren, Michael has one son, Cathell has two daughters, Darnell has two children, Jeannie also has two children and Alex's marriage is still young and they are yet to have children. Each one of the young parents speaks of his or her desire to be as good a parent to his or her children as their parents were to them. Therefore, they try to emulate their parents by being as available and supportive as possible to their families and to guide them in their education.

Since the apple rarely falls far from the apple tree, Darnell's children are, like their father, both talented and athletic. He remembers that his parents were always there to support his athleticism and his siblings', so he tries to be there for them as often as he can. In this regard, he can in fact think of several similarities as well as contrasts in the way that his parents guided my siblings and himself and the way that he tries to guide his own children now.

As far as his own education, and his siblings', Darnell feels that his parents did the best that they could in their circumstances. It is quite easy to speak to your children of about the importance of education and to encourage your children to focus on their education. However, talking is one thing but teaching your children to do well in their education is something else. Unless you went through the same educational stages that your children are going through, you are handicapped in your ability to actually help them through their education. It is actually difficult, even impossible, to sit and assist your children with their homework when you really have no idea what the work is about. However hard you try, experience in that kind of work still matters.

Sylvester and Billie were not immune from the handicap to which I have just alluded here, since they had little education themselves. In the circumstances, what they emphasized to their children was hard work, structure, respect, and developing the qualities that would make their children good people. As far as the specifics of the children's education, however, they all had to work very hard to develop themselves, since their parents' levels of education ensured that they could not help their children with their homework most of the time. The children had to work very hard by applying to their education the value of hard work that their parents emphasized so much.

In everything that they do, the McClearn children apply that value of hard work and expect good results. This is what Richard has done with his career, Michael in his pro football career, Darnell, Alex and Jeannie in the corporate world and Cathell in his own chosen field where he works with children who would otherwise fall through society's cracks.

The McClearn family has had great triumphs, one of which is certainly their success in escaping society without serious injuries. The overwhelming stereotype of African American males as criminals does not include the McClearn children. They have been fortunate enough to avoid accumulating any criminal records against them, despite the fact that negative impressions regarding African American males were certainly on the rise while they were growing up. This is significant, considering the percentage of young African American males who sit in America's jails today. It also speaks to the great value that is inherent in being raised by both parents in the same home. As we all know, this is increasingly become alien to the African American family.

The fact that some of Sylvester's children do not have as high a level of education as they could is somewhat disappointing to at least one of them. It is certainly not what he expected, nor is it what he believes his parents envisaged. He is conscious of the fact that his father left the fields of North Carolina to help himself. From nothing, he rose to become something and he gave his family everything. Yet, some, in the family have failed. But this McClearn son is not discouraged. As he puts it: "My father succeeded and yes, some of us (his children) have also done well. But, really, I think we are really trying to break out. My father has always spoken of the importance of giving everyone the opportunity to grow at his or her own pace. He has also always felt that, even when you give everybody an equal opportunity to move, some will move out faster than others, and there will be others who will break out after everyone else has left the gate".

Again, the testimony that this is true is clear in the accomplishments of his children. Some people hit bumps on the way up and break down. In this family, people hit bumps but they ride it along and find their way to their destination. Much of this has to do with the attitude that they developed as a result of the foundation that was laid by their father, the pillar. With such a strong foundation, it is always possible to thrive, even when much of the immediate future looks bleak.

This pillar of strength was also sometimes human. He was a huge "people person" with a great personality. So, football fans often flocked around him at big tailgate parties that he began to participate in when Michael played football at Temple University, and dad seemed to really increasingly enjoy the tail gate parties. Being a big teenager or young adult at this time, the last thing Michael wanted was to have people pointing out his father in the middle of a tailgate party. It began to get embarrassing. Now when he looks back, Michael realizes with joy that his father did what he did because all of those actions now combine to make his football years much more memorable in his mind than it would otherwise have been.

Sylvester's involvement went beyond game attendance and encouragement. He even became a very active participant, as all parents should, in the scouting that was done of his for the professional teams of the National Football League (NFL). As it turned out, Michael was drafted by the Cleveland Browns and played for the Washington Redskins.

As a human being who has been through a lot in his life, Sylvester McClearn continues to stand tall both in his physical body and in his spirit. He has no concerns at all about his spiritual state or his life because he knows the God that he believes in. As pillars come, Reverend Sylvester McClearn is a giant whose strength is beyond any that is imaginable against the background that he had. But that is more so when we look at him with our human eyes and think of him with our human minds. But this Reverend is not your everyday person. He is different. When Darnell was requested to sum up his father in a few words, he said quite aptly, "When I think about my father, and the life he had lived, I think of someone who, deep in his heart, must perceive of himself as God's discipline who will become an angel. How deep!

HONOR THY FATHER AND MOTHER:
THAT THY DAYS MAY BE LONG
UPON THE LAND
WHICH THE LORD THY GOD GIVETH THEE.

EXODUS 20:12

TWENTY

A PEEK AT THE NEXT GENERATION

On various pages in this book, the children of Billie and Sylvester have expressed their thoughts about their parents but have not directly spoken to their parents, or to one another. This is the chapter in which they do so. It is important because this is the generation that nature has bequeathed with the responsibility of taking the mantle from their parents and running with it. Whatever they do with that responsibility will determine the survival and strength of the McClearn name long after their parents have left the stage. This is not because they are McClearns but because this is the way it is with every name and every giant who has lived and moved on.

The readiness of the McClearn children to step into the giant shoes of their parents and to lead the next generation of their family further into the land of opportunity can be gleaned from the degree of appreciation and commitment that they express as they speak below:

RICHARD

TO MY PARENTS:
Dad and mom, I hereby commend you for a job well done. You have run your race with remarkable endurance and now I wish you would relax. In your life, you have worked very hard and right now I believe that you still work too hard, though you say you are retired. My great wish is that you would just listen to us (your children), select a place where you would like to go and live and just relax. I love you very much and I thank you for being there for me all my life.

TO MY BROTHERS AND SISTER:
Though we may not always see eye to eye, you are my brothers and sister, and forever will be. We are all alike but also different. I love you all for both our similarities and our differences but, even more than that, I love and thank you for making my life more complete.

TO OTHER YOUNG PEOPLE:
You can pick anything else in life but you can never pick your family. So you must learn to get along with them. You may not always agree with your parents but in the long run, you will realize the benefits of the work that they have done. If you feel the need to disobey the rules established by your parents, think of me and believe what you are reading right now. I know now that my parents were not just right, but that they were in fact always right all along. At my age, you tend to look back often at your childhood and feel the need to thank your parents. The time to do so is when they are still alive. The best gratitude you can give them is to obey them now that they are parenting you. If you are in obedience, you will prosper.

MICHAEL

MESSAGE TO MY PARENTS:

Dad and mom, you are my heroes. Dad, you are an excellent provider, a motivator, and a man who very rarely makes mistakes in judgment or in decisions. There are many things I am waiting to find out about your life but I know that you have given your children a better life than you had growing up. You are a great dad and a great guy. I wish I could be like you.

Mom, you are a strong woman and the greatest mother on the face of the earth. Your strength and your support for my father made our family what it is today. I will forever love you both and thank God for making you my parents.

CATHELL

TO MY PARENTS:

I owe everything I own to you. The efforts that you have invested in me are not in vain. In my darkest and deepest moments, I know you are holding, nurturing, and praying for me. I love you with everything that is in me, and your grandchildren love you very dearly also. I hope you can forgive the mistakes that I have made in my life. Never in my life have I intended to bring shame to you, and I hope you will read this and forgive me for disappointing you as much as did when I did. I have always loved you and I will love you forever. Please be patient with me; God is not through with me yet.

TO MY SIBLINGS:

We have come from a heritage of pride, respect and integrity. Let us keep that consistent. Even if all else fails, we must always remember that God is in our parents and grandparents. When things get rough, remember that generations before us have prayed for us and brought us into a life of destiny.

DARNELL

TO MY PARENTS:
What you did for us is nothing short of spectacular. You have done it all, and more. Despite where you came from, you focused on yourselves and worked together as a great team to give the best to your family. I don't think you know how much you did for us but, thanks to your love and hard work, you have created a family with an unbelievable story. I am forever grateful to you for everything, and I thank you for giving me hope.

TO MY SIBLINGS:
We have a very strong historical tradition but we lack in some areas. Our challenge is to take the old model of what the McClearn name used to be and transition those values into a more conventional model. By not doing that, we are losing sight of staying close to one another, even in an era of high technological advancement.

JEANNIE

MESSAGE TO MY PARENTS:
I thank God for blessing you with hearts of forgiveness and I thank you for allowing God to lead you in all the ways that He has, not the least of which is the way you have raised my brothers and me. As parents, you are full of love and you are the examples of how God wants us to be. I have benefited from your hearts of forgiveness and I hope I never hurt you again. I am eternally grateful to you for the quality of life you have given me and I want you to know that you are always in my thoughts. I love you very much.

MESSAGE TO MY BROTHERS:
RICHARD: My big brother, my teacher, my power, I respect and love you from the bottom of my heart. You are a great example for me, and you are a brother who is like a father. I pray that God should continue to bless you with more strength and wisdom.

MICHAEL: My shoulder, my great listener. Thanks for your ever-ready willingness to listen. I commend you for your ability to understand and relate to pain and I am grateful to God for your compassionate nature.

CATHELL: My brother who, like me, understood teenage fun and tried to live it, I am very proud of you, as I know you are of me. I am happy that I have you as a brother and I want you to know that you have a special place in my heart.

DARNELL: My great reminder that hard work still pays off. You are a role model for me and I am thankful to God for what He is doing in your life. I look up to you and I pray for more successes for you. The Lord is indeed your strength.

ALEX: My best friend and confidant. Thanks for being you. There are no words to describe your place in my heart and the role you have played in my life. Without you, I don't know what life would be like but, with you, I know that life is sweeter than it might have been. It is always great to know that your love and support are unshakable, and I am glad that you are a brother that who sticks close even when times are tough. My brother, I love you, and always will.

ALEX

MESSAGE TO MY PARENTS:
I love you for everything you have done for me. I realize now more than ever that you did not have to do for me as much as you did, but you chose to do it all because of the tremendous amount of love that you have for your family. You believed that being a parent must never stop at having children. You went through the most difficult aspects of parenting, which is the nurturing, caring, and teaching - and you did a tremendous job at each. For every single thing that you have done for me in my life, I am grateful and I love you.

MESSAGE TO MY BROTHERS AND SISTER:
I love you all very much and I am thankful for the role you have all played in my life. I appreciate growing up with you in this blessed family of ours and I hope we can continue to be the close-knit family that we have always been. We must maintain our bonding and keep the strong relationship that we have among us, and extend that to our children, grandchildren, and cousins. We come from a great family, and we should rise up to the challenge of maintaining our strength by keeping our family heritage and traditions. I have no doubt that we can do it in love. Our parents taught us how.

TWENTY-ONE

REFLECTIONS

BY REVEREND SYLVESTER MCCLEARN

    As I reflect on a life during which I came from the bottom of our country's social ladder to obtain an Associates Degree from New York University (NYU), and a Bachelor's degree from a seminary, what I see is the hand of God guiding me through the journey of my life. This journey has led me through five years as the Associate Pastor of the United Methodist Church in Newburgh, New York, and seventeen years as the pastor.

    During this time, I had the kind of pastoral experience that many people can only dream of. The church that God blessed me to pastor underwent a tremendous transformation under my leadership. To see a church that was an entirely Caucasian church go through such a complete transition, to the point where it is now a thriving African American and Latino church, was certainly not my dream when I became the pastor of the church. In fact, I was a little concerned about how these changes would be perceived when they began to occur. But I learned very quickly that it was very essential that I let go and allow God to do with His church exactly what He desired.

    In the process of God getting His will done, there were some hurts and pain but the energy that God was capable of providing His people became the soothing comfort that I needed to be able lead the church as God directed me. Even now, I can say with my whole heart that it was God that built the United Methodist Church in Newburgh as it now is. He gave me the strength to be the church leader that He wanted me to be, and I am aware that there was certainly no way that I could have developed or executed any vision, unless it flowed directly from Him.

Even when I knew that I was working from a position of educational weakness, I never felt inferior. This character held up even in the midst of crisis that was initiated and orchestrated by people in the church who were uncomfortable with my appointment as the pastor of this great church> They were uncomfortable because they were afraid that the church would go from being all-white to being all-black. I guess they had foresight, but I believe that they should have allowed God's people to inhabit His temple, regardless of their race. As it turned out their fear did in fact become reality, but only because they left the church rather than be in the same sanctuary with people of a different race.

On my part, I was confident that the battle was not mine to fight, so I gave it all to God. I felt as though the church was a tall mountain that God had given me to scale because He knew that what He wanted me to do was to move mountains. Although there were several sleepless nights and periods of frustration, my God was always taller than the tall mountains that He put before me and He has continued to keep me fresh and blessed as I have done the work He has placed in my hands.

People who remember my experiences and struggles in those early years of my services as pastor of the United Methodist Church would be surprised that I do not perceive of the opposition to my appointment as a racial issue. I do not believe that my detractors were upset because I was black. In my mind, it was not about me as a person. Instead, I simply believe that they were just naturally afraid that the church would become an African American church under my leadership. That change would have produced something very different from what they had been accustomed to.

It is not very often that a man born on a North Carolina farm, as I was, gets the opportunity to reflect on his life from my current position. As I look back on my life, I see a man who has had a long walk on a road that was not always paved with gold, but was full of lessons to be learned. One of the major lessons that I have learned from this journey is that, although the road of life may be very long and difficult, humility, perseverance, and determination can be great virtues capable of heralding remarkable blessings.

Regardless of what we think of ourselves, we are mere mortals who can accomplish great tasks only by God's special grace. I believe that it was only by the special grace of God that I came out of the circumstances of my birth and my family background to travel the road that I have thus far traveled in the manner in which I have done so.

When I dropped out of school as a child and worked as hard as I did in North Carolina and Washington, D.C., and later moved to Newburgh, New York, I thought I knew where I was and exactly what I was doing. Now I realize that every move was specially orchestrated by God to fulfill His plans for my life.

In the years before I gave my life to Christ, I did not always do what was right by His word. Yet, even at that time, He had His plans for me, and I have no doubt that He was always there to protect me from the dangers that could have befallen me as a young man in a fast world. God's grace is forever powerful and His plans for our lives sometimes unfold in ways that we can never fully explain. That is exactly what has happened to me.

In my life and walk with Him, God has blessed me with a wife who remains as beautiful inside and outside today as she was on the first day I met her. Billie has been an unparalleled partner to me and I am certain that there is no way that I could have done all of what I have done for over four decades now without her. She is the best wife that I could ever have hoped for and she is the best mother that my children could have had. Through our marriage, we have also had the opportunity of having some of my siblings live with us. About five years into our marriage, my sister, Estelle, died. Estelle was a wonderful woman who had taken over as mother of the family after my mother's death. In that role, which she handled with great competence, Estelle took in my sister Alice and my brother, Jesse.

Following Estelle's death, her family was broken up and Alice and Jesse came to live with Billie and me. Alice lived with us until she graduated from high school and moved to Washington, DC where she still resides with her family. Jesse also lived with us until he graduated from high school and went to the military.

I carry with me memories of my mother and my siblings who have passed on. My mother's death was a very huge loss for me, but I have also never been good at dealing with the death of any of my siblings. My brother Thomas was like a father to me and his death, when it occurred, completely broke my heart. He was the closest thing that I had to a father, and I looked up to him for stability. Randolph's death was such a sad loss for me that I had great difficulty with even the thought of his burial. I have similarly sad memories regarding the death of each one of my siblings who is no longer here. The pictures of my mother and my siblings that have passed on are all over the place, downstairs, in our home. My wife calls the place a memorial.

Sometimes, I recall the challenges of parenthood and of being an entrepreneur. I am never left in any doubt that there would have been absolutely no way to achieve what we did, had I not have a partner at who was always willing and able to handle the challenges with me. Both in triumph and in crises, Billie's support has consistently been invaluable. However, there is no way that a true tribute can be paid to Billie without some focus being placed on the role that she has played as pastor's wife in all the years that I have been in the ministry.

I suspect that only people who know what it's like to be a committed pastor's wife can truly appreciate the role Billie has consistently played in the ministry – in addition to her own responsibilities as the executive director of a community agency. I understand that there are pastors whose spouses are not involved in their ministries. The pastor perceives of the ministry as his job while his spouse's life is considered to be separate from that of the pastor. Pastors who are in situations like this may defend themselves by making the assertion that this is an arrangement that is convenient, acceptable, and right.

Whereas I cannot pass judgment on this approach to the ministry, I can whole-heartedly say two things: First, ministers and their spouses are better served and perhaps more highly blessed, when they put God's work first and put their own convenience last. Secondly, a pastor is more complete in his ministry and attains more respect from other ministers and church congregation when he and his spouse can be seen working together for God's purpose.

In my own work and walk as a pastor, Billie has in fact put herself last every time and allowed the work of God to be first. This has required a tremendous amount of sacrifice on her part, as well as a remarkable degree of humility and grace. I am eternally thankful to God for placing Billie by my side and I know that my Christian walk is made easier because of her presence in my life.

Couples who desire lasting relationships must learn to display mutual respect for each other. The love that they profess must be genuine and they must understand that mutual respect requires that they see each other as partners, rather than as superior or inferior beings to each other. From my experience, I know that love can be the foundation upon which a marriage relationship is based, but mutual respect must be an ever-present ingredient if the relationship is to be sustained.

Regardless of the upbringing that I received, I have been able to go through life with remarkable accomplishments, but not without the encouragement of people like my brothers who saw something in me and supported me with their love. Thus far, I have tried to do the same for my children and others in my community. In doing so, I have tried to impart in my children the value of love for others and support for those in need.

It is impossible to mandate society, church, or government to love and help others. Yet, it is a value that we could really use in this and every society in the world. I am convinced that our world becomes a much better place when each of us who has been blessed takes the hand of someone else and helps lift that person up from a state of difficulty. I submit that this is a responsibility that we should all take on for the sake of humanity.

As I reflect on my life, I am very thankful for the opportunities that I have had and I can only hope that my journey from birth on that farm along Angel Highway in North Carolina has been worth the walk. I am highly convinced that there is still a lot of work left for me to do as I continue my journey to glory. For as long as God gives me the power to do what He has laid up for me, I desire only one thing: that I may do it all to His glory.

TWENTY-TWO

THE SERMON TO END IT

BY REVEREND SYLVESTER MCCLEARN

I wish to share with you today two scriptures in the Holy Bible. The first is from the sixteenth chapter of the Gospel of Matthew, beginning at the thirteenth verse. It reads like this:

> When Jesus came into the coasts of Caesarea Phillipi, he asked his disciples, saying, Whom do men say that I the Son of man am? And they said, Some say that thou art John the Baptist: some, Elijah; and others, Jeremiah, or one of the prophets. He saith unto them, But whom say ye that I am? And Simon Peter answered and said, Thou art the Christ, the Son of the living God.

My second scripture is found in the first epistle of John, chapter 4, beginning at the eighteenth verse. That is, 1 John Chapter 4, starting at verse 18:

> There is no fear in love; but perfect love casteth out fear: because fear hath torment. He that feareth is not made perfect in love. We love him, because he first loved us.
> If a man say, I love God, and hateth his brother, he is a liar: for he that loveth not his brother whom he hath seen, how can he love God whom he hath not seen? And this commandment have we from him,

That he who loveth God love his brother also."

Fear is related to punishment. The one who fears is not made perfect in love. We love God because He first loved us. Without God, we have no capacity to love. With God, we have the capacity to love everyone, even those who disagree with us. If anyone says he loves God and hates his brother, he is a liar. Anyone who does not love his brother who sees daily cannot possibly love God who he has not seen. God has given this commandment to us, that whosoever claims to love Him must also love his brother.

The thought that I want to share in this sermon today has to do with a very important question that I feel a need to ask everyone who is reading this sermon today. The question is: What are people saying about you? If this is not an important question to you, it should be.

We should take time every now and then to examine and call ourselves into question. But we should not just be satisfied with our own self-evaluation. Instead, we should also be concerned about our fellow brothers and sisters, and what they think of us. How they feel about you can hurt you. How they feel can close doors in your face. They can close the bowels of compassion against you. In your mind, you might not have done anything very bad, but that is never all that matters. If people have a bad perception of you, the only way you will find out and know how to explain yourself is if you know how they perceive of you. If you have this important piece of information about others and yourself, perhaps you can help them overcome some of their negative perceptions of you. Otherwise, those perceptions can become the basis for creating a wall of obstacles that can keep them from loving you.

We know that it is not everybody that will speak well of us, even if we consider ourselves to be great people. That is how life is. However, everybody should not be speaking badly of us. The saying is true today as it has always been that a good name is better to be desired than material things. The Bible makes clear that Jesus grew in favor of God and in favor of man. This is according to Luke chapter 2 verse 52. According to that Bible verse, *"And Jesus increased in wisdom and stature, and in favor of God and man."* We should strive to be like Jesus. Proverbs chapter 22 verses 1-2 tell us that, *"A good name should be more desired than riches. Having favor is better than silver and gold".*

A good name can open doors for you. If you have a good name, you can get money, receive commercial credit, and get many things that you need. Sometimes, at the mention of your name, the boss will come out of his office and shake your hands. If you have a good name in your community, people will want to meet you. People will feel good about you because they know only good things about you. We should be concerned about the state of our names. As old folks often said, we should always treat our neighbors well, treat our friends and even our enemies well, so that God can use us anytime, anywhere.

Jesus saw that His church was in need of some investigation. He wanted to know what kind of reputation He had in the community. So he asked His disciples, "What are people saying about me? How am I coming across to the people? Are they reading me the way I want them to?" This had to be very important to Jesus. It was something that Jesus wanted to know. This reminds me of a former New York City Mayor, Ed Koch, who used to ask every now and then, "How am I doing?"

You have to be open-minded enough to be willing and able to ask such a question about yourself and you have to be ready for the good and the bad in terms of the response that you might get. You may choose not ask the question if you only want to hear good things about yourself. Otherwise, the news that you might get may not be so good. Yet, we need to ask the question anyway. Look at somebody and ask: "How am I doing? What do you think about me? What kind of job am I doing? How am I coming across to my community?"

I like what Jesus did because it tells me something very special about Him. He was human and He had feelings. He loved people and He wanted them to love Him too. This is the impression I get from reading about Christ in this part of the scriptures.

I have met people who say that other people's opinions do not mean anything to them. Such people often say: "I don't care what the world says about me, I am going to heaven". To me, I am not sure how that can be true. I really don't know about that. I am glad that Jesus was not like that. He cared about what people were saying about Him. He was not only concerned about what the world was saying about Him, but also about what people close to Him were saying about Him. He cared about that. Therefore, He asked them: "What do you say about me?" Jesus did not have to go there.

You may say to yourself, "Why did Christ ask a question like this?" What if I asked you to ask those who you work with and those who live with you in your home: "How am I doing? Am I doing right? Am I coming across to my brothers and sisters the way I should be?" Never forget that Jesus turned to those with whom He worked everyday and asked them: "How am I doing? Who do you say I am?" This is a question we need to ask, even in our family setting. We should not be afraid to ask the question of even people that are very close to us. Jesus showed us that He is concerned about what the world says about us. He told us to go out into the world and let our light so shine that people would see our good works and give God the glory for the works that they see being done in our lives.

My sermon may seem hard or strong to you but it is my responsibility to remind us that we have a duty to each other and to God. Let me ask you today: What are members of this greater community saying about you? What are your friends saying about you? What are the two greatest commandments that God gave to us?

1) That we should love God with all our heart, mind and spirit.
2) That we should love our neighbors as ourselves.

It is important that our neighbors be cared for. As we do this, people will see and say the right things about us. Some of us have separated the two commandments. Some of us want to love God and hate our fellow people. Some of us think that we can love God - and God only. Their attitude is: "All I need is to walk with God and have God walk with me". We seem to have forgotten how important that second commandment is - that we should love and care for other people, and be concerned about how we deal with one another.

Listen to a typical attitude that some people display: "I love you Lord. O God, I love you....I love you with all my heart." But what about your brother and sister? Some may say, "Preacher, don't go there". But I have to go there because John said: "How can we love a God we have never seen and not love each other." How can we hold on to God and say, "I love you, I love you, I love you" without loving each other? How can we truly love God who we have not seen and hate our brother who we see everyday?

This may all sound tight, but it is right. God loves the truth and the truth will set us free. This speaks to the genuineness of Christian life. It is the commandment that God has given to us and all of us who say we love God – to love our fellow man. Not only should we love God, but we should also love our family members, our friends, and our enemies. God has called us and given us the power to fly like an eagle, to go where no one has dared to go, and to do the impossible. We need to fight the foe that seems unbeatable to the human mind, and to reach heights that are otherwise unreachable.

I heard someone say: "I will trust in the Lord till I die; I will stay on the battlefield; I will do what the Lord God has commanded me to do". Yes, I want Jesus to walk with me. Also, I will walk with my brothers and sisters through life's journey and I want them to walk with me.

Some day, by and by, when life's journey is over, I will, as the old folks say, fly away. I will fly away to be at rest. I heard David say: "If I had wings like an eagle, I would fly away to be at rest. One good morning, when this life is over, I can see the Lord standing with His arms wide open, saying: "Well done, you have fought a good fight; you have kept the faith. There is a crown waiting for you. Come up. Come, sit up and rest a while. Come bathe your soul in the Jordan River. Come where the wicked will cease to trouble you, where all the Saints and God's angels will sit at my feet and be blessed."

God bless you, God keep you till we meet again in that great getting-up morning, in that great getting-up morning. Farewell, farewell.

ABOUT THE AUTHOR

Ohiro Oni-Eseleh has authored several articles and two other books, *In Pursuit of Dreams: The Truth About Immigration,* and *Thy Will Not Mine, Accepting the Will of God.* He also travels and lectures extensively.